Queer TV i

Queer TV in the 21st Century

*Essays on Broadcasting from
Taboo to Acceptance*

Edited by KYLO-PATRICK R. HART

McFarland & Company, Inc., Publishers
Jefferson, North Carolina

ISBN (print) 978-1-4766-6440-8
ISBN (ebook) 978-1-4766-2560-7

LIBRARY OF CONGRESS CATALOGUING DATA ARE AVAILABLE

British Library cataloguing data are available

Front cover image of Megan Mullaly (as Karen Walker), Eric McCormack
(as Will Truman), Debra Messing (as Grace Adler), Sean Hayes (as Jack
McFarland) in *Will & Grace* (NBC/Photofest)

Printed in the United States of America

McFarland & Company, Inc., Publishers
  Box 611, Jefferson, North Carolina 28640
  www.mcfarlandpub.com

For A, E, I, O, U, and Z^3 plus T

Table of Contents

Introduction

Media Representation and Sensitive Subjects

KYLO-PATRICK R. HART

When making his 1957 film *The Seventh Seal*, an allegory of humankind's never-ending search for the meaning of life, Swedish director Ingmar Bergman was forced to confront not only his longstanding fear of death—which he has described as being a "source of constant horror" (*Images* 238) during his childhood and early adulthood—but also the challenge of how to most effectively depict death visually within that cinematic creation (*Images* 238–240).

Early in that work, the knight Antonius Block (played by Max von Sydow) and his squire, Jöns (played by Gunnar Björnstrand), come upon an individual resting against a rock, of whom they ask directions. After a few seconds of silence, Jöns taps the man on the shoulder, wondering if he is sleeping or simply shy. Dead is more like it. When Jöns gazes at the person's face, it is half rotted away, with no eyes in their sockets—a haunting representation. Chalk one up for the plague. A bit later in the film, as the knight and squire watch two actors performing a song about the Black Death, an eerie religious procession moves through the streets, interrupting the on-stage action. The variety of marchers, weakened and even crippled by the plague, are a hideous lot. Several truly call to mind images of the "walking dead." It is apparent at such moments that Bergman's various life experiences—such as befriending a hospital caretaker who allowed him to see numerous corpses in varying stages of decay (*Magic* 12), or vacationing near an upscale nursing home for syphilitic aristocrats which exposed him to half-dead zombies in different stages of deterioration (*Images* 343)—have paid off handsomely in terms of creative inspiration.

But Bergman faced an even bigger challenge when making *The Seventh Seal*: how also to visually depict Death, with a capital "D," effectively within that same cinematic creation. To achieve this end, the director says that he found inspiration in the various altarpieces, murals, and stained-glass windows he encountered as a child when visiting various churches with his preacher father, which featured images such as "The Knight playing chess with Death; Death sawing down the Tree of Life, a terrified wretch wringing his hands in the top of it; Death leading the dance to the Land of the Shadows, wielding his scythe like a flag, the congregation capering in a long line, and the jester bringing up the rear" (Bergman, *Images* 231) as well as countless "saints, prophets, angels, devils, and demons" (*Images* 232). At the same time, he recalls that he made a recklessly daring decision that he would not have had the confidence to make later in his career: he decided that "Death should have the features of a white clown, an amalgamation of a clown mask and a skull" (Bergman, *Images* 236). About this decision, the director recalls:

> The knight performs his morning prayer. When he is ready to pack up his chess set, he turns around, and there stands Death [played by Bengt Ekerot]. "Who are you?" asks the knight. "I am Death." ... It was a delicate and dangerous artistic move, which could have failed. Suddenly, an actor appears in whiteface, dressed all in black, and announces that he is Death. Everyone accepted the dramatic feat that he was Death, instead of saying, "Come on now, don't try to put something over on us! You can't fool us! We can see that you are just a talented actor who is painted white and clad in black! You're not Death at all!" But nobody protested. That made me feel triumphant and joyous [Bergman, *Images* 236].

Certainly, Bergman was not the first, nor the last, artist forced to wrestle with the complexities of visually depicting death, both with a lowercase "d" (as in the phenomena of dying and death) and an uppercase "D" (as in death personified), effectively in his creative works. Writing in the century before the director was born, poet Emily Dickinson (1830–1886) devoted a great deal of her creative output to depicting death in visual terms, using only words to accomplish this challenging task, in her handwritten poems. Literary experts report that Dickinson, who wrote primarily for personal pleasure rather than publication and became a recluse in the later decades of her life, was fascinated with the possibility of death and therefore wrote about it quite regularly (Ellmann and O'Clair 21–22).

One subset of Dickinson's poetry deals with the phenomena of dying and death directly. In Poem 341 ("After great pain, a formal feeling comes"), for example, Dickinson provides vivid imagery of what she believes happens to the human body after it dies, offering the reader visions of a body initially in a state of disbelief about what has happened to it—its nerves and heart on edge, searching for clues about what has occurred; its feet thrashing about, from the earth toward the sky and back again—before experiencing the leaden and freezing states associated with the final letting go that is dying and death (Johnson 162). Similarly, in Poem 547 ("I've seen a Dying Eye"), Dickinson provides very visual language about a dying eye that searches around for an image of *anything* before it clouds over, becomes foggy, and ultimately becomes sealed shut for all eternity—without ever revealing what it was blessed to see as the body it is attached to passes into death (Johnson 266). A second subset of Dickinson's poetry addresses the locations where bodies dwell after they have passed into death and their possible interactions in the afterlife. In Poem 51 ("I often passed the village"), for instance, Dickinson explores the peaceful and solemn nature of a local graveyard as an eternal resting place. The picture that emerges from her words is one of a calm, relatively silent location with a beauty that is enhanced by flowers scattered about and birds flying calmly all around. In the concluding stanza of this poem, Dickinson emphasizes the graveyard's eternal appeal of such a loving, welcoming setting for individuals who are at the point that they can no longer go on living (Johnson 28). In Poem 261 ("Put up my lute!"), Dickinson fantasizes about bringing a deceased individual, or perhaps even several such individuals, back to life by playing the same sort of music that was used to lead him/them into death (Johnson 120). In a related way in Poem 24 ("There is a morn by men unseen"), she envisions a possible world in which the dead come back to life to engage together in dance and play each spring, her words calling to mind visions of the spirits of various individuals, undetectable to the human eye, whose feet are now used only occasionally for revelry, dancing and frolicking together on their special day each year. Here, Dickinson proffers images of a playful celebration that is even more wondrous than what is experienced by the living and suggests the narrator's enthusiastic willingness to one day experience such revelry, once his or her life is through (Johnson 17–18). The dead come back to life as well in Dickinson's Poem 607 ("Of nearness to her sundered Things"), within which the grave's various "robberies" are unburied and allowed to dwell about once more, wearing their jackets and other clothing items of old and appearing in much the same form as they did before they passed away, seemingly having been enjoying themselves in the years since they left their human bodies behind (Johnson 298–299).

Arguably the most intriguing subset of Dickinson's poetry pertaining to death, however, is composed of her poems that feature the personification of Death, the being that comes to claim a human life and lead an individual into the eternal afterlife. Among her most impressive creations in this regard is Poem 712 ("Because I could not stop for Death"), in which the poet places herself in the position of the character that is the poem's narrator. In this creation, Dickinson represents Death as a male figure who is kind enough to stop his carriage and take her for a ride to her eternal slumber when she is too busy, or perhaps simply unwilling, to wait around for him. From her words, the reader receives a powerful vision of an individual being led to revisit key moments from her life, such as those at recess in the schoolyard when she was just a child playing games such as ring around the rosie (an early, playtime reenactment of death), as well as special attributes of her life's setting, in which the fields of grain appear to be "gazing" back at her and her driver—Death himself—in a sort of respectful recognition, before the setting sun overtakes them both and she grows colder, until she is ultimately delivered by Death to her graveyard resting place. The concluding stanza of the poem, which refers to centuries that seem to pass in less than a day and horses that are aimed toward eternity, reinforces both the civil nature of Death as he led his latest victim to her grave by again calling to mind the trotting horses moving in the direction he guided them as well as the notion that deceased individuals may not really engage in an all-encompassing eternal slumber (Johnson 350). Similarly, in Poem 390 ("It's coming—the postponeless Creature"), Dickinson personifies Death as a being (this time with no specified gender) that approaches first from afar, then from down the block, and then from outside the door before entering, greeting its victim respectfully and identifying itself boldly and briefly, and then, without offering any opportunity for postponement, carrying the person out of the world of the living (Johnson 186). Poem 1686 ("The event was directly behind Him") further personifies Death, again with no clearly specified gender, as a being that sneaks up on its victim, wraps its arms tightly around the unsuspecting individual whose time has come, and then separates that individual's eternal soul from its earthly body (Johnson 688).

What has likely become evident from these examples of Dickinson's various depictions of death in visual terms, accomplished solely through the use of her carefully selected and arranged words, is that many of this poet's creations were highly conceptual in nature as they explored topics such as immortality, passing centuries, deceased beings returning to life, and the afterlife. As such, she provides adequate detail to instill various sorts of images in the reader's mind without providing such extensive detail that she ends up dictating the specific forms that those images must necessarily take. This leaves a good part of the creative process up to each individual reader, working in collaboration with Dickinson's words and following her lead.

In dramatic contrast to Dickinson's textually flexible 19th-century approach, and materializing nearly half a century after Bergman's playfully innovative 20th-century approach, HBO's highly acclaimed, 21st-century drama series *Six Feet Under* (2001–2005) also represented the sensitive subject of death on a continuous basis, albeit in shockingly graphic, provocative, and frequently highly realistic ways, regularly offering, as I have argued elsewhere, "psychological realism and philosophical rigor that are rarely encountered on popular television" through its "dark tone, dramatic intensity, and characters who refused to let the fact that they are dead prevent them from talking to the living" (Hart 163). That last part about recently deceased individuals refusing to stay dead is particularly relevant here. The typical *Six Feet Under* episode begins with a death—caused by anything from sudden infant death syndrome to murder—and the dead body then usually ends up at the Los Angeles funeral home run by the Fisher family, where it frequently (and freakishly) comes back to life and converses with the employee who is embalming it, or sometimes with the individual who is coordinating its funeral arrangements. This series stood out right from the start of its premiere episode when it defied television conventions by killing off the family's patriarch, funeral home owner and father Nathaniel Fisher (played by Richard Jenkins), during the first four minutes, on Christmas Eve when the new hearse he is driving collides with an oncoming bus. At the time of his death, Nathaniel was singing "I'll Be Home for Christmas" and, indeed, he does not stay far from home for long. For in addition to all of other dead people who pay unexpected visits to the Fisher sons, Nate (played by Peter Krause) and David (played by Michael C. Hall), and others as they continue to run the family business, the viewer soon comes to realize that Nathaniel Fisher also

> refuses to go quietly into the afterlife; instead, he appears from time to time over the show's five seasons to his various family members, most commonly to his two sons, to offer advice and help guide them in leading what he believes will be successful, fulfilling lives. Whenever the ghost of the father materializes to talk to his family members, therefore, he represents both the patriarchal social order generally as well as their internalized versions of its social expectations [Hart 167].

By continually confronting audience members with recurring images of death in various forms, *Six Feet Under* endeavored intentionally, at least in part, to assist its viewers in coming to terms with their fears associated with the phenomena of dying and death and the corresponding acceptance of their own morality. In addition, unlike most other series in the history of U.S. television, this one opted to provide a true sense of closure to its viewers, in the aftermath of Nate's unexpected death and during the closing minutes of the series' final episode, by providing a series of flash-forwards that vividly present, along with a few future milestone events, each of the main characters' future death. To provide a sense of the representational impact of these final images on viewers for those who have not yet personally encountered them, Adam David has titled his recap of this emotionally powerful concluding sequence "Reminder: Nothing Will Ever Traumatize You as Much as the *Six Feet Under* Finale."

The logic behind all of the aforementioned representational approaches appears to be that sensitive subjects become easier to deal with, and ultimately less foreign and threatening, the more media consumers are confronted with them. As they demonstrate, individuals have clearly been obsessed with the (unpleasant) topic of death for centuries. It is this sort of fascination that captivated Emily Dickinson, who wrote numerous poems about the phenomena of dying and death, as well as the personification of Death, during her lifetime, as well as Ingmar Bergman, who admitted that it was quite difficult for him to accept the notion that "one [can] be transformed from *being* to *not-being*" instantly and that he has lived a life filled with "constant anxiety about death" (*Images* 241, original emphasis). "That I plucked up my courage and depicted Death as a white clown," Bergman has stated, "a figure who conversed, played chess, and has no secrets, was the first step in my struggle against my monumental fear of death.... First you *are*, then you are *not*. This I [now] find deeply satisfying" (*Images* 240–241, original emphasis). That is why so many talented individuals, past and present, have devoted such extreme amounts of time and care to depicting death visually in words and images: to begin addressing their anxieties and fears by producing images of death that they find to be somewhat reassuring and palatable—which enables them to work through their thoughts, concerns, and fears related to this sensitive subject until they (ideally) ultimately become more comfortable with its existence—and to help others do the same through the process of being exposed to their words and images.

The same sort of argument can be made with regard to media representations of queerness in its various forms, the subject of this collection of essays. Individuals who are already familiar with *Six Feet Under* know that, in addition to its eye-opening representations of death, this series was similarly noteworthy for its groundbreaking representations of sexual orientation, perhaps most notably in regard to the lived realities of character David Fisher, a gay man who worked alongside his father at the family's funeral home for more than a decade prior to the man's untimely passing. As Robert Tobin notes, the series "attempts to provide a positive answer to the question of how society should develop without patriarchal guidance" (87), as do several of the essays included in the present collection. The impulse underlying many of the examples of queer television in the 21st century that are analyzed at length herein is that, like other kinds of subject matter that have at one time or another been culturally regarded as controversial or taboo, regular exposure to a range of boundary-pushing televisual representations of queerness in its various forms can result in this historically sensitive subject matter becoming easier for audience members to encounter, accept, and no longer feel threatened by. Such representations can be communicated through the contents of a television series such as *Will & Grace*, or *Queer as Folk*, or *The L Word*, or *RuPaul's Drag Race*, or, even more ideally, in cumulative exposure to all of these various series and many more (e.g., *Buffy the Vampire Slayer*, *Modern Family*, *Queer Eye for the Straight Guy*, *Spartacus*—you get the point!). For as Rachel Griffiths, who plays the character Brenda Chenowith in *Six Feet Under*, insightfully expressed, the time is long overdue for all individuals to "take sex out of the ethical and moral way we appraise people" and stop judging others on the basis "of what they choose to do with like-minded people who are choosing to do it with them" ("Why").

WORKS CITED

Bergman, Ingmar. *Images: My Life in Film*. Trans. Marianne Ruuth. New York: Arcade Publishing, 1994. Print.

_____. *The Magic Lantern*. Trans. Joan Tate. New York: Penguin, 1988. Print.

Davis, Adam. "Reminder: Nothing Will Ever Traumatize You as Much as the *Six Feet Under* Finale." *BuzzFeed*. 21 August 2015. Web. 19 December 2015. http://www.buzzfeed.com/adamdavis/i-am-crying-thanks-six-feet-under#.uvozEdNOI.

Ellmann, Richard, and Robert O'Clair. "Emily Dickinson." *Modern Poems: A Norton Introduction*, 2d ed. Ed. Richard Ellmann and Robert O'Clair. New York: Norton, 1989. 20–22. Print.

Hart, Kylo-Patrick R. "Keeping the Intelligent Woman 'In Her Place' within the Patriarchal Social Order: Containing the Unruliness of Genius Brenda Chenowith on *Six Feet Under*." *Common Sense: Intelligence as Presented on Popular Television*. Ed. Lisa Holderman. Lanham, MD: Lexington Books, 2008. 163–172. Print.

Johnson, Thomas H., ed. *The Complete Poems of Emily Dickinson*. New York: Little, Brown, 1951. Print.

Tobin, Robert. "*Six Feet Under* and Post-Patriarchal Society." *Film and History* 32.1 (2002): 87–88. Print.

"Why Rachel Griffiths Is Going All the Way." *Australian*, 14 June 2003: B1. Print.

Gay It Forward

How Will & Grace Made Gay
Male Couples Okay on Television

ZACHARY SNIDER

On May 21, 2014, 10.45 million viewers tuned in to ABC's immensely popular, Emmy Award–winning situation comedy *Modern Family* (2009–) to watch neurotic Mitchell Pritchett (played by Jesse Tyler Ferguson) and flamboyant Cameron Tucker (played by Eric Stonestreet) exchange vows and become man and wife (Kondolojy). Husband. I mean husband, not wife; man and *husband*.

For a same-sex wedding plot, this U.S. television viewership figure is impressive. Also impressive is how greatly ABC publicized Mitch and Cam's wedding to *Modern Family*'s fans, considering that same-sex marriages, especially male pairings, have not always received so much positive publicity. Back on December 12, 1995, viewers of *Roseanne* (1988–1997) watched Roseanne's Barbra Streisand-and-drag-queen-hating boss Leon (played by Martin Mull) "marry" (same-sex marriage was not yet legal in the state of Illinois, where the series took place) his girlishly friendly boyfriend Scott (played by Fred Willard); ABC moved this episode from its regular 8 p.m. time slot to 9:30 p.m. hoping to avoid viewer objection and inevitable media controversy ("Roseanne Adult").

Years later, on May 11, 2008, stoic Kevin Walker (played by Matthew Rhys) got hitched to overdramatic Scotty Wandell (played by Luke Macfarlane) on the season-two finale of ABC's *Brothers & Sisters* (2006–2011). When Kevin and Scotty became husband and wife—er, husband and husband—the turnout for the *Brothers & Sisters*' same-sex wedding actually bested *Modern Family*'s ratings, with 11.02 million viewers tuning in ("Weekly"). However, during the six years between Kevin and Scotty's and Mitch and Cam's weddings, recordable viewership for television ratings decreased due to DVR and

9

on-demand viewing, which suggests that more people presumably caught the Pritchett–Tucker ceremony than were effectively measured by ratings systems (Ulin 281–282).

On April 2, 2013, after viewership for sensationalist Ryan Murphy's *The New Normal* (2012–2013) had rapidly dwindled, not many people stuck around to watch doctor-jock David Sawyer (played by Justin Bartha) say "I do" to hyper-effeminate Bryan Collins (played by Andrew Rannells) on NBC, thereby making Bryan his loving wife. On ABC's *Desperate Housewives* (2004–2012) in 2008, the sports-loving, beer-chugging guy's guy Bob Hunter (played by Tuc Watkins) and his wife, Lee McDermott (played by Kevin Rahm), were bitchily married and trying to adopt a baby, but Lee—HAHAHA!—just could not stop drinking Chardonnay and gossiping all the time with the other gals on the series' heteronormative Wisteria Lane. On cable, Professor Ben Bruckner (played by Robert Gant) of *Queer as Folk* (2000–2005) played dad to teenage hustler James "Hunter" Montgomery (played by Harris Allan), whose mommy figure, the wimpy Michael Novotny (played by Hal Sparks), cooked and cleaned just like any good housewife. Ben eventually took Michael as his bride, too. Even on HBO's *Six Feet Under* (2001–2005), notoriously moody David Fisher (played by Michael C. Hall) refers to mega-manly cop Keith Charles (played by Mathew St. Patrick) as his "husband" even before they wed, and even when he was *so* upset that Keith would not go to brunch with David's gay friends, who call themselves "the leading ladies."

I am obviously using words like "wife," "bride," and "housewife" sarcastically here, in order to illustrate how heteronormatively these male-male same-sex marriages are represented in their respective series. I am also not using these female-connoted words derogatorily. Likewise, I am certainly not antagonizing male-male same-sex marriage as a farce of opposite-sex marriage. Rather, these recognizable images and gender signifiers are simply the ones that audience members regularly encounter(ed) on these television shows.

Back in 1998, just before David Kohan and Max Mutchnick's sitcom *Will & Grace* (1998–2006) debuted as part of NBC's popular "Monday night comedy lineup (*Suddenly Susan* [1996–2000], *Conrad Bloom* [1998], *Caroline in the City* [1995–1999])," the advertisement for these various series "included four photos featuring each series' primary male-female couple" (Becker 172). In other words, just looking at this lineup, one would never know that the character of Will Truman (played by Eric McCormack) was gay, as he was pressed up to his lady companion in a typical boyfriend-girlfriend–style pose. Things have come a long way since then, considering that the print promos for *Modern Family*'s debut in the fall of 2009 featured a tri-level divide of its key families: Jay and Gloria Pritchett with her son Manny Delgado at the top (i.e., the geriatric patriarch who remarried a Latin trophy wife and legally adopted her son); Claire, Luke, Haley, Alex, and Phil Dunphy placed comfortingly in the middle (i.e., the "normal" family of a mom, dad, and their three kids); and, on the bottom, Mitchell Pritchett, Cameron Tucker, and Lily Tucker-Pritchett (i.e., the affluent white gays and their adopted Asian baby). Admittedly, when I saw this advertisement on a New York City subway in the late summer of 2009, I rolled my eyes at ABC's audacity to segregate these clichéd character types and lifestyles on the poster. Looking back, though, I have reconsidered that, hey, at least the gays made it on there, and, unlike Will Truman, they were snuggled up to each other, rather than cuddling up to some woman in between them.

In Evan Cooper's research pertaining to viewer reception of *Will & Grace*, he found that "the popularity of [the series] signifies a degree of acceptance from the larger culture, even if … it does not necessarily lead to greater acceptance.… [The series also was] useful in making gays more familiar and less the Other to a heterosexual audience" (531). Such media visibility in 21st-century television shows is possible *because* of the clever trickery that *Will & Grace* worked so hard at, in its efforts to make gays and "gay lifestyles" (the plural here is definitely intentional, considering that there is not *just one* gay lifestyle; more on this later) more acceptable to heterosexual American viewers.

While the imposition of traditional gender roles in real life can certainly limit one's identity composition and the healthiness of a same-sex relationship, on television, gender-role representations are safe. They are marketable. They are formulas for financial profit and viewer sustainment. This is, of course, not to say that such heteronormativity is *positive*, or *productive*, or *right*. However, in the case of *Will & Grace*, the series engaged viewers for years with heteronormative conventions; hooked these viewers with its characters, silly plotlines, and uncommon character relationships; and then, in its last couple of seasons, abandoned heteronormativity for its characters'— namely Will's—happiness. For *Will & Grace*, the exploitation of gender roles and gay stereotypes tricked audiences into laughing along with its characters. Specifically, by juxtaposing Will's "everygay" lifestyle with the stereotypically showy gay lifestyle of Jack McFarland (played by Sean Hayes), which effectively fooled viewers into thinking of Will as an everyman, *Will & Grace* created appreciation for and accessibility to the following: (1) male same-sex couples and marriage; (2) friendships with and among gay males; (3) "alternative" urban families; and (4) gay humor.

Will and Grace and Jack and Karen's Trickster Heteronormativity

Like nearly all male-female married couples on television, the same-sex television marriages I mentioned earlier suggestively feature one partner as the masculine husband and the other as the effeminate wife. Not presenting them in this way is simply too threatening for many viewers, heterosexual and homosexual alike, because television's married couples, especially in situation comedies, have always featured heteronormative pairings. In sitcoms, that's what marriage *is*. That's where the comedy comes from: opposition, misunderstanding, misinterpretation, and incompatible character differences, which are quite often based on gender expectations and misperceptions. Thus, in order to defy such gender expectations and roles, a sitcom must first employ them; only then can they be challenged and, hopefully, changed. The viewing threat of *not* presenting a heteronormative coupling is not particularly a sociopolitical statement on series that feature same-sex partnerships, nor is it executive-producer ignorance. Rather, a non-heteronormative couple does not mesh with the established comfort to which most viewers have grown accustomed when watching married couples on television spar about kids, bills, and neighbors.

Most of these sitcoms are billed as romantic comedies, too, a genre that historically requires a dominant partner who pursues a submissive (or, for laughs, a problematically non-submissive) partner. The dominator has always (comfortably for viewers) been male, while the female is submissive. A few rare exceptions to this are Samantha Jones (played by Kim Cattrall) on *Sex and the City* (1998–2004), Gwen Leonard (played by Sharon Lawrence) on *Fired Up* (1997–1998), and, arguably, Monica Geller (played by Courteney Cox) on *Friends* (1994–2004). This genre of the sitcom regularly features an "odd" couple or an "opposites attract" couple, also produced for laughs, who can romantically join together in union despite their massive differences and yin-yang personality traits. On U.S. television, these romantic-comedy pairings historically have been—and still are—traditional male-female couplings, so it is expected and understandable that, for viewers' interest and attention spans, *behavioral* heteronormativity is *necessary* for a successful romantic-comedy sitcom. Series such as *Friends, How I Met Your Mother* (2005–2014), *Marry Me* (2014–2015), *The Mindy Project* (2012–), *Sex and the City*, and even *Will & Grace* have relied on these gender-oppositional "odd couplings" for the sake of comedy, romance, and viewer understanding and empathy.

In Rodger Streitmatter's book about the increase of sex and "alternative" lifestyles on television, he points out that "Will [was] so lacking in effeminate mannerisms that focus group members who previewed the pilot episode refused to believe that he was gay" (145). In other words, this heteronormativity is not solely a visual aspect but also a *behavioral* one; it is dependent upon an actor's performance. Based on the successes of more recent male-male pairings in mainstream television series, such as *Brothers & Sisters* and *Modern Family*, it has indeed become okay to film two men intimately next to one another, even if they might be holding hands or walking closely side by side. These signified male-male pairings are not as much of a threat nowadays as they were ten years ago, when *Will & Grace* was at the height of its run yet still often visually featured male-female pairings for viewer approval and comfort.

Just as television sitcoms need, and certainly thrive on, archetypal characters like the comedic fool and court jester, the raging-lunatic boss, the creepy roommate slob, the fuddy-duddy neighbor, and the ditzy-blonde single best friend, most viewers *need* to see married partners acting in these heteronormative roles, regardless of gender. The married couple itself has become an archetypal duo, one that, like all other television archetypes, is comfortably confined to sitcom conventions. One married partner must always be the irresponsible, overemotional spouse who is always getting her husband and her family and/or friends into trouble (i.e., the woman/wife), while the other partner must always play the role of the stern "straight man" who is a paternal figure to all of the other characters (i.e., the man/husband). By "straight man," I am referring here to the comedy term for one partner in a comedic duo who has silly things done to him, or directed at him, or that coincidentally yet unwantedly involve him, by the more outlandish, cuckoo partner (the woman/wife). Thus, television series that feature same-sex pairings are not necessarily even succumbing to negative heteronormative clichés; they are instead simply borrowing from the standard character, plot, and laugh-line blueprints of some of television's most successful and memorable shows, specifically with regard to their marital relationships and how their heteronormative spouses behave toward one another.

Will & Grace's Happy Modern Family: Two Gays, a Jew and a Drunk Pill Popper

While the sitcom's title suggests that *Will & Grace* focuses on just a male-female duo who have supporting players visit their exclusive plotlines, the series quickly unfolded as a quartet program featuring the dependable yet obsessive-compulsive Will Truman, the neurotic and self-centered Grace Adler (played by Debra Messing), the flamboyant and goofy Jack McFarland, and the drunk, high, and fabulous diva Karen Walker (played by Megan Mullally). Soon, Jack and Karen had complex plotlines that received almost equal screen time as Will's and Grace's. The storyboarding became a quadrant rather than focusing on just Will and Grace as a "couple." In the series finale, Jack and Karen even poke fun at this reality with self-aware meta-dialogue, confessing to each other how all of these years they have felt like they "were on the Will and Grace show."

These four characters were their own modern family of sorts, who interacted with each other's immediate family members (parents and siblings and, later, aunts, uncles, cousins, nieces, and nephews) during extended family functions and holidays. Will, Grace, Jack, and Karen all had children and spouses by the end of the series, too (with the exception of Jack on the spousal front, though he did have a son; Karen went through a few spouses), which made them even more of an extended modern family, one that was not related by blood but rather by location, experience, sexual orientation (for Jack and Will), and their collective desire to be part of a supportive urban family unit. The focus on family is prominent throughout the series' entire eight-year run, with countless examples: Will and Grace each wanting a family; Grace's Jewish mama pressuring her to get married and have kids; Grace's husband, Leo (played by Harry Connick, Jr.), wanting kids; Jack finally coming out to his mother on his thirtieth birthday; Jack finding out that he has a preteen son as a result of a sperm donation he provided years ago; Jack dating Stuart Lamarack (played by Dave Foley), his only brief true love in the series, who also has a teenage son; all of Will's family members coming to visit New York City on separate trips (including his mother, father, and brothers); Will and Jack mentoring Will's flamboyant nephew, Jordy (played by Reed Alexander); etc. The list is endless, and solidly rooted in a collective desire to be a non-traditional yet supportive family unit.

It is also important to note that most of the other series mentioned earlier—*Brothers & Sisters, Modern Family, The New Normal, Six Feet Under*—took place in family-friendly, bright and sunny suburban California. While the tone of *Six Feet Under* (and sometimes *Brothers & Sisters*) was not particularly bright, sunny, and supportive, the family aspect of all these shows was emphasized as being of prime importance to their characters. Even *Desperate Housewives*, which took place in a fictional locale referred to as "the Eagle State," had visual signifiers of Californian suburban purity, safety, and wholesome family values (albeit with an attempted ominous tone). *Will & Grace*, in contrast, was set in hedonistic, not-so-family-friendly New York City, predominantly in Manhattan, until Grace moved to Brooklyn with her husband.

In film, television, music, real life—you name it—New York City is hardly the place for the traditional American family. Rather, most sitcoms about New York City—*Friends, The Mindy Project, Sex and the City* to name a few—typically feature adults who, although financially and professionally successful, were outcasts in their immediate families and/or are characters who want nothing to do with the family-friendly suburbs. The core quartet on *Will & Grace* is just as progressive and alternative as the city itself, meaning that these individuals, too, do not have an overwhelming need for a traditional family like the characters of the California-based shows. New York City television families, nuclear and alternative ones alike, are built on fundamental elements such as financial security and social greed, plus fashion, style, cynicism, pastiche, a shared frustration with everyday metropolitan problems, and, especially, a desire to fit in together because none of these people particularly fit into their own families.

Will, Grace, Jack, and Karen—plus their partners, lovers, children, maid, butler, driver, cook, deliverymen, and/or other synonymous friends—are all of these things, which is why they have formed their own urban modern family. This, in a way, makes their familial connection even stronger than those of other television series: they have *chosen* to group together as a family, rather than having to stay together out of traditional family obligation like, for instance, the melodramatic Walkers of *Brothers & Sisters* or the snarky Pritchetts (plus the Tuckers and Dunphys) of *Modern Family*. For *Will & Grace*'s characters (and, after eight seasons, for its viewers, too), "alternative" same-sex marriage seems "normal" in their version of New York City. For people like Will Truman and Grace Adler, marrying someone of the same or opposite sex is part of the process of bringing another member into their urban, carefully chosen family. This is precisely why, whenever Will meets a new dating partner, Jack and Karen repeatedly ask, "Has Grace met him? No? Then how do you know if you like him?" Jack and Karen ask these questions like they are small children, which, in their family unit, is precisely what they are. Grace is the kooky yet self-obsessed Jewish mama, while Will is the WASPy patriarch who recovers for his "wife" and "kids" whenever they make fools of themselves. As childish characters, Karen and Jack get away with essentially anything and everything in their family, while Grace emptily scolds them. Will, the gay "straight man," must therefore repeatedly pay the consequences for his eccentric family's actions, just like in so many other sitcoms. Even in *Will & Grace*'s conclusion, Will, now married to a man, remains the responsible patriarch; Grace, married to a different man, is now the middle-aged, doting Jewish mama; and Jack and Karen remain wholly free of responsibility, as aging children at play.

In the New York City that is represented in *Will & Grace*, and even in nearby Connecticut (where Will was raised) and upstate New York (where Grace is from), same-sex marriage and "alternative" families are never viewed by any character, main or supporting, as icky or problematic or something that an entire family must melodramatically overcome. This is so dissimilar to most other television shows that have same-sex marriage plots, in which the members of the entire family typically must all sob together about their tragic, socially outcast gay characters. In *Will & Grace*'s NYC, being in love, being monogamous, and wanting to get married is weirder than being a homosexual. Having an alternative family is so commonplace in *this* New York City that when characters outside of *Will & Grace*'s quartet view their family dynamic, they seem jealous of this bond (examples include millionaire socialite "pocket gay" Beverley Leslie [played by Leslie Jordan], or Will and Grace's unhappily married friends Rob and Ellen [played by Tom Gallop and Leigh-Allyn Baker]). Many viewers also envy their "alternative" family unit.

In the third season of *Will & Grace*, and before gay marriage was legal in the state of New York, Will, Grace, Jack, and Karen attend the civil union ceremony of their friends Joe and Larry (played by Jerry Levine and Tim Bagley). Here, when most of the guests assume that Grace is Will's wife, Will realizes that he spends far too much time with his lady friend and, more importantly (both for him and for viewer acknowledgement), that he wants what Joe and Larry have: a loving male-male relationship that all of their family members, friends, and onlookers (*Will & Grace's* viewers, in this meta-narrative case) unabashedly *accept*. The episode can be viewed as Will making this realization for himself about his own love life and personal shame about being gay, which cleverly transposes this realization of shame and prejudice onto the episode's viewers, too. By season three, many are so invested in these characters that, now, *they want Will to be that happy, too*. In terms of this same-sex couple's heteronormativity, Larry can be perceived as more "female" on-screen than is Joe, namely because he is more outspokenly dramatic than his "husband" and because his voice is a bit higher (again, stereotypes are necessary here for viewer identification). Ultimately, however, for these supporting characters, their gender does not matter when audience members watch their civil union ceremony. Joe and Larry adopt a baby soon after their ceremony, an act that Will also uses for personal realization about how much he wants his own traditional family in addition to his alternative urban one. And, again, *viewers want Will to be happy*. It took another five seasons for Will to find love, get married, have a baby through surrogacy, and freely reference his "in-laws," but it is rather telling—both for his character development and for viewer acceptance—that Will looked up to and envied the lives of this same-sex married couple for the duration of the series.

A Family of Interchangeable Heteronormative Couplings

During its eight-season run, the criticism against *Will & Grace*, from both popular media outlets and scholarly publications, focused primarily on the series' clichéd gayness or, in some cases, its absence of gayness. Some critics claimed that the show was offensively too gay (namely with regard to Jack's character) or offensively not gay *enough* (namely with regard to Will's character). Gay activist groups complained that Will was not living enough of a "gay lifestyle," that there was never any man-on-man sexual activity, that Will was too straight, and, especially, that the on-screen character pairings were so visually heteronormative that *Will & Grace* was not about gays at all, nor did it do anything to progress gay characters' positive and accurate representation on-screen. From a purely visual standpoint, this might be true, considering that if you tune in to an average episode, Will and Grace are often paired together, dealing with their dating and career woes, while Jack and Karen get themselves into hysterically over-the-top shenanigans, ones that oftentimes result in their practicing sexual gratification techniques on each other. During moments when the four characters all come together, you can certainly view them as the central protagonist "couple" (i.e., Will and Grace)—à la Ricky and Lucy Ricardo of *I Love Lucy* (1951–1957)—joining their supportive players (i.e., Jack and Karen)—their Fred and Ethel Mertz—for cocktails and ongoing bitchfests, most of which take place in Will's apartment (which is sometimes Grace's or sometimes Jack's home, too).

Most often throughout the series, Will, Grace, Jack, and Karen trade off scene partners in various storylines, giving them near-equal opportunity to affect each other, and near-equal opportunity to visually serve as rotating, gender-suggestive pairings. While I cannot deny that Will and Grace, and Jack and Karen, do spend quite a bit of time together, the series presents this more as a matter of its characters' personal tastes and social pleasures (in terms of whom they most enjoy spending their time with). Will and Grace love to chat about how ridiculous Jack and Karen are, while Jack and Karen genuinely enjoy poking fun at Will and Grace—so, we as the audience do, too. The personality traits of these four characters, however, would prohibit them from being together in different partnerships for very long. For example, Karen and Will jest about severely disliking each other for the duration of the series. As a result, it makes sense that the romantic-fantasist duo (Will and Grace) and the absurdist-fool duo (Jack and Karen) are heteronormatively paired up in storylines for viewers. Every time Jack and Grace spend much time together, they start bickering and run to Will to complain about each other. Alone, their friendship just does not work.

Consider as comparison: Monica Geller (Courteney Cox's character) and Joey Tribbiani (played by Matt LeBlanc) of *Friends* have hardly anything in common and simply would not make sense as stand-alone friends, so it is logical that they rarely (if ever) have a solely shared plotline. Likewise, on *Sex and the City*, Carrie Bradshaw (played by Sarah Jessica Parker) had her own GBFF (gay best friend forever), Stanford Blatch (played by Willie Garson), while Charlotte York (played by Kristin Davis) had her own preferred yet immensely different GBFF, Anthony Marantino (played by Mario Cantone). As per their writers' purposeful creation, these characters' personalities and their respective plotlines meshed, so it makes perfect sense that these women never traded GBFFs. They would hate them. Heteronormatively visually speaking, those pairings do not go together emotionally, socially, or logically. Ergo, why would Grace and Karen trade GBFFs when they clearly enjoy spending so much time with their own chosen GBFF? I am, of course, not suggesting that obtaining a GBFF as a fun new toy means that a woman's social life is stronger. Rather, I provide these examples in order to comment on the visual heteronormativity for which the show was so regularly criticized.

Will, Grace, Jack, and Karen trade partners quite often, actually, and whenever they do, regardless of what resulting genders the on-screen partnerships have (male and male, male and female, female and female), one scene partner always represents the masculine role while the other represents the feminine. Kooky Grace and cuckoo Karen typically represent the female roles in these heteronormative pairings—unless they are paired together. Whenever this happens, either Karen or Grace can be the "male," depending upon who is acting less crazy, which means that usually Grace is the male, as Karen is frequently drunk, high, or both. This is not always the case, however, because Karen must occasionally—and rather shockingly, which is when more laughs occur—be the sensible "man" in various ludicrous situations that Grace gets them into. Karen is also the "man" whenever money comes into play within these plots, which, in New York City storylines, it often does. Class, more so than gender, in *Will & Grace* seems to dictate who has the heteronormative power in each scene. For example, whenever Karen is buying Jack presents or controlling situations with her bottomless cash flow, she is the heteronormative "man" to giddy Jack, who flounces around in each scene like a schoolgirl, thanking her and telling her what other expensive possessions he desires. Will, in contrast, has his own money, so he has no need for Karen's manliness. Whenever Will is paired with Grace or Karen, he always remains the man, not because of visual gender identification or because Eric McCormack is, in fact, male in real life, but rather because Will's conservative, paternal behavior must repeatedly calm down these two lunatic women (or perhaps three, if you count Jack).

This also means that whenever Will and Jack are paired together on-screen—something that happens more as the series progresses, presumably as a result of all the complaints about the show never featuring two men together—Will is nearly always the "man." Will-the-patriarch also has money, while little-boy-Jack never does, thus further positioning Will as "the man." Hardly (if ever) on *Will & Grace* is there a non-heteronormative pairing on-screen because, behaviorally speaking, one partner in each pairing is always doing something a bit nutty and therefore automatically assumes the classic television female/wife role (see Edith Bunker of *All in the Family* [1971–1979], Samantha Stephens of *Bewitched* [1964–1972], Vivian Banks of *The Fresh Prince of Bel-Air* [1990–1996], Rachel Green of *Friends*, Jeannie of *I Dream of Jeannie* [1965–1970], Lucy Ricardo of *I Love Lucy*, Peg Bundy of *Married with Children* [1987–1997], Mindy Lahiri of *The Mindy Project,* Gloria Pritch-ett of *Modern Family,* Roseanne Conner of *Roseanne* [1988–1997], and Kitty Forman of *That '70s Show* [1998–2006]). This odd-couple pairing of sane husband/cuckoo wife is nothing new to television. Furthermore, a 1998 issue of *Entertainment Weekly* surmised that this odd-couple married pairing his-torically changed just prior to the turn of the millennium:

> Gay men and straight women are to the 1990s what Oscar and Felix were to the 1970s. They're certainly the dream odd couple for nervous networks. On one hand, there's enough gayness to grab some hipster cred and lots of Oscar Wilde-ish repartee. On the other, the straight gal keeps the scripts from drifting into Joe Six-pack alienating territory [qtd. in Tropiano 250].

While television's actual *Odd Couple* (1970–1975), Felix Unger (played by Tony Randall) and Oscar Madison (played by Jack Klugman), were both male, because *Will & Grace* is billed as a romantic-comedy sitcom, one in which the two characters agreeably *use* each other for companionship while looking for love in the big city, all oddly coupled pairings on the show must be viewed through a heteronormative lens. While this statement may not give viewers enough cognitive psychological credit to be able to switch back and forth between male-male, male-female, and female-female pairings (and therefore be okay with the disparity of these pairings), *Will & Grace* is *about* gay males and their female friends. The series frequently features bawdy, sex-ualized jokes that fly out of all four characters' dirty mouths, commentary that is so rooted and referenced in gay culture that heterosexual viewers run the risk of being appalled or, worse for long-term viewership, feeling isolated and incapable of understanding these jokes. About this frank sexuality, Evan Cooper suggests that

> *Will & Grace* makes the idea of a gay man with a real sexual life more palatable for future network series…. The appearance of the sexually explicit *Queer as Folk* on the pay cable network Showtime was made possible, in part, by the pop-ularly of *Will & Grace* [531].

While *Will & Grace* might shy away from male-male pairings in which both partners are definitively "male acting," it never shies away from witty banter about homosexual lifestyles, behaviors, and stereotypes.

Sociopolitical Responsibility: Too Gay Yet Not Gay Enough

Much of *Will & Grace*'s gay-reference-littered dialogue is delivered in crossfire between Will and Jack, the former of whom represents the average "everygay," while the latter represents the hyper-effeminate "faggy queen." In her critique of *Will & Grace*'s gay characters, Suzanna Danuta Walters states that

> Jack makes gays safe for middle America through his outrageousness, his snappy repartee. It might be easy to see Will as the perfectly integrated gay man (straight with a twist) and Jack as his opposite, the snap queen girlfriend who loves *la vida loca*.... Both are integrationist images (not that there's anything wrong with that). If Will is the perfectly integrated gay man through his recognizability to straights (like them and one of them), then Jack is also perfectly integrated through his recognizability as the charming, narcissistic, witty, flitty fag next door. Neither one of them seems to live in any political gay world [108–109].

Stated bluntly: Jack is there for heterosexual viewers—but not in a productive sociopolitical way that furthers gay representation, because that is why Will is there. While Walters' analysis accuses Will's character of being just as politically devoid as Jack's narcissistic dunce is, it is important to note that the careful construction of Will's character was an eight-year-long process. In addition, most of Will's political happenings on the show were emotional, psychological, and familial prejudices and misunderstandings, rather than Will protesting out in the streets like in-your-face Jack has no fear of doing.

Will is used as a sociopolitical vehicle for gay identity formation and self-acceptance more than for widespread public protests and grand-scale social issues. For example, when Will dates a straight-acting sports commentator who will not come out of the closet and even gay bashes homosexuals with his brutish boss, Will proudly announces that he is gay and leaves his date. Another example of this self-acceptance during Will's quest to find love is when his three-episode boyfriend James (played by Taye Diggs) asks Will to marry him so that he can obtain his green card, rather than being deported to Canada. In this same-sex marriage example, Will makes a last-minute realization that he still loves Vince (played by Bobby Cannavale), and wants to live happily ever after with Vince, so he turns down James' marriage offer. In an episode from the final season, Vince half-jokingly defines "traditional" marriage as "two men who live together and have a baby who looks nothing like either of them."

Jack McFarland is also not entirely devoid of any sociopolitical interest or urgency. Jack, like Will, in equally small doses of disguised social commentary, serves as a minor vehicle for *Will & Grace*'s producers to engage with current events, issues, and outcries within gay culture. Rodger Streitmatter notes that "as the series evolved, [it was] Jack [who] repeatedly stood tall against gay oppression" (148), while Evan Cooper writes, "Though Jack may be hailed as a subversive presence for his uninhibited sexuality, a key question is whether heterosexual audiences merely regard him as a slightly different version of the standard fool on many situation comedies" (520).

Both assertions about Jack's more-complex-than-it-seems character ring true. More so than fear-filled Will, lazy Grace, or intoxicated Karen, it is Jack who repeatedly gets riled up when he feels that a social injustice has been committed against him and/or his community. However, because his reputation on the show has long established him as the funny screaming queen, when Jack becomes impassioned, his sociopolitical rants are always costumed with his screeching voice and goofy shaking fist, thereby undermining his valid political platforms. Jack is *always* played for laughs.

Most critical research pertaining to *Will & Grace* focuses on the second-season episode "Acting Out," in which Jack convinces an unbothered Will to protest NBC by appearing in the live audience of *The Today Show* (1952–), after a highly publicized male-on-male kiss was cut from the episode that was supposed to air it. (This episode was actually *Will & Grace*'s tongue-in-cheek meta-response to criticisms about how its own gay characters similarly never show any physical affection.) "Acting Out" was not rare in its passive-aggressive handling of the show's criticism, considering that *Will & Grace* often tackled its complaints in the form of clever sociopolitically charged storylines rather than by its creators directly and discursively responding to critics and hecklers. This episode concluded with Jack screeching to *Today*'s Al Roker that it was unfair for NBC to have removed the male-on-male kiss, and then Will grabbing Jack and planting a huge, comically elongated smooch on Jack's lips for all of America to see live.

Thus, Will emerged the hero of this momentous (at the time) episode, but not necessarily as a *gay* hero; the kiss between friends was so unromantic, so nonsexual, and so played-for-laughs that it may as well have been any straight yet dutiful everyman smooching his gay friend's horrified lips to make an emotionless yet highly political statement. (The kiss was about as passionate, and about as sensually homosexual, as a man planting a kiss on his dog's lips, which, oftentimes, is how Will and Jack interact: Jack begs for money and toys, Will feeds Jack, etc.) About this now-famous gay on-screen kiss, Walters suggests that "Will's motivation to finally help Jack seems premised more on his friendship than on any stated political position. And this was [*Will & Grace*'s] one foray into the political arena, their one reckoning with institutional homophobia!" (109). Walters' assessment was published in 2001, when *Will & Grace* was only three years old and had another five seasons to go. Her quotation also exemplifies how quickly mainstream news critics and scholars alike attacked the series for its lack of a political agenda, thereby insinuating that its job was to change the world's opinion of gay rights and acceptance rather than to make its viewers laugh.

In his study of the series' gender stereotypes, Richard Conway states that Jack's character "poses little threat to masculinity; the more camp Jack is, the less camp normative masculinity is.... Unlike Will, Jack is constantly man-hungry and sexual" (80). Jack is *so* stereotypical and *so* proudly promis-cuous and *so* flamboyant and *so* over the top that he, of course, reinforces gay stereotypes for viewers, regardless of their sexual orientation. However, Jack's presence also allows heterosexual viewers to be *in* on all the gay jokes because they can *get* how incredibly gay Jack is. They can identify the stereo-types that he exemplifies and perpetuates and then (wrongfully) assume that they now know everything there is to know about the "gay lifestyle," an over-used term in *Will & Grace* criticism that is wholly problematic. While viewers can identify with super-duper-gay Jack (not identify themselves with, in most cases, but rather identify his archetype), the problem with Jack is that he is only *one* representation of a gay lifestyle, albeit the most stereotypical one.

Today, years after the series ended, it is amusing to consider the stylistic and fashion signifiers of Will, Jack, Grace, and Karen. As per gay clothing stereotypes, it is "straight man" Will who dresses in tightly ribbed muscle t-shirts, khakis that hug his gym-sculpted buttocks, pricey alligator loafers, and trendy leather jackets. At the same time, however, the colors of Will's attire are always dulled and subtle, communicating everyman-ness. Anna McCarthy notes, in her research about the visual gay culture signifiers on *Will & Grace*, that new gay characters on popular sitcoms are "on the air because, after *Will & Grace*, gayness is the most surefire ingredient for sitcom success. Or rather, as I hardly need to note, a particular kind of middle-class gay white man, ideally with a haircut like Will's" (97). Jack, in comparison, is always dressed in conservative Oxfords and sweater vests, typically wears unflattering light-washed denim jeans, and runs around the city in clunky sneakers. For the most flamboyant character on-screen, it is ironic now to see that Jack actually looks like a Midwestern tourist stuck in the big city. For any viewer who watched the series in its heyday but is now in his or her mid-thirties or older, it is nostalgically embarrassing to intentionally consider both Will's and Jack's late 1990s to early 2000s fashion choices.

In contrast, the straight women in the series dress far more flamboyantly than the gay men do. Karen wears so many furs, animal prints, feathers, and dominatrix getups that she practically looks like a drag queen at some point in each episode. When she is not festooned in these elaborate costumes, she wears conservative Jackie O/rich-lady businesswoman suits and pretty socialite dresses, thereby balancing out her circus attire. Grace, however, is chastised in nearly every episode—mostly by Karen, but also regularly by Jack and Will—for the clothing that she wears, which is so mismatched in color, so blindingly out of style, so culturally misguided, and/or so gaudy and garish that she seems to be dressed up in various alien-lady Halloween costumes. Visually speaking, in terms of costume design Jack is the most conservative and plain character, with Will coming in a close second.

In his analysis of *Will & Grace*'s heteronormativity, Denis Provencher compares these characters' family unit to another groundbreaking television family when he writes, "In a sense, *Will & Grace* attempts to present fresh and positive images of homosexuality and gay men in everyday situations, analogous to how *The Cosby Show* [1984–1992] normalized African Americans on television during the 1980s" (178). When Cliff Huxtable and his classy, sweater-wearing black family debuted, their program received complaints similar to those of *Will & Grace*'s critics. The Huxtables of *The Cosby Show* were viewed as being "too white" or "not an identifiable black family" (read: for white people) because they were successful, not put upon, and did not use race as a reason for victimhood or for the sole definition of their identities. They were wealthy, loving, and caring without succumbing to an abundance of black stereotypes. To white viewers, the Huxtables' lifestyle was *white*; so, after this facet was accepted by viewers, only then was *The Cosby Show*'s family allowed to "act black" on certain episodes that featured black history lessons, praised black entertainers, or explored sociopolitical issues that affected African Americans. Likewise, to heterosexual viewers, Will Truman (mostly) lives like a heterosexual so, once viewers are tricked by (and buy into) this idea, Will can "act gay" later in the series—just not as gay as Jack.

This conversely suggests that Will's "gay lifestyle"—being a klutzy, self-deprecating yet financially successful career lawyer who is also a romantic, longing for a monogamous relationship—is, initially, threatening to viewers because he is not readily identifiable as what viewers have (stereotypically) come to know to be "a gay." While Jack is the flighty "female" partner in his heteronormative scenes with Will, Will is just as much of a parental, collected "male" partner with Jack as he is when partnered in scenes with Grace or Karen.

Conway suggests that "Will's masculinity is rendered pseudo-heterosexual and his homosexuality transformed into a nominal joke. He can be just like everyone else and still be labeled homosexual" (78). Will's masculinity was, hopefully, not purposefully constructed to be laughed at, as this would imply that any gay man who is not just like Jack is not engaging in a "proper" gay lifestyle. Rather, Conway suggests that Will has a "pseudo" sexuality, and therefore a boring love life, in efforts to showcase how tacky and elaborate his friends' love lives are: "His sexuality becomes a harmless foible, a quirky characteristic that lands him in humorous situations, his sexual eccentricity a comedic analogue to Karen's postmaterialist superficiality or Grace's neurotic competitiveness" (78). Until he meets Vince, Will's dating life is bound by caricatures and silly types, yet types that are no less authentic than New York City offers anyone (viewers see these Manhattanite types regularly on *Sex and the City*, yet no one complained whenever Carrie and her girl gang met these circus freaks—they were feminists, while Will Truman's writers supposedly entrapped him in heteronormativity!). Will dates an elderly sugar daddy who wants to buy him cowboy apparel and art all of the time, a dancer from the musical *Cats* who is always stretching and jumping in public places, a codependent man who cares for his elderly mother and clearly has an Oedipal complex, Karen's bisexual pastry chef who is also sleeping with Karen and Rosario, and an obsessive-compulsive police detective, among other oddballs. In other words, Will as the "straight man" dates weirdoes who are as strange as his own friends.

As such, it is no coincidence that Will's marriage to Vince is unquestionably the healthiest of the four main characters' long-term relationships. Karen has been married four times, purely for money—which she is perfectly okay with. Grace's husband, Leo, cheats on her, leaves her for another woman, moves across the world, and does not even know she is pregnant with his baby—yet she still takes him back in the end. Jack's longest relationship, with Stuart, lasts only a few months—until promiscuous Jack cheats on him. In contrast, Will and Vince break up a first time because Vince is depressed about his unemployment and needs time to collect himself; neither partner commits crimes of infidelity, dishonesty, or anything else. The worst problem they face together, which causes them to break up a second time, emerges when Will admits that he places importance on Grace above anyone else, including himself, which then makes him realize what a terrible issue this has been for him his entire life. In other words, Will's realization that his engagement in heteronormativity, in relation to his own life's stagnancy as well as viewers' understanding of his character, is another meta-plot technique that is cleverly disguised to make viewers feel empathy for Will: he *had to* act heteronormatively in his life with Grace, and for viewers, so that audience members could also participate in his character's cathartic reformation. Will's awakening allows him to get Vince back, marry him, have a child with him, and live happily ever after without television's conventional heteronormativity. By this point in the series, viewers already know Will as the straight man; the father; the homosexual who lives his life similarly to how heterosexuals do (which we also now know is not a requirement but a choice, a lifestyle that Will genuinely wants for himself). By now, to viewers, Will is "no different than straight people." Accordingly, he cannot be the flighty "woman" character in his marriage. Nor can Vince, though, as Vince is a rough-and-tumble, manly Italian police officer whom, although a sweet teddy bear at heart, no viewer would want to run into in a dark Manhattan alley. They are just two regular dudes in a loving marriage, without a woman necessary for their happiness.

It is also fitting that the series' final moment features a middle-aged Will, a middle-aged Grace, a middle-aged Jack, and Karen (thanks to "touch-ups," plus her materialistic eternal soul, she never ages, despite the eighteen years that have gone by) meeting up in a nondescript Manhattan bar. When the four hold up their glasses, Will toasts "To family," and they all clink happily. Although Will and Grace now have their own traditional/"traditional" families back at home with their own respective husbands, viewers know that the family they are toasting here is the proud urban one they have assembled over the years, one that features a "Truman" in love with another "true-man," and that is just fine by us.

Works Cited

Becker, Ron. *Gay TV and Straight America*. New Brunswick: Rutgers University Press, 2006. Print.

Conway, Richard J. "A Trip to the Queer Circus: Reimagined Masculinities in *Will & Grace*." *The New Queer Aesthetic on Television*. Ed. James R. Keller and Leslie Stratyner. Jefferson, NC: McFarland, 2006. 75–84. Print.

Cooper, Evan. "Decoding *Will & Grace*: Mass Audience Reception of a Popular Network Situation Comedy." *Sociological Perspectives* 46.4 (2003): 513–533. Print.

Kondolojy, Amanda. "Wednesday Final Ratings: 'Survivor,' 'The Middle,' and 'Modern Family' Adjusted Up; 'Survivor' Reunion Adjusted Down." *TV by the Numbers*. Zap 2 It, 22 May 2014. Web. 12 January 2015.

McCarthy, Anna. "Crab People from the Center of the Earth." *GLQ: A Journal of Lesbian and Gay Studies* 11.1 (2005): 97–101. Print.

Provencher, Denis M. "Sealed with a Kiss: Heteronormative Narrative Strategies in NBC's *Will & Grace*." *The Sitcom Reader: America Viewed and Skewed*. Ed. Mary M. Dalton and Laura R. Linder. Albany: State University of New York Press, 2005. 177–190. Print.

"'Roseanne' Adult Humor Forces Change." *Washington Post*, 11 December 1995. Web. 12 January 2015.

Streitmatter, Rodger. *Sex Sells! The Media's Journey from Repression to Obsession*. Boulder: Westview Press, 2004. Print.

Tropiano, Stephen. *The Prime Time Closet: A History of Gays and Lesbians on TV*. New York: Applause Theatre and Cinema Books, 2002. Print.

Ulin, Jeffrey C. *The Business of Media Distribution: Monetizing Film, TV, and Video Content in an Online World*, 2d ed. Burlington, MA: Focal Press, 2014. Print.

Walters, Suzanna Danuta. *All the Rage: The Story of Gay Visibility in America*. Chicago: University of Chicago Press, 2001. Print.

"Weekly Program Ratings." *ABC Medianet*. ABC, 13 May 2008. Web. 12 January 2015.

Skeletons in the Closet

The Contradictory Views of the Queer
in the Works of Joss Whedon

DON TRESCA

The scene opens with two beautiful, young women in a bedroom. They are getting dressed, beaming lovingly at each other. As one, a petite redhead, pulls on a white blouse, she says to the other, a willowy blonde, "Hey, clothes," to which the other woman responds, "Don't get too used to them." They share an intimate moment, an embrace, a kiss. As they pull away and face one another, preparing for a lifetime of bliss and love, a window cracks with a sharp tinking sound. Suddenly, the crisp white blouse is spattered with blood. The blonde woman stares at her lover uncomprehendingly. "Your blouse..." is all she manages to say before she collapses dead at the other woman's feet, the victim of a stray bullet meant for another.

Thus ends the romance of Willow and Tara. For two-and-a-half seasons on the WB/UPN hit series *Buffy the Vampire Slayer* (1997–2003), they were the longest-lasting, most realistically depicted lesbian couple in the history of network television. The LGBT community had showered series creator Joss Whedon and his writing staff with numerous accolades for the portrayal of the Willow–Tara relationship, and the actresses who played Willow and Tara (Alyson Hannigan and Amber Benson) became superstars within that same community for their sensitive and loving performances. All of that changed in an instant when a random gunshot fired by Warren Meers (played by Adam Busch) pierced Tara's heart and plunged Willow into a chaotic state of vengeance and dark magic.

It was a dramatic and suspenseful piece of television storytelling, but the backlash that Whedon and his colleagues experienced as a result from the LGBT community was unlike anything that had ever been seen before. The writers and producers who previously had been praised beyond reckoning were now reviled and endlessly criticized in the press, in academic circles, and, perhaps most importantly, in online blogs. Although these critical discussions focused almost exclusively on the dark outcome of the Willow–Tara relationship, what is clear is that decision was only one in a long line of story decisions by Whedon and his staff that have sent a decidedly mixed message about homosexuality within the "Whedonverse," the collective name of the various properties created by Joss Whedon (which include, in addition to *Buffy the Vampire Slayer*, *Angel* [1999–2004], *Firefly/Serenity* [2002–2003/ 2005], *Dr. Horrible's Sing-Along Blog* [2008], and *Dollhouse* [2009–2010]).

Incorporating Homosexuality in the Whedonverse

Before discussing the controversy surrounding Willow and Tara, let us first go back and look at some of the earlier incarnations of homosexuality within the Whedonverse. The first openly gay character in the Whedonverse was Larry Blaisdell (played by Larry Bagby), who initially appeared in the second-season *Buffy* episode "Phases." When viewers are introduced to Larry, he comes across as a stereotypical sexist, high school jock who hangs out with his friends ogling girls and bullying the meeker kids. When Buffy (played by Sarah Michelle Gellar) and her "Scooby Gang" (made up of her best friends, Willow and Xander [played by Nicholas Brendon], and her Watcher/ mentor/school librarian, Giles [played by Anthony Head]) begin to suspect that a werewolf is stalking residents of their town of Sunnydale, Xander spots Larry with a bandage on his arm (courtesy, Larry claims, of a dog attack) and comes to believe that Larry is the werewolf. Xander decides to confront Larry with his suspicions and gets a big surprise: the secret Larry has been hiding is not that he is a werewolf but rather that he is gay. As the scene plays out, it juxtaposes the empowerment of Larry (as he is finally able to come out of the closet to another person) and the discomfort of Xander when the latter realizes that not only has he inadvertently "outed" Larry, but Larry believes Xander, too, is gay (because he told Larry that "I know what you're going through because I've been there").

Larry then vanishes from the show and does not appear again for another sixteen episodes. His next appearance, however, is rather extraordinary. In the third-season episode "The Wish," viewers are given a glimpse into what Sunnydale would have been like if Buffy had never come to town, in the form of a wish-generated, alternate-reality Sunnydale. Among other events differing in the new reality, Buffy's season-one nemesis, The Master (played by Mark Metcalf), has succeeded in his plan to take over the town and has transformed Buffy's two most important allies, Willow and Xander, into vampires. Giles continues to fight the good fight with the help of a trio of "white hats," one of whom is Larry. Although Larry's sexual orientation is never explicitly mentioned in this episode, the fact that Whedon and his staff (in this case, writer Marti Noxon) chose to make the homosexual Larry a member of the good guys' team suggests that, in contrast to the dominant approach prevalent in most films and television programs of portraying the homosexual as deviant and evil, they intentionally made the homosexual a hero, a positive image for public consumption (Booth).

That positive image is mitigated somewhat during Larry's next appearance, in the third-season episode "Earshot." In this episode, Buffy gains the ability to telepathically hear the thoughts of others and discovers that someone in her school is planning a Columbine-style massacre. She enlists the help of the Scooby Gang to figure out exactly which member of the student body she psychically "overheard" making the threat. The first person Xander chooses to interview is Larry, believing that his secret of being gay is "frustrating [and] filling [Larry] up with resentment, unexpressed rage waiting to burst out," only to learn that Larry is not only thoroughly comfortable with his newfound sexual identity, but also that he is "out" to the extent that "I got my grandma fixing me up with guys." Xander's immediate suspicion that Larry is the source of the threat suggests his own homophobic tendencies (no doubt fueled by his geeky fascination with pop cultural products such as movies and television shows) to equate homosexuality with "monstrosity" and "evilness" (McAvan, par. 19). The scene also reiterates Larry's belief that Xander, too, is gay. Xander's discomfort at being labeled "gay" is clearly played here for laughs. Although he makes no direct attempt to correct Larry's perception of his sexuality, Xander is clearly unnerved at the idea of being "outed" and having his heterosexuality and/or masculinity called into question. A similar situation occurs earlier, in the fourth episode of season three, "Beauty and the Beasts," in which Xander assumes the task from Willow of watching over Oz (played by Seth Green), her werewolf boyfriend who has locked himself in the library cage overnight to keep from harming others. Willow tells Xander that she has put up a towel to ensure Oz's privacy, because he is nude when he transforms back into human form. To this, Xander casually responds, "No worries. I can handle the Oz full monty." Then, realizing the double entendre he has inadvertently uttered, Xander becomes nervous and panicky, quickly responding with, "I mean … not 'handle' … like 'hands to flesh' handle." Clearly, at this point in his development, Xander is highly uncomfortable with giving anyone the opportunity to question his masculinity or sexual proclivities.

Larry's final appearance in the series occurs during the third-season finale episode, "Graduation Day: Part Two," in which his character is brutally killed by the local mayor (played by Harry Groener), who has transformed into a giant demon. This appearance dovetails nicely with Tara given the fact that both characters—the two most blatantly gay characters in the first six seasons of the show—are killed without any chance of redemption or a happy life, which, as Scott Matthewman notes, "sends a terrible message to the audience ... sex is bad, but gay sex is worse" (par. 17).

In later seasons, Xander, perhaps as a result of his experiences with Larry and his friendship with Willow, becomes more comfortable with his own sexual identity. Although his romances with Cordelia (played by Charisma Carpenter) in seasons two and three, Anya (played by Emma Caulfield) in seasons three through six, and Renee and Dawn (in the season-eight series of comic books that continued the story after the television series went off the air) code him as strictly heterosexual, he has no qualms about making comments (albeit jokingly) about his own sexual orientation. In the fourth-season episode "Goodbye Iowa," for example, after his first glimpse of the Initiative (of which Buffy's current boyfriend, Riley Finn [played by Marc Blucas], is a member) military base below UC Sunnydale, an awestruck Xander tells Buffy, "I totally get it now. Can I have sex with Riley, too?" Later, in the sixth-season episode "As You Were," Xander's fiancée, Anya, upset by his constant talk about Riley and Riley's marriage to his new wife, Sam (played by Ivana Milicevic), tells Xander, "You know, if you love Riley Finn so much, maybe you should marry him." To this, Xander responds, "He's taken," which is not so much a denial of his "love" for Riley as it is a statement about Riley's lack of availability as a potential love interest. In the fourth-season episode "Superstar," both Xander and Anya clearly become sexually aroused while watching Jonathan Levinson (played by Danny Strong), their former high school classmate who has used magic to transform himself from a loser into the most powerful and respected man in Sunnydale, during a musical performance at the local nightclub The Bronze. Both cannot take their eyes off of him as they head toward the exit to have sex. And then, in the episode "First Date" during the series' final season on television, Xander becomes exasperated by his inability to find a normal girl while he attracts only female monsters and demons. As a result, he decides he is going to be gay and demands to Willow: "Gay me up.... Tell me what to do.... Let's get this gay show on the gay road. Help me out here!"

Xander is clearly not the only character who notices his occasional lapses into a more queer sexual identity. The fifth-season episode "Intervention" contains a scene in which Xander waxes eloquent on the physical characteristics of Spike (played by James Marsters), a vampire who serves as an occasional ally to the Scoobies and harbors a secret romantic infatuation for Buffy. Xander and Anya have spotted Spike having sex with whom they believe is Buffy (in reality, it is a sex robot created to be a perfect replica of Buffy). When Xander confronts Buffy about the liaison, he tells her, "No one is judging you. It's understandable. Spike is strong and mysterious and sort of compact but well-muscled...." His detail is such that Buffy responds with, "I am not having sex with Spike, but I'm starting to think you are." In the seventh-season episode "Beneath You," Xander shares an embarrassed (and somewhat guilty) look with Spike in response to a question posed by Nancy (played by Kaarina Aufranc): "Are there any of you who haven't slept with each other?"[1] Like Xander's own self-deprecating comments about his sexual orientation, such scenes are meant to serve primarily as sources of humor (as well as to whet the appetites of the members of the viewing audience who engage in slash, a genre of fanfiction in which two same-sex characters in a popular film or television series are shown to be involved in a homosexual relationship).

The use of homosexuality as a source of humor is a double-edged sword, however. Frequently, it can be used to accentuate a character's comfort or discomfort with his or her sexual identity (as is the case with Xander, as detailed previously) or to reveal a character's hidden sexual desires. One character in *Buffy* who uses humor to reveal his hidden sexual identity is Andrew Wells (played by Tom Lenk). Andrew was introduced during the show's sixth season as a member of the Trio, a group of geeks composed of Andrew, Jonathan, and Warren who imagine themselves as supervillains and wish to use their powers (Andrew's demon summoning, Jonathan's magic, and Warren's technology) to defeat Buffy and take over Sunnydale. Although initially Andrew (along with the rest of the Trio) is coded as heterosexual (for example, he and the others are excited that their new status as conquering supervillains will allow them access to "naked women" and "free cable porn" and that the Cerebral Dampener that Warren has invented will allow them to make any woman their willing sex slave), by the end of the season his sexual orientation becomes muddled and fluid. In the sixth-season episode "Entropy," the Trio catches Anya and Spike on a secret camera having sex. In response, Andrew states, "He is so cool," but then, realizing that he has just made an inadvertent slip, he adds, "And, I mean, the girl is hot, too." In "Seeing Red," Andrew's queer desires for Warren ("Man, I can't wait to get my hands on his orbs") manifest so strongly that he is genuinely crushed when Warren abandons him and Jonathan to police custody in order to pursue vengeance against Buffy: "How could he do that to me? He promised we'd be together. He was just using me. He never really loved—[realizing that Jonathan is listening to his rant]—hanging out with us." By season seven, when he has chosen to seek redemption and joins Buffy's Scooby Gang in their fight against the First Evil, Andrew's queer desires are completely front and center. In "Storyteller," the writers jokingly refer to Andrew's homosexuality in a scene during which he is filming the interior of Buffy's house, which the Scooby Gang is using as a headquarters. As Willow and her new girlfriend, Kennedy (played by Iyari Limon), engage in kissing and heavy petting on the couch in front of him, Andrew narrates to his unseen audience, "There's something here I think you're going to be interested in, gentle viewers," but then, rather than focusing on Willow and Kennedy as most typical heterosexual males would, Andrew chooses instead to focus on the window, commenting, "Look at the fine work Xander did on replacing the window sash. It's undetectable!" Clearly, Andrew is much more interested in the home design (and Xander's contributions to it) than he is in the sexualized female scene playing out before him.

Humor can also be used at times to expose a character's overt or hidden homophobia. Most of the major characters in the Whedonverse appear, a majority of the time, to be very accepting of homosexual relationships; however, homophobia does inevitably creep into even the seemingly most sympathetic of characters. In the fifth-season episode "Real Me," Buffy's mother, Joyce (played by Kristine Sutherland), reveals some homophobic tendencies after Buffy's little sister, Dawn (played by Michelle Trachtenberg), tells her, "I wish they'd teach me some of the things they do together" (actually referring to Willow and Tara's use of magic); in response, Dawn says that Joyce "got really quiet and made me go upstairs." In the sixth-season episode "Gone," when a social worker discovers that Willow is living with Buffy and Dawn, Buffy is very quick to make it clear that the relationship is not romantic: "It's not a gay thing. Well, she's gay. But we don't … gay." Buffy's reaction here is one of almost instantaneous homophobia, for she believes that even the slightest appearance of a queer relationship between herself and Willow will cast her in a negative light.[2] As well, Cordelia, a former member of the Scooby Gang who relocates to Los Angeles to join Buffy's former vampire love, Angel (played by David Boreanaz), in his quest to assist the helpless and gain redemption, has her own moment of homophobia in a second-season episode of *Angel*, "Disharmony." During a conversation with Willow about Harmony (played by Mercedes McNab), Cordelia's former best friend who was transformed into a vampire on graduation day, Cordelia says, "Oh, Harmony is a vampire? … All this time I thought she was a great big lesbo!" This offensive statement is immediately followed by contrition when Cordelia discovers that Willow is now a lesbian: "Oh, yeah? Really? Well, that's great! Good for you!"

Humor in television series such as *Buffy* and *Angel* is a necessity, for it breaks up the dark tension and introduces a level of camp that is essential in shows about teenagers and young adults battling demons and vampires on the sunny streets of Southern California. However, including jokes about homosexuality (hypothetical or not) is problematic. Ridiculing an individual's sexual orientation is a relatively safe and easy source of humor. Jokes about turning gay (or being "gayed up," to use Xander's words) are funny to straight audiences, for whom being gay is typically funny. But for many gay men and lesbians, especially

for those whose living space is threatened by legislated homophobic violence, for those who are looking for representations of themselves in popular television and finding nothing, and for those who look up to *Buffy* [and/or *Angel*] as a show that rhetoricizes tolerance and inclusion, these ironic asides can appear patronizing at best, and insulting at worst [Battis 54].

Humor at the expense of members of other minority groups (such as racial or religious groups) is not tolerated in nearly the same way, and the differences are clearly delineated even within the Whedonverse. Andrew's attempts to "pass" as straight and to remain closeted are a source of a great deal of *Buffy*'s humor in the latter part of season six and throughout season seven; in contrast, Judy Kovacs (played by Melissa Marsala), an African American character attempting to "pass" as Caucasian in the second-season *Angel* episode "Are You Now or Have You Ever Been?" is portrayed as a serious character with virtually no humor leveled at her situation. Certainly, while there are some who would argue that *Buffy* and *Angel* are in many ways comedy series that use humor to deflate all of their characters (including gay or hypothetically gay ones) equally, the plight of gay characters in other comedy–drama series do not typically suffer as sharply from targeted humor. The television series *Glee* (2009–2015), for example, which is generally regarded by critics and fans as a musical comedy, featured the plights of both out (Kurt, Blaine) and closeted (Santana, Brittany) gay characters without resorting to such easy humor at the characters' expense.

Another character whose theoretical homosexuality is a source of humor, but of a slightly different bent, is Angel, the heroic vampire with a soul. While Angel is coded as heterosexual through his relationships with a wide variety of characters (including Buffy, Cordelia, the vampires Darla and Drusilla [played by Julie Benz and Juliet Landau], and the werewolf Nina [played by Jenny Mollen]), Paul Shapiro, in his quantitative analysis of the vampire biting patterns in *Buffy*, reveals that Angel "is much more likely to engage in homosexual biting behaviors" than is Spike, the only other major vampire character in the show, despite the fact that "Spike is often considered the less masculine, less heterosexual, of the two vampires" (par. 23). The Angel–Spike relationship is rife with homoerotic undertones. In the fifth-season *Angel* episode "Destiny," the audience is treated to a scene between Angelus (Angel's former evil alter ego) and the newly sired Spike during which Angelus thrusts his hand into the sunlight and watches it burn as he tells Spike, "I do love the ladies. It's just lately I've been wondering what it'd be like to share the slaughter of innocents with another man. Don't think that makes me some kind of a deviant, hmm? Do you?" The irony here is that Angelus is equating deviance with his homoerotic desire to be with another man while his true deviance is what he wants to do with that man: not to engage in sexual activity but rather to slaughter innocent people. In fact, the only reference to any kind of sexual contact between Angel(us) and Spike is in the second-to-last season-five *Angel* episode, "Power Play"—the penultimate episode of the series—when Spike tells Illyria (played by Amy Acker), "Angel and me have never been intimate. Except that one [time]...." The one time is left deliberately vague and may even reference their exchange from "Destiny" (detailed earlier), but Spike's comment does indicate that he, at the very least, acknowledges a queer connection with Angel even if Angel does not acknowledge it. For his part, Angel himself is deeply homophobic, a remarkable flaw evident in the main hero of a series created and written by individuals who claim to have no homophobic agenda in their shows. Early in the *Angel* series, Angel's homophobia was not apparent, and he seemed in fact to have no problem with homosexuality at all. While he is clearly uncomfortable and somewhat irritated in the series' first episode, "City of...," when a talent agent gives him his business card and tells him, "Call me. This isn't a come-on. I'm in a very serious relationship with a landscape architect," he does not seek to correct the man about his sexual orientation or respond in any sort of angry or violent way. Nor does he seem anything but slightly exasperated when a man in a singles bar that he is investigating in the series' second episode, "Lonely Heart," walks away from him as Angel assures him, "No, seriously, I wasn't hitting on you!" And he does not appear to be upset at all when Cordelia's friends refer to him and his associate, Wesley (played by Alexis Denisof), as gay in the first-season episode "Expecting," telling Wesley that it "adds mystery."

All of this changes, however, in later episodes. Beginning in the first episode of season two, "Judgment," viewers get an indication of Angel's homophobia when Angel considers joining a gym until Cordelia reminds him, "You shower with a lot of men." Angel is further taken aback later in season two, in the episode "Belonging," when Lorne (played by Andy Hallett), a male telepathic demon who serves as the host of a demon karaoke bar named Caritas, asks him out on a date to an Elton John concert, where they can sit in "back-row seats." Despite Angel's insistence that he does not "do big and crowded," it is clear that his discomfort stems from the knowledge that he has just been asked out on a date by another man. Later, in the third-season episode "Couplet," Angel must accompany Groosalugg (played by Mark Lutz), a warrior from another dimension whom Cordelia has been dating, to a demon brothel in order to obtain a potion that will enable Cordelia and Groosalugg to have sex without Cordelia losing her psychic visions of people in danger as a result. When Anita (played by Fanshen Cox), the demon madam of the brothel, sees Angel and Groosalugg wearing matching outfits (thanks to Cordelia choosing to raid Angel's closet for suitable clothing for Groosalugg to wear), she assumes they are "together," suggesting a potential sexual relationship. Angel very quickly and vehemently points out that he and Groosalugg are "not 'together' together. Just 'get the potion' together." When Groosalugg tells Anita that he wants the potion to "com-shuck [have sex with] my princess," Angel feels the need to reiterate that he is most definitely "*not* the princess." Finally, in the series' final season on television, in the episode "Just Rewards," Spike introduces himself to the necromancer Magnus Hainsley (played by Victor Raider-Wexler) as Angel's "date," which causes Angel to roll his eyes in annoyance and frustration. Whedon's decision to increase Angel's homophobia (or, at the very least, his distaste and discomfort over being mistaken as homosexual) as this series progressed indicates a likely desire to show that an individual can be uncomfortable with homosexuality and still be a good person—a world-saving hero, in fact. It is important to note that the beginnings of Angel's behavioral change in this regard took place during the same television season (2000–2001) when the decision was made to kill Tara's character at the end of the following television season (2001–2002).[3] Such a coincidence is unlikely. It is entirely possible that Whedon and his writers anticipated the outrage that would erupt at the end of *Buffy*'s sixth season and sought to mitigate it in some way through the use of Angel's mild (though apparent) homophobia. Regardless, its presence indicates a remarkable shift away from the "gay-friendly" storytelling apparent on *Angel*'s sister show, *Buffy*.

Which brings us back to the controversial decision by Whedon and his writing staff to kill off Tara, one-half of the most endearing and longest-lasting lesbian couples in the history of U.S. television, which ended up sending the other half of that couple, Willow, into a dark chasm of vengeance, murder, and dark magic. At the start of their relationship (which began "officially" at the end of the season-four episode "New Moon Rising," although Tara had been in the series as Willow's Wicca friend since "Hush," nine episodes earlier), both fans and critics alike were convinced that the decision to make Willow gay was nothing more than a ratings stunt. However, Whedon denied this and made it quite clear that the decision was an organic one, designed to further develop Willow's character (Gunther 79; Whedon, "At the Bronze"). Whedon had always intended for one of his main characters, either Willow or Xander, to be revealed as gay ("Willow or Xander" 1). He set up foreshadowing for both characters (e.g., Willow's revelation in *Buffy*'s third-season episode "Dopplegangland" that Vamp Willow is "kinda gay"; Xander's conversations with Larry in *Buffy*'s second-season episode "Phases" and third-season episode "Earshot" in which his sexuality is questioned). However, the decision as to which character would end up pursuing a gay storyline was made for him when Seth Green, the actor playing Oz, decided to leave the series midway through *Buffy*'s fourth season. "I really think what we're doing with Willow and Tara is interesting," Whedon expressed in a 2000 radio interview. "That might not have happened if we hadn't lost Seth" (Whedon, "Interview"). He continued:

We had to do something with Willow, and it seemed like a good time for her to be exploring [her sexuality]. Then the question just became how much do we play in metaphor and how much do we play as her actually expanding her sexuality? And you're walking a very fine line there. The network obviously has issues [Whedon, "Interview"].

Willow's coming out and beginning a relationship with Tara were celebrated by many. Scott Seomin, the entertainment media director for the Gay and Lesbian Alliance Against Defamation (GLAAD), stated that the relationship would be highly beneficial toward gay and lesbian partners gaining acceptance in the real world: "These representations can educate potential gay bashers. If Willow is lesbian and all the characters accept her, maybe the straight viewers will accept the lesbian sitting next to them in homeroom" (qtd. in Rice).

Initially, Whedon and his staff took the responsibility of presenting a balanced lesbian relationship very seriously. They basked in the glory of their success with the story arc (e.g., receiving numerous GLAAD media awards and Whedon being presented with an engraved toaster, a reference to the coming-out episode of *Ellen* [1994–1998], which contained a running joke about the LGBT movement awarding every newly out individual a toaster for "joining") but also received criticism from certain elements of the LGBT community for not making the couple "gay enough." This concept was one that was explored more fully by various scholars who argued that, by denying Willow and Tara the same kind of visible romantic subplot that the series had provided to Buffy and her various lovers and by couching Willow and Tara's romance in metaphoric rather than literal terms, Whedon and his writers were rendering Willow's and Tara's lesbianism invisible and "un-depictable" (Beirne). Farah Mendlesohn argues that this invisibility actually undoes all of the work Whedon and his writers put into establishing Willow's new sexual identity, "first by neutralizing her sexuality and then by rechanneling thoughts of lesbian relationships in a safe direction" (59). Granted, the decision to reduce the visibility of Willow and Tara's relationship was largely out of Whedon's hands; he was constrained by the standards and practices demands of the network (Whedon, "Interview"). However, the decision to couch their relationship in the metaphor of witchcraft and magic was entirely Whedon's idea, and it generated a whole new set of problems in and of itself. By aligning Willow's and Tara's lesbianism with witchcraft, Whedon and his writers remove their experiences as lesbians from the realm of everyday life and move them into the realm of the mysterious and the supernatural. This "positions lesbian desire and sexuality as mysteries that can only be represented as magic.... It leaves a large space for reading this desire as being unnatural, frightening, and potentially evil" (Bartlem), especially when it is contrasted with the more physical and natural views of heterosexuality in the series.

This "potential evil" of lesbianism progresses into *Buffy*'s sixth season, as Willow begins her descent into magic addiction. She starts to use magic for more nefarious purposes, including altering Tara's memories (in the episodes "All the Way" and "Tabula Rasa"), which summons images in the minds of viewers of lesbians as "manipulative and obsessive; they can and will use their 'unnatural' influence on anyone that will not bend to their will" (Wilts 49). This dark addiction, which many critics and viewers equate with drug addiction (see, for example, Bartlem; Latham, par. 15; Ryan 65; Tresca 163), can also be viewed as a fixation or obsession with her "excessive [and] perverse" sexuality (McAvan, par. 19).

This "perversion" thus moves both Willow and Tara into the clichéd realm of what is known as the "dead/evil lesbian." This cliché relates to the tendency in most novels, films, and television shows that portray lesbian relationships to eventually have one of the lesbians end up dead (usually right after a scene in which the couple has sex) and the other driven into madness (Booth).[4] This cliché is considered to be one of the most homophobic because it communicates that lesbians "can never find happiness and always meet tragic ends" (Booth). The LGBT audience was given numerous assurances by *Buffy*'s writers that things would be different, including Doug Petrie's comment in the February 21, 2000, issue of *Sci-Fi Universe* that

> we definitely don't want to touch on "being a lesbian is bad." We've all seen shows where if you have any kind of gay tendencies, you must be killed or made to suffer for no other reason than you're gay. We're hyperaware of that, so we're more predisposed to have things work out for Willow and Tara [qtd. in Booth].

Nevertheless, "they did it anyway" (Booth). Tara is murdered immediately in the aftermath of the first intimate sex scene between the pair in the episode "Seeing Red," and Willow is driven into a violent, murderous, dark-magic-induced rage that culminates in her brutal murder of Warren and her near destruction of the world. What is worse for many members of the LGBT community is that Willow is pulled from the brink of her destructive madness by an admission of love from a man, Xander, which suggests that all lesbians need to save themselves is the love of a good man.

Exploring Gay and Lesbian Issues in the Post-Tara Era

Whedon and his writers seem to have learned their lesson about dealing with gay and lesbian issues in their post–Tara work. Whedon's next television series, *Firefly*, debuted in September 2002, just months after the furor over Tara's death began (with the broadcast of "Seeing Red" in May 2002). Set in the far future and concerning a band of anti-heroic space pirates, *Firefly* features very little in the way of queer subtext. The only overt example occurs in the episode "War Stories," in which the companion/prostitute Inara (played by Morena Baccarin) "entertains" a female client, The Councillor (played by Katherine Kendall). The scene unfolds beautifully, with Inara and The Councillor agreeing that their encounter need not be filled with playacting and artificiality because "one cannot always be oneself in the company of men," suggesting a natural and honest bond between women that does not exist between women and men. But even in this more positive portrayal of a sexual relationship between women, Whedon cannot help but indulge in what Jonathan Last calls his penchant for "pornographic humor." Jayne Cobb (played by Adam Baldwin), the ultra-masculine mercenary, upon witnessing Inara and The Councillor together, is clearly sexually aroused by the prospect of two women being intimate and tells the rest of the crew, "I'll be in my bunk," thereby countering the positive aspect of the women's encounter with a reaction of male prurient interest.[5]

Another of Whedon's subsequent television series, *Dollhouse*, featured no overtly gay or lesbian characters or content, despite the claim by Eliza Dushku (the star of the series) that in the show's second season there would "definitely be some storylines following gay and lesbian characters" (Schwartz).[6] The series was cancelled by the Fox television network before such storylines could be implemented.

Whedon's Internet miniseries *Dr. Horrible's Sing-Along Blog* includes some queer subtext in its merging of the hypermasculine genre of the superhero movie with the queer aesthetics of musical theater, a threat of homosexual rape,[7] and a movement of the character Dr. Horrible (played by Neil Patrick Harris) from effeminate to masculine as well as a reverse movement of the character Captain Hammer (played by Nathan Fillion), Horrible's archnemesis, from masculine to effeminate (276–287). Nevertheless, the homosexual subtext was deeply layered within the foundation of the miniseries and secondary to the more gender- and genre-busting concerns.

One thing that both camps—those who find Whedon's view of homosexuality to be largely positive and those who regard his view as being largely negative—agree on, however, is that Whedon and his writers are, at heart, not deliberately homophobic (Booth; Black, "It's Not Homophobia"). Each side maintains that a homophobic group of writers would never have been able to produce the loving and caring relationship of Willow and Tara in the first place. But ultimately, all pop cultural products, whether they be music, movies, or television programs, are subject to cultural factors. The reality that homophobic imagery can rear its ugly head even when the producers of the text have nothing but the best intentions merely shows how ingrained such beliefs have become within our culture. Until we can rid ourselves of the notion that homosexual love is somehow humorous, prurient, and/or alien (from the type of love that heterosexuals share), we will never be entirely rid of these inadvertently homophobic images that pop up in our entertainment media. Only when each person in the media and in real life is able to fully and honestly love whomever he or she wants, without fear of mockery or cliché, will we truly feel free to celebrate.

NOTES

1. The shooting script states that Spike and Xander "barely glance at one another," but the actors in the scene, James Marsters and Nicholas Brendon, clearly signal that there is more to the glance than viewers are told in the scene.

2. Buffy has a very similar homophobic-style reaction in the season-eight comic book *Wolves at the Gate* in relation to her "experimental" lesbian relationship with Satsu, a fellow Slayer. She immediately requests that Satsu not mention their sexual encounter to anyone. The next panel shows Buffy entirely boxed in, trapped within this situation and trying to figure her way out (Call, "Slaying" 113), assuring Satsu that she is not "ashamed or anything" (Goddard 40).

3. In a July 27, 2002, appearance at the Toronto Trek convention, Amber Benson stated, "I knew [about Tara's impending death] like in the middle—pretty much the middle to the end of season five—that it was going to happen. In fact, Joss was really excited about it" (qtd. in Black, "Message").

4. Examples include Radclyffe Hall's 1928 novel *The Well of Loneliness*; the films *The Children's Hour* (1961, directed by William Wyler), *The Fox* (1967, directed by Mark Rydell), *Basic Instinct* (1992, directed by Paul Verhoeven), and *Mulholland Dr.* (2001, directed by David Lynch); and television programs such as *Quantum Leap* (1989–1993), *Northern Exposure* (1990–1995), and *Law & Order* (1990–2010).

5. This idea of lesbianism as a male erotic fantasy is not limited in the Whedonverse to this scene alone. Xander, on three separate occasions in *Buffy*, engages in this same sort of behavior (although each occasion is within a dream sequence). In Willow's dream in the fourth-season finale, "Restless," Xander tells Oz, "Sometimes I think about two women doing a spell … and then I do a spell by myself." Later, in Xander's own dream sequence in the same episode, he has an erotic-fantasy moment in which Willow and Tara, dressed as ultra-femme "lipstick lesbians," make out in front of him and attempt to entice him into a sexual threeway. Finally, in the seventh-season episode "Dirty Girls," Xander has an erotic dream about several of the young potential Slayers in which some of them proposition him sexually, including a statement about how "I've never been with her [referring to one of the other potentials] in front of a man before." Like Jayne Cobb's statement," each of these instances reduces lesbian relationships from positive and loving to prurient and pornographic.

6. One of the few exceptions took place in the second-season episode "Vows" when the doll Sierra (played by Dichen Lachman), on her way to a mind-wiping "treatment," tells Dollhouse tech Ivy (played by Liza Lapira), "If you were to tie me down and spank me, I could hardly be expected to resist, could I?" Although both Ivy's expression at this rather blatant lesbian proposition and the timing of the scene suggest that the viewer is meant to regard this as humorous, Lewis Call suggests that the scene is actually a rather clever way of suggesting that the sexual nature of the dolls is "playful," while the sexual games engaged in by the non-dolls (such as Hearn [played by Kevin Kilner] and Kinnard [played by Vincent Ventresca]) are "morally

repugnant sexual abuse" (*BDSM* 192), a theme that is dealt with in various significant ways throughout the series.

7. The master supervillain, Bad Horse, leader of the Evil League of Evil, threatens Dr. Horrible that if he fails to commit a "heinous crime" in order to prove his worthiness to join the League, Bad Horse will "make [Dr. Horrible] his mare."

WORKS CITED

Bartlem, Edwina. "Coming Out on a Hell Mouth." *Refractory: A Journal of Entertainment Media* 2 (2003): n. pag. Web. 29 August 2011.

Battis, Jes. *Blood Relations: Chosen Families in* Buffy the Vampire Slayer *and* Angel. Jefferson, NC: McFarland, 2005. Print.

Beirne, Rebecca. "Queering the Slayer-Text: Reading Possibilities in *Buffy the Vampire Slayer.*" *Refractory: A Journal of Entertainment Media* 5 (2004): n. pag. Web. 29 August 2011.

Black, Robert A. "It's Not Homophobia, but That Doesn't Make It Right: Creative Freedom, Responsibility, and the Death of Tara." *The Other Side.* 2002. Web. 17 December 2007. http://www.xtreme-gaming.com/theotherside/homophobia. html.

_____. "The Message Is 'Pay Attention to the Message': More Thoughts on the Craft of Writing and the Death of Tara." *The Other Side.* 2002. Web. 17 December 2007. http://www.xtreme-gaming.com/theotherside/themessage.html.

Booth, Stephen. "The Death of Tara, the Fall of Willow, and the Dead/Evil Lesbian Cliché." *Stephen and Kath's Place,* n.d. Web. 13 September 2011. http://www. stephenbooth.org/ lesbiancliche.htm.

Call, Lewis. *BDSM in American Science Fiction and Fantasy.* New York: Palgrave Macmillan, 2013. Print.

_____. "Slaying the Heteronormative: Representations of Alternative Sexuality in *Buffy* Season Eight Comics." *Sexual Rhetoric in the Works of Joss Whedon: New Essays.* Ed. Erin B. Waggoner. Jefferson, NC: McFarland, 2010. 106–116. Print.

Goddard, Drew. *Buffy the Vampire Slayer: Wolves at the Gate.* Milwaukie, OR: Dark Horse Books, 2008. Print.

Gunther, Lisa. "Worth the Wait: *Buffy* Season Eight." *Curve,* April 2011: 78–79. Print.

Last, Jonathan V. "Joss Whedon: Sexist Monster?" *Galley Slaves.* 26 March 2008. Web. 20 September 2011. http://galleyslaves.blogspot.com/2008/03/joss-whedon-sexist-monster.html.

Latham, Jo. "'[I]s It Dangerous?' Alternative Readings of 'Drugs' and 'Addiction' in *Buffy the Vampire Slayer.*" *Watcher Junior: The Undergraduate Journal of Whedon Studies* 4.2 (2010): n. pag. Web. 29 August 2011.

Leonard, Kendra Preston. "'The Status Is Not Quo': Gender and Performance in *Dr. Horrible's Sing-Along Blog.*" *Buffy, Ballads, and Bad Guys Who Sing: Music in the Worlds of Joss Whedon.* Ed. Kendra Preston Leonard. Lanham, MD: Scarecrow Press, 2011. 275–292. Print.

Matthewman, Scott. "Ta-ra Tara, Hello Homophobia?" *Scott Matthewman: A Personal Blog,* 8 May 2003. Web. 29 August 2011. http://matthewman.net/2003/05/08/ta-ra-tara-hello-homophobia/.

McAvan, Em. "'I Think I'm Kinda Gay': Willow Rosenberg and the Absent/Present Bisexual in *Buffy the Vampire Slayer.*" *Slayage: The Online International Journal of Buffy Studies* 6.4 (2007): n. pag. Web. 29 August 2011.

Mendlesohn, Farah. "Surpassing the Love of Vampires; or Why (and How) a Queer Reading of the Buffy/Willow Relationship is Denied." *Fighting the Forces: What's at Stake in* Buffy the Vampire Slayer. Ed. Rhonda V. Wilcox and David Lavery. Lanham, MD: Rowman & Littlefield, 2002. 45–60. Print.

Rice, Lynette. "*Buffy*'s Willow Takes a Female Lover." EWwww. *Entertainment Weekly,* 3 February 2000. Web. 20 September 2011. http://www.ew.com/article/2000/02/ 03/buffys-willow-takes-female-lover.

Ryan, Brandy. "'It's Complicated ... Because of Tara': History, Identity Politics, and the Straight White Male Author." *Buffy Goes Dark: Essays on the Final Two Seasons of* Buffy the Vampire Slayer *on Television.* Ed. Lynne Y. Edwards, Elizabeth L. Rambo, and James B. South. Jefferson, NC: McFarland, 2009. 57–74. Print.

Schwartz, Terri. "*Dollhouse* Star Eliza Dushku Reveals Gay Storylines, Possible Cameo by Nathan Fillion." *MTV News.* 16 June 2009. Web. 20 September 2011. http:// hollywoodcrush.mtv.com/2009/06/16/exclusive-dollhouse-star-eliza-dushku-reveals-gay-storylines-possible-cameo-by-nathan-fillion/.

Shapiro, Paul D. "Someone to Sink Your Teeth Into: Gendered Biting Patterns on *Buffy the Vampire Slayer*—A Quantitative Analysis." *Slayage: The Online International Journal of Buffy Studies* 7.2 (2008): n. pag. Web. 30 August 2011.

Tresca, Don. "Images of Paraphilia in the Whedonverse." *Sexual Rhetoric in the Works of Joss Whedon: New Essays.* Ed. Erin B. Waggoner. Jefferson, NC: McFarland, 2010. 146–172. Print.

Whedon, Joss. "At the Bronze, May 4, 2000." *Buffyguide,* n.d. Web. 29 August 2011. http:// www.buffyguide.com/extras/josswt.shtml#ixzz2HAJvD0gt.

_____. "Interview with David Bianculli." *Fresh Air.* National Public Radio. KQEI, Sacramento, 9 May 2000. Radio.

"Willow or Xander, Who Should Be Gay?" *Slayerverse News.* 2 December 2004. Web. 20 September 2011. http://slayerverse-news/willoworxander.html.

Wilts, Alissa. "Evil, Skanky, and Kinda Gay: Lesbian Images and Issues." *Buffy Goes Dark: Essays on the Final Two Seasons of* Buffy the Vampire Slayer *on Television.* Ed. Lynne Y. Edwards, Elizabeth L. Rambo, and James B. South. Jefferson, NC: McFarland, 2009. 41–56. Print.

Beyond Golden Gardenias

Versions of Same-Sex Marriage
in Queer as Folk

Gael Sweeney

The American version of *Queer as Folk* (2000–2005), which aired on the premium-cable network Showtime, was noted for tackling many issues important to the LGBT community, including coming out, gay bashing, HIV and AIDS, drug usage, anti-gay politics, and same-sex marriage. In 2005, *Los Angeles Times* critic Kate Aurthur called the series "arguably the most politically engaged drama on television" (Aurthur). American adaptors/producers Ron Cowen and Daniel Lipman have said that *Queer as Folk* is "the story of boys becoming men" (Rowe 49), specifically gay boys becoming gay men. However, "CowLip" (the name of their production company and also how they are referred to in the fandom) never detailed what kind of gay men they mean: resolutely separatist and queer, in the manner of queer theorists such as Michael Warner; assimilated and accepting of the heteronormative narrative espoused by cultural critics such as Andrew Sullivan; somewhere in the middle? Or, is the series not quite sure what kind of gay manhood it envisions for the 21st century? And what about its lesbian characters? How do they fit, or not really fit, into the story?

One continuing element evident throughout all five seasons of *Queer as Folk* is the question of marriage. This is not surprising because same-sex marriage was the primary gay issue during the years the show aired, with the walls barring marriage equality falling, beginning in Canada (where the series was filmed) in 2003, then the state of Massachusetts in 2004, with other states soon to follow. The series frames this topic as a debate between assimilationists to heteronormative mainstream culture and those holding out for a uniquely queer, homonormative alternative. Andrew Sullivan, in his 1995 book, *Virtually Normal: An Argument about Homosexuality*, and his 2005

New Republic article, "The End of Gay Culture: Assimilation and Its Meaning," argues that marriage equality is the primary political issue for gays and lesbians, and that same-sex marriage and a traditionalist lifestyle that downplays gay sexuality and the more extreme visible elements of the gay community (e.g., drag queens, leather daddies, over-the-top pride parades, drug-fueled dance clubs, etc.) are the keys to acceptance and equality in the wider straight world. Countering Sullivan's thesis is Michael Warner's response to Sullivan, *The Trouble with Normal: Sex, Politics, and the Ethics of Queer Life*. Warner contends that the single-minded focus on marriage equality forgets that queer culture has always been an alternative to the status quo that long rejected and marginalized homosexuals, and that the gay community has developed its own distinct culture that does not reject sexuality or alternative ways of living and loving, ways that do not need to conform to the expectations of straight people and their institutions. While Sullivan posits a safe gay world that mirrors a conformist version of heterosexuality, Warner celebrates a queer culture that is not ashamed of its own sexuality or even of its own excesses because they are the products of a specific transgressive history.

All three of the major couples in *Queer as Folk* deal with this issue of marriage and its consequences: Lindsay Peterson (played by Thea Gill) and Melanie Marcus (played by Michelle Clunie) in season two; Michael Novotny (played by Hal Sparks) and Ben Bruckner (played by Robert Gant) in season four; and Brian Kinney (played by Gale Harold) and Justin Taylor (played by Randy Harrison) in season five. Each of these relationships represents a different philosophy and view of marriage in the LGBT community, and comparing how their stories unfold represents the swiftly changing views toward same-sex marriage, both within the gay community itself and also in straight-media discourse of the same period.

"The lesbian Lucy and Ethel": Lindsay and Melanie

Lindsay and Melanie are a long-term lesbian couple who have a baby fathered by Lindsay's gay friend, Brian. In many ways they are almost a television cliché, that of the lesbians (one femme and one butch) with a baby (see *Friends* [1994–2004], etc.). But their relationship is also turbulent, with multiple breakups and make-ups, and plenty of angst, which is a *Queer as Folk* specialty. Much of the first half of season two deals with Lindsay and Mel's attempt to have the "perfect wedding," an event that they can ill afford and which seems jinxed from the start by Lindsay's homophobic parents, the meddling of one of Mel's ex-girlfriends, and even the alignment of the stars. Lindsay and Melanie are presented as the "romantics" of the series, and their struggle for public acknowledgement of their relationship is a centerpiece of its second season. But looking at their story over the course of all five seasons, the real question is whether they are the poster girls for lesbian marriage or instead for the bitter possibility of gay divorce.

In the ten-episode UK version of *Queer as Folk*, which preceded the American version, the two lesbian characters, Romey Sullivan (played by Esther Hall) and Lisa Levene (played by Saira Todd), exist primarily to have and raise Stuart Jones' baby (the offspring of the equivalent of the Brian character, played by Aidan Gillen), but over the cumulative five seasons of the American version, Lindsay and Melanie have a number of story arcs of their own, most centering on either marriage (and separation) or babies, as each woman has a child during the run of the series. But while expanding the roles of the two lesbian characters, gay partners/producers Cowen and Lipman and their overwhelmingly gay male writing staff often present them as the most irritating and even duplicitous characters on the show. As the long-term, "stable" couple among the Liberty Avenue gang—über-stud advertising executive Brian Kinney, his best friend Michael Novotny, fashionista Emmett Honeycutt (played by Peter Paige), and accountant Ted Schmidt (played by Scott Lowell), with the later additions of teenager Justin Taylor and college professor Ben Bruckner—Lindsay and Melanie are portrayed as being passive-aggressive, judgmental, and cowardly. They are ardently assimilationist, constantly lecturing the men about the gay community's responsibility to fit in, set a good example, and be seen in a positive light by the straight world. They are also big supporters of the local Gay and Lesbian Center, run by the insufferably self-righteous Philip (played by Clinton Walker) and Tannis (played by Maggie Huculak), and their favorite television show is *Gay as Blazes*, CowLip's fictional anti–*Queer as Folk*, in which there is no fucking or sucking, and the politically correct gay men are all monogamous and spend their spare time reading Jane Austen to the blind. Lindsay, a tall, blonde WASP from a wealthy family, is a classic entitled know-it-all who is almost always wrong about everything, while her partner Melanie, a thin, dark Jewish lawyer, is paranoia personified, seeing homophobia, anti–Semitism, and misogyny even in their best friends. Their usual target for correction is bad boy Brian, who, despite his admitted promiscuity and substance abuse, is the most honest character in the series, in contrast to the two women, who lie, manipulate, and cheat on each other despite their pretense of monogamy and domestic bliss.

Lindsay is the more marriage-minded of the pair, and also of all the characters in the series (both gay and straight). She was Brian's college girl-friend/beard and, although they had sex—the resolutely queer Brian calls it "Midsummer Madness" in a sly shout-out to the gay classic *Auntie Mame* (1958, directed by Morton DaCosta)—it obviously meant more to Lindsay, who is clearly bisexual (even though the series shies away from that label). In the first episode, after she has given birth to their son, Lindsay compares her relationship with Brian to that of Peter Pan and Wendy, the boy who never grows up and the girl who loves him but must find a life beyond Peter's Neverland (in this case Babylon, the dance club at the center of gay social life in the Liberty Avenue "gayborhood"). This trope is repeated again in season three, and for the last time in the series finale. Brian as the queer Peter Pan is an obvious analogy, but Lindsay plays on it, seeing herself as the most important woman—the only woman, the only "Wendy"—in Brian's life.

But beyond Brian, Lindsay also wants a heteronormative life, which she has established with her partner of five years (as the series begins), Melanie. They have a house, mainstream careers (Lindsay is an art teacher, Mel a lawyer), and a son, Gus (played by identical twins Kegan and Logan Hoover). The paternity of Gus is a contentious issue between the partners: Melanie detests donor/dad Brian not only for his take-no-prisoners club-boy ways but also because it is clear that Lindsay is still in love with him. Lindsay refused to use an anonymous sperm donor, as Melanie wished, and would only have a baby if Brian agreed to be the father. Because of this, Mel tends to blame everything that goes wrong in their relationship—from an interrupted bris (in the third episode of the first season) to her own cheating (in the thirteenth episode of that same season)—on the ubiquitous Mr. Kinney, who in turn mockingly calls the women, who are in a constant emotional uproar, "the lesbian Lucy and Ethel" (in the third episode of season two).

Along with all of the other perks of hetero life, Lindsay dreams of a wedding with all of the traditional trappings. During a separation from Melanie in the latter half of the first season, she plans to go through with a green-card marriage to Guillaume (played by Noam Jenkins), a gay Frenchman who is about to be deported. Even though the proposed wedding is a complete sham, Lindsay preens in front of the mirror in a garish wedding dress, posing for the skeptical Brian and trying to get him to see her as a potential bride. "You're marrying the wrong person," he states bluntly. "You never asked me," she gushes. "I meant Melanie," he says in disgust at what he considers to be a "horror story." But in order to get the women back together and ensure that his son has a stable home with "two parents who love each other," the supposedly selfish Brian agrees to give up his parental rights to his son, reuniting the lesbians.

In season two, only a few episodes after Lindsay and Mel's commitment ceremony (see below), Lindsay coaxes Brian into pretending to be her husband for an interview at an exclusive preschool for Gus, who is not yet even out of diapers. "I want you to be my husband," Lindsay says, to which Brian responds that she already has one: Mel. "You want to pass him off as the product of a happy hetero home life?" asks Brian, the noted heterophobe.

"Well, fuck that shit!" Nevertheless, he goes with Lindsay to the school, awkwardly playing the part of doting dad and husband. As they wait to speak to the principal, Lindsay muses, "There was a time when we first met that I thought this could be reality. Did you ever feel that way?" When Brian flatly says no, the look on Lindsay's face reflects her true feelings: although she identifies as a lesbian and is supposedly committed to Melanie, she still loves and continues to dream about a life with Brian.

Although throughout the first season Lindsay and Melanie wear rings and refer to being married, during season two they become fixated on having an elaborate wedding, which in the Pittsburgh of the early 2000s means a commitment ceremony, as same-sex marriage was not yet legal there. In the first episode of season two, Lindsay's straight sister, Lynnette (played by Heather Hodgson), marries for the third time, and Lindsay and Melanie attend with Ted and Emmett as their beards. Lindsay is warned to "play it straight" in front of the guests and not cause any embarrassment to the wealthy and proper Petersons. But Lindsay, sick and tired of being treated like a pariah by her own family, interrupts the proceedings to publicly propose to Mel. In the following episodes that lead up to their ceremony, Lindsay tries again and again to convince her homophobic parents not only to accept the marriage but also to help pay for it, as they did for her sister. She even takes them out for an expensive dinner in an attempt to soften them up. However, Nancy Peterson (played by Pixie Bigelow), Lindsay's mother, states flatly that they will not give the women a dime and adds that they paid for Lynette's wedding "because her wedding was real." That Lindsay and Melanie, two supposedly independent lesbians in their thirties, would still "give a shit about what straight people think" (as Brian comments), let alone be begging Lindsay's dismissive parents for money, is typical of the series' attitude toward the women: "the girls" are presented as the adult and stable couple while simultaneously maddeningly incapable and incompatible, dishing out platitudes about responsibility and good behavior while they are unable to stay together or take care of their own business for longer than a few episodes at a stretch. Brian constantly comes to their rescue with money (for life insurance, school fees, daycare, even a lawyer for Lindsay's custody battle in the final season) while Lindsay croons "I love you" and Melanie calls him an "unfeeling asshole," even as he is writing them a big check.

When "The Wedding" episode finally arrives, the event is played for laughs. The women, in the spirit of Lucy Ricardo and Ethel Mertz (played by Lucille Ball and Vivian Vance in the television sitcom *I Love Lucy* [1951–1957]), cannot get anything right as their big day approaches. At a wild lesbian bachelorette party hosted by Mel's Kinney-like ex, the biker-dyke Leda (played by Nancy Anne Sakovich), the trouble begins with a reading by Mysterious Marilyn, the resident drag-queen psychic of Liberty Avenue: Mercury is in retrograde, which means that disaster is inevitable. Consequently, the rings are lost, the caterer and hall are shut down by the health department, Lindsay's wedding dress is ruined, and Lindsay begins to have panic attacks: "Somebody up there doesn't think we should get married.... Maybe that's because people like us aren't supposed to get married," she states. Always looking for someone to blame for every misfortune, Lindsay now decides that fate (along with right-wing politicians and the religious establishment) is also against same-sex marriage.

It is only when the desperate Melanie traps Brian (who else?) in his tanning bed—where he is preparing for the trip he has won to the White Party in Miami, thereby fulfilling his destiny as the "luckiest fuck" in Pittsburgh, retrograde Mercury be damned—that things finally come together. Even though she loathes Brian, Mel knows he is the only person able to get anything done in the "QAF Universe." Accordingly, the marriage-hating Brian gathers the gang, including Michael's ubiquitous mother, Debbie (played by Sharon Gless), and tells them, "We have precisely twenty-one hours to get 'the munchers' married," pointing out that no one knows weddings like queers, who are the florists, caterers, planners, designers, servers, performers, and even the priests at countless straight weddings. He assigns everyone a task to help pull the wedding off on schedule while he himself works on his basecoat. Of course, under Brian's direction, things fall neatly into place. Lindsay, in a not-so-fluffy femme white dress, and Melanie, in a black butch faux-tux, exchange rings (perhaps the same ones they were wearing in season one?) to a k.d. lang soundtrack in front of their friends, but with no sign of the Petersons—or even Brian, who is seen dancing at the White Party in South Beach, having metaphorically caught the thrown bouquet all the way from Pittsburgh.

But a commitment ceremony does not calm the drama between the two women. Lindsay's conflicted sexuality moves beyond her singular obsession with Brian in season three, when she has a brief affair with the male artist Sam Auerbach (played by Robin Thomas). Although Melanie herself had an affair with Marianne (played by Angela Asher) in season one, and both she and Lindsay had encounters with Leda in season two, sex with a man is something Melanie cannot forgive. Melanie is pregnant with a baby fathered by Michael (after she rejected Brian as a possible sperm donor), but she refuses to forgive Lindsay. The two women pretend to be together because they are aware of their status as the poster girls for marriage and a stable relationship, even though that is far from their reality. The public breakdown of their marriage following the birth of their daughter, Jenny Rebecca (or "J.R.," played by twins Kate and Megan McDonald), ignites a furious custody battle in season five between Melanie and Michael, who feels betrayed by their lies and is convinced that he and his husband, Ben, would make better parents than the feuding lesbians. This fight frays all three of the major relationships in the series, and only a major hate crime—the bombing of Club Babylon during an anti–Proposition 14 fundraiser during the tenth episode of the final season—brings them all together again (to a point).

At the end of the series, Lindsay and Melanie, in arguably the most controversial move of all of the controversial moves in season five, decide to leave Pittsburgh for Toronto, where they believe their children will be safe from the homophobes who are pressing for the anti-gay Proposition 14 and are responsible for the bombing. When they realize that a woman they know was among those killed, Melanie decides Pittsburgh is now analogous to Nazi Germany and, like her grandfather who escaped Hitler in the 1930s, the best course of action is for her, Lindsay, and their children to flee. The realities that the women have only been reconciled for a few days (following a bitter separation of almost a year), neither has a job (as Melanie cannot practice law in Canada), and they have never been able to get by without Brian's financial support do not dissuade them, nor does the fact that they have often lectured others about their responsibility to the local gay community. The wishes of Brian and Michael, the fathers of Gus and baby J.R., are also disregarded. Her love of Brian finally trumped (apparently) by her fear, Lindsay convinces her Peter Pan to let his Wendy go. In a heartbreaking scene, Brian says goodbye to his son in a manner that feels like forever, especially as it comes just minutes before the end of the entire series. To say this plot twist made Lindsay and Melanie the most hated characters among fans (e.g., the Showtime boards, Yahoo, LiveJournal, and other active *QAF* fan boards exploded with vitriol toward the "cowardly 'munchers'") is an understatement. Their shaky commitment to each other and their supposed desire to assimilate to a heteronormative lifestyle translates here into an escape from the reality of the struggle for equality and gay rights in Pittsburgh. And, looking back at these developments a decade later, their defection seems even more a pointless gesture—gay marriage became legal in Pennsylvania by court order in May 2014 without subsequent backlash. If the primary message of the final scene of *Queer as Folk* in the resurrected Club Babylon is one of the triumph of the "thumpa-thumpa"—the heartbeat of queer survival—the counter message seems to be that those who do not have the stomach for the fight will cut and run. That those two people turned out to be Lindsay and Melanie, the series' central lesbian characters, remains extremely problematic.

"Stepford fags": Michael and Ben

Michael and Ben, two men in a serodiscordant relationship, have been together for approximately two years when they legally marry in Toronto at the end of season four. They are presented as a couple that longs for a mainstream family life, including a house in a gay-friendly suburb ("Stepford Avenue" as the cynical Brian calls it), a son (an adopted former hustler who, like Ben, is HIV-positive), and a legal (at least in Canada) marriage. Although Brian is skeptical, Michael and Ben do not feel they are trying to replicate heteronormative behavior but rather merely claiming the rights (including marriage) that should be available to everyone, gay and straight, denied them up to then (i.e., the year 2004).

Michael grew up in a rundown neighborhood in Pittsburgh, where he was raised by his single mother, Debbie, a PFLAG mom who works as a waitress at the Liberty Diner in the local "gay ghetto," Liberty Avenue (portrayed in the series by the Church Street Gay Village of Toronto). As a child, Michael was obsessed with two things: comic books and his best friend, Brian Kinney. As an adult, little has changed. Michael's love for Brian remains unrequited yet informs his friendships with flamboyant Emmett and conservative Ted, who tolerate the snarky, arrogant Brian for Michael's sake, as well as his two major romantic relationships, with chiropractor Dr. David Cameron (played by Chris Potter), who hates Brian, in season one, and with college professor Ben Bruckner, who is one of Brian's former tricks, in seasons two through five.

Short, puppy-doggish Michael is the series' POV character, providing voice-over commentary in the early episodes of season one, and then again in the season-five series finale. He describes himself in the premiere episode as a "semi-cute, boy-next-door type," but he is also supremely insecure, especially as compared to the super-confident stud Brian. Michael is a mama's boy who longs to be like his superhero idol, Captain Astro, but more often finds himself in the role of Lois Lane to Brian's Superman. He longs for a boyfriend and a "normal" life, including a job somewhere other than the Big Q-Mart, where he is deeply in the closet. But Michael's romantic life is constantly blocked by Brian, whose Ayn Randian philosophy of "no apologies, no excuses, no regrets" includes a rejection of anything that smacks of heteronormativity, including "romantic bullshit" like love and monogamy. Throughout the series' first season, the tug of war between Brian and Dr. Dave over Michael's time and affection throws the conflicted Michael into an emotional turmoil. While the fantasy of Brian represents sex and excitement, Dr. Dave offers everything Michael has always wanted: a stable relationship, an upper-middle-class home, and a family, as Michael bonds with the chiropractor's twelve-year-old son, Hank (played by Ryan Cooley), another comic book fan.

But Brian, who has made it a policy to fuck every guy in Pittsburgh *except* Michael, is ever-present: his jealousy of Dr. Dave is palpable, and, although he loves Michael, he understands they will never be a couple except, as Brian tells Debbie in the first-season episode "Surprise!," "Who knows?

Maybe we'll end up a couple of old queens in Palm Springs." The product of an abusive Irish Catholic family, Brian has always regarded Michael, Debbie, and Michael's gay, HIV-positive Uncle Vic (played by Jack Wetherall) as a refuge from his father's drunken outbursts and his mother's prayers, which makes it difficult for him to let go of the only safe emotional space he has ever known. Michael's love for Brian, on the other hand, is both emotional *and* erotic, but the sexual side, other than an interrupted handjob when the boys were fourteen years old, has never been fulfilled. Dr. Dave offers not only emotional and sexual love but also marriage. The fortysomething David (Michael is twenty-nine years old when they meet), who has been in a heterosexual marriage and also a long-term gay relationship before meeting Michael, is an advocate of same-sex marriage. Late in season one, David and Michael, who are by now living together, hold a fundraiser for a pro-gay-rights state representative who remarks that one day she would love to attend their legal wedding. Almost on cue, the event, which is packed with conservative Pittsburgh A-list gays, is crashed by the gang (who had been excluded for being too déclassé)—decked out as gay stereotypes including Jackie-O drag (Emmett), a leather daddy (Ted), a twink (Justin), and Quentin Crisp (Uncle Vic)—with Brian, in leave-nothing-to-the-imagination ostrich-skin pants, leading the way. Michael begins to realize that, although he represents everything he has always wanted in terms of material things, David is also controlling and condescending, treating him the same way he treats his twelve-year-old son. As a result, Michael begins to have second thoughts as he prepares to leave Pittsburgh, and Brian, in order to move to Portland with David. In the final moments of season one, Justin is attacked at his prom and Michael's decision is temporarily postponed, but in the first episode of season two, Michael is back in "the Pitts." The loss of his family, his friends, and Brian was too much to sustain, so Dr. Dave sent the miserable Michael back home. "There's never a right time to admit you've failed," Michael tells Emmett and Ted, "that you had this great opportunity to start your life over with someone you loved, or thought you loved, and you blew it." Without the safety of Liberty Avenue, and the approval of Brian, Michael's dream of a heteronormative life collapses. Nevertheless, he does not abandon his search for love—or for his own personal superhero to give him the relationship for which he so desperately longs.

Early in season two, Michael finally comes out to his coworkers at the Big Q-Mart and promptly quits in order to follow his dream of owning a comic-book store, with the help of Brian and a rare Captain Astro first issue. It is there that he meets Ben Bruckner, a professor of gay and lesbian studies at Carnegie Mellon/Yale grad/product of the Iowa Writers' Workshop (his memoir is titled *R-U-1-2?*), unlike Michael, who only made it through high school because Brian did his homework, and who dropped out of community college after just two semesters. But Michael is attracted to opposites: men who are not only intellectually more sophisticated (e.g., Brian is an advertising executive, David a chiropractor, and Ben a professor) but also physically larger and more dominant sexually (of all the gay characters on the show, Michael is the only one who is never shown topping, even though he insists he is "not a total bottom"). Ben is the visual embodiment of Michael's super-hero fantasies: tall, square-jawed, and pumped up. He is also HIV-positive, and Michael contemplates dating him without the approval of either Brian, who has already had (safe) sex with Ben ("Handle it, kiss it, jerk it off, just don't fall in love with it," he warns), or Debbie, who nursed her brother Vic through the complications of AIDS and fears for Michael's health. "I don't want him getting anything! I never thought I'd say this, but for the first time in my life I wish my son wasn't gay," she tells Vic, who reacts with righteous anger, in the second-season episode "The Leper (Hath the Babe Not Eyes?)." But Michael defies both his mother and Brian and, after a rocky start, enters into a relationship with Ben.

From the beginning, it is obvious that Michael and Ben have similar expectations: they both want monogamy, a home, and perhaps even a family, although Ben's HIV-positive status complicates the situation. The difference between Michael's relationships with Ben and Dr. Dave, and what makes the former a success and the latter a failure, is, as usual, their attitudes toward Brian. David, older and having lost his partner to AIDS, fears Brian's in-your-face sexuality and tries to separate Michael from the bad influence of Liberty Avenue. Ben, however, moves easily between Babylon and the world beyond the gay ghetto. As a writer and student of queer culture, Ben is connected to the gay community politically and intellectually, and he is not intimidated by Brian or the sexual ethos he represents. In other words, Brian is not the mystery to Ben that he was to David: Brian and Ben tricked a number of years earlier, and Brian understands that while Ben was more sexually active before he became positive, he does not condemn those who still are. In the second-season episode "One Degree of Brian Kinney," the always emotional Michael (who once described himself as being "half Italian and half drag queen") finds out that his lover and his best friend have had sex and he cannot deal with it. He imagines seeing Brian and Ben together everywhere, includ-ing their bed; the reality that Ben has experienced what Michael has always desired but will never have—sex with Brian—is too much for him to handle. Finally, Brian confronts Michael in his comic store and presses him to have sex: "I know your secret identity," Brian confirms. But Michael declines. He now knows what he wants: a life with Ben. He and Brian are too different in their philosophies of life and love and would never be happy together, some-thing Brian has been trying to convince Michael of for years. That night, before he and Ben make love, Michael imagines Brian walking out of the bedroom, shutting the door behind him. Michael's unrequited fantasy love is finished, opening a new door to a real relationship.

In season three, Michael and Ben settle down into monogamous domesticity. They move in together and become foster parents to Hunter, the former hustler (played by Harris Allan). Despite a few rocky patches, including Ben's steroid abuse and being stalked by a bug chaser who wants his HIV, their relationship deepens. A trip to Toronto for the Liberty Ride, an AIDS charity bike-a-thon, gives Ben the opportunity to propose in the fourth-season episode "Proposal of Two Kinds," knocking Michael off-guard. There is little suspense about whether or not Michael will accept—the entire trajectory of the relationship has been leading to this moment—but it gives Cowen and Lipman, along with teleplay writer Shawn Postoff, a direct opportunity to rehearse the marriage/anti-marriage debate within the gay community. Lipman said in an interview with Lynn Elber that "Michael's entrenched view of marriage as unattainable reflects real-life gay attitudes" (Elber) and he hoped the show would change perceptions, in both the gay and straight communities. In Moosie's, the Toronto alter ego of Pittsburgh's gay bar of choice, Woody's, Michael ponders Ben's proposal, as Brian, who has decided to join the Liberty Ride despite recently recovering from cancer, serves (as usual) as the dissenting voice. Although Michael comments that Ben's proposal is heartfelt and beautiful, he is holding back from accepting it, anticipating Brian's objections. As expected, Brian expresses that the idea of such a marriage is pathetic. In response, Michael states that his hesitation is not because he does not want to get married, but rather because it "wasn't a story I told myself like straight kids did. You know, that someday I'd meet that special person and we'd fall in love and have a big wedding. It was never real for me." Brian, however, digs in, pointing out that marriage is not all about love, but more about registering at Pottery Barn and then having an "acrimonious divorce": "We're queer. We don't need marriage. We don't need the sanction of dickless politicians and pederast priests. We fuck who we want to, when we want to. That is our God-given right." But rather than dissuading Michael, the debate ultimately convinces him to accept Ben's proposal. Brian has no reply to this except to tell Michael that he is a writer, so he will have to rewrite the story to include himself and, by implication, all queers.

Of course, Michael (like the writers) elides the fact that he has been thinking about the possibility of marriage as far back as season one; Dr. Dave, like Ben, was also a strong advocate of the institution. But for the purposes of the series and the debate, Michael, the fatherless boy who has always yearned to belong, is made to see that a legal marriage is what he has wanted all along, and, ironically, the one who helps him to realize it is the anti-assimilationist Brian. In contrast to his usual fierce demeanor when railing about "pseudo-breeder bullshit" like love and marriage, in this scene Brian is resigned, as if he knows this is not only what Michael wants but also what he needs. Brian even stands as Michael's best man and throws the newlyweds a reception, complete with cake and klezmer band. Although he teases Michael about still loving him best, Brian knows that is no longer true. They have both moved on, and Michael's future is the kind of life that Brian has always rejected: one of monogamy and assimilation—at least as far as the law back in the United States will allow. In the next episode, the fourth-season finale, Michael and Ben attempt to enter the States as a married couple and are rejected by a customs agent placed in the narrative for the sole purpose of being a homophobic jerk. That Officer Butz (played by Scott Wickware)— yes, that is his name—is following U.S. law at the time does not negate the painfully obvious scene in which Michael's mother reams him out. "Did you bring any fruit into the country?" Butz asks Debbie, who replies: "Two hundred fifty of them. On bicycles." What follows is a typical Debbie-preaching- to-the-choir speech about gay versus straight marriage, referencing everyone from the Queen of England to Britney Spears, that does not do much to advance the debate but gives actor Sharon Gless an opportunity to go over the top. As Michael and Ben return to Pittsburgh and settle into marriage, their progression into a more assimilative lifestyle disconnects them further from Brian, leading to a season-five clash between the recalcitrant Brian and the so-called "Stepford fags."

"A palace for my prince": Brian and Justin

The most improbable pairing on Queer as Folk is also the one viewers are introduced to first, at the beginning of the series' premiere episode, when the twenty-nine-year-old backroom sex god Brian picks up the seventeen- year-old virgin and budding artist Justin under a Liberty Avenue lamppost. Michael's voice-over clues viewers that this is not simply one of Brian's usual tricks: "And that's when it happened," he intones. "When *he* came along." Justin's arrival changes the dynamic of the four friends—Brian, Michael, Ted, and Emmett—but especially of best friends Brian and Michael, driving the primary narrative of the series until the final minutes of its last episode. This relationship also sets up the circumstances of the series' most problematic "marriage," primarily because, throughout the eighty-three episodes of Queer as Folk, Brian has been the loudest voice against assimilation and, specifically, against marriage. But a string of traumatic events, including the bombing of Babylon, causes him to reverse himself completely and propose to Justin. This mind-numbingly out-of-character plot twist was extremely controversial among fans and critics, but how it plays out brings Queer as Folk—and Brian—full circle, for better or for worse.

As the series opens, Brian is "the most fabulous fag in Pittsburgh": hedo-nistic, promiscuous, heterophobic, entirely fucked up—and proud of it. Able to have any man he desires, he is the king of Babylon's dance floor and back-room. Brian is also the poster boy for anti-assimilation, a gay man who will, as expressed in the first-season episode "Smells Like Codependence," "Do anything, say anything, fuck anything, no apologies, no excuses, no regrets." His Irish Catholic background, with an alcoholic father and a rigidly religious mother, has left him deeply suspicious of hypocritical "traditional" straight values and institutions, a view confirmed when he has an encounter at the baths with his mother's priest, and again later when his mother, after finding out that Brian has cancer, tells him it is God's judgment for his homosexuality. Outspoken in his individuality and independence, Brian hates the straight institution of marriage the most, seeing it as joining together two people (like his own parents) who will only end up hating each other and destroying their children in the process. Besides, marriage implies monogamy, which gets in the way of his "God-given right" to fuck as many hot guys as he can man-age—and Brian can manage quite a lot. As Paul Robinson notes in his book *Queer Wars: The New Gay Right and Its Critics*, "In his idiosyncratic way Brian is an extraordinarily radical figure, the dramatic counterpart, one might argue, of Michael Warner" (159). Brian's radical individualism does not apply only to his attitude toward his own family and the straight community it rep-resents, however—he rejects the notion of belonging to the gay community as well. He sees his essentialist sexuality as his own and not connected to any larger political movement or culture. When Lindsay urges Brian to attend a fundraising event at the Gay and Lesbian Center (a place he reviles) in the first-season episode "The Art of Desperation," she also lectures him about his responsibilities to his community as a gay man. Brian insists that he is not part of some larger community just because he sleeps with guys. When Lindsay points out that they all need to take care of one another, Brian again disagrees, emphasizing that he does not need anyone to take care of him. Lindsay mentions that one day he might, tiptoeing around the AIDS issue, a taboo subject for the promiscuous Brian. "Fuck groups!" he retorts. When Lindsay responds that she thought Brian did just that, he replies, in classic Kinney mode, "Occasionally, but it's by invitation only."

But Brian's anti-assimilationist position is under siege from the first episode. Although high and having picked up a teenager, he is interrupted from the process of Justin's de-virginization by a telephone call: his son has just been born and he is expected at the hospital. The man who hates families is about to become a father. However, the contradictions of Brian's life are only beginning. When Brian has sex with Justin, he actually believes that will be the end of it. But Justin, an upper-middle-class, private-school boy who does not understand the meaning of the word no, is idealistic and imagines that because they had sex, they are in love. A novice to gay culture and expectations, Justin sees in Brian "the face of God" (as he explains in the series premiere) and believes they are destined to be together. Although Michael warns Justin, in the series' second episode, that "Brian's not your boyfriend; Brian doesn't do boyfriends," Justin nevertheless seeks out Brian at his loft, where he is entertaining a trick he met on the Internet. Brian is, as always, brutally honest with the boy whose virginity he took only twenty-four hours before. He states that he believes in fucking rather than love, insisting that the latter is just something heterosexuals convince themselves they are in so they can have sex—after which they end up hurting each other, because the sex is based entirely on lies. Brian reads the romantic hope in Justin and then shoots it down by telling him, "If that's what you want, then go and find yourself a pretty little girl ... and get married."

Justin, however, refuses to take the hint, certain that he can force Brian to love him. "I told you, I'm not your lover, I'm not your partner, I'm not even your friend. You're not anything to me," Brian tells him in the first-season episode "Now Approaching ... the Line." "I could be, if you gave me a chance," Justin persists, adding, "I *need* you." "No, you *think* you do," Brian replies, "because that's what you're taught to think: 'We all need each other.' Well, it's a crock of shit. You're the only one you need. You're the only one you've got." Brian's painful childhood has taught him to trust only in himself and to present a fuck-all façade to the world. At the same time, he constantly undercuts this don't-give-a-damn self-sufficiency with quiet acts of self-sacrifice: donating his sperm to Lindsay, giving money to his odious parents, getting the hapless Ted a job, arranging Lindsay and Mel's wedding, driving his best friend Michael away so that he can have a relationship, playing sleuth to flush out the killer of a murdered young hustler, and taking Justin in when his father kicks him out in season one, again after he is gay bashed and his mother cannot deal with him in season two, and yet again in season three after Justin cheats on him, only to see that other potential "romantic" relationship fall apart. It is after Justin is attacked that Brian realizes, like it or not, he is in a relationship, and perhaps even in love, although he cannot acknowledge those things in words. Brian is determined to redefine their relationship on his own terms, making it clear to Justin that, as gay men, they live by a different set of "rules." But Justin, as an equal partner, also has some demands of his own, which he and Brian negotiate in the second-season episode "Mixed Blessings." Brian warns Justin not to start thinking of them as a married couple because that is not what they are. In contrast to straight people, Brian emphasizes, "We're queers, and if we're together, it's because we want to be, not because there's locks on our doors." He adds that if he is out late, Justin should simply assume that he is out fucking, but when he comes home, it will be to Justin and only Justin. Justin agrees, but he makes

Brian also agree to some terms, including never fucking the same guy twice, never exchanging names or numbers with other men, always coming home by 3 a.m., and never kissing anybody else on the mouth. They seal their deal with a decidedly unchaste kiss.

But being in a relationship, even an "undefined, unconventional" one, does not mean Brian has reconciled himself to any faux-hetero rituals. When Lindsay and Melanie have their commitment ceremony, he opts out, preferring to attend the White Party in Miami, even though the ceremony was only accomplished under his direction. Both women rail at him for being a selfish asshole until he reminds them that his hatred of marriage will cause him to misbehave accordingly. As he explains in the second-season episode "The Wedding":

> I'll be drunk, I'll be bored, not to mention better looking than the brides. I'll offend all the dykes, I'll heckle the ceremony, table dance at the reception, and inevitably fuck every good-looking guy—gay, straight, or undecided—in the place. Finally, I'll pass out, naked, bitching about the cheap booze. You'll lose your dignity, your friends, and your shirts paying for the damages. Hell, I'm doing you a favor getting out of town.

The women exchange glances and wish him a safe trip.

Slowly, the influence of Justin begins to change Brian. He opens up emotionally and pursues a stronger relationship with his son. He also reconciles himself to the idea of Michael and Ben as a couple, although he still mocks their monogamy whenever he gets the chance. And he begins to see himself as part of the gay community, especially in season three, when the culture of Liberty Avenue is threatened by the "family-friendly" policies of Jim Stockwell (played by David Gianopoulos), an anti-gay mayoral candidate who closes the backroom of Babylon and all of the local bathhouses in the name of "family values." Brian, the queer who hates group unity, works on Stockwell's election campaign while secretly undermining him, eventually putting himself more than a hundred thousand dollars in debt in order to defeat the politician under the guise of "Concerned Citizens for the Truth." Brian's modus operandi is stealth, especially when he is doing things that seem out of character, such as helping his community. In that regard, he is the perfect model for Rage, the gay comic-book hero written by Michael and illustrated by Justin: arrogant, hedonistic ad exec by day, defender of the queers of Gayopolis by night. Label-queen Brian, whose possessions define his success, maxes out his credit cards and even sells his Mies van der Rohe table and Italian Moda furniture in his efforts to defeat Stockwell. When Justin asks him why he behaved in such an uncharacteristic manner, Brian replies, in the episode "The Election," "Some asshole told me that if you believe in something strongly enough you have to be willing to sacrifice everything." Justin grins, understanding that he is the influential asshole. But the notion of sacrifice is one that will return to haunt both men.

Prior to the start of season four in 2004, Robert Greenblatt, the new president of entertainment at Showtime, discussed the network's "re-launch" of *Queer as Folk*, including making the show more appealing to a "broader audience," reversing the previous philosophy of "No Limits," and catering to niche (e.g., gay, Hispanic, African-American) viewers with offerings targeted directly to them. While formerly focused on sexuality, this new direction would include the "maturation of the characters, shifting focus from the perils of promiscuity to the complexities of relationships" (Wallenstein). I would argue that the "perils" of gay sex were never a "focus" of the series, at least for the character of Brian Kinney. Instead, Brian's sexuality was celebratory, revolutionary, and in-your-face queer. I would also argue that Brian's distinctly independent character and the relationship of Brian and Justin were major factors in the attraction of large numbers of female viewers: fifty-two percent of the audience in the first season and approaching seventy percent by the last. But the new regime at Showtime, as well as a more conservative political climate under George W. Bush, seems to have fueled this pursuit of a more "mainstream" (read: assimilationist and/or straight) viewership, signaling a shift in the narrative from pride in a distinct and even angry queer culture to a much safer view of what it means to be gay: "Greenblatt acknowledged that less clubbing and more cuddling will appeal to more viewers" (Wallenstein). Ten years later, Ron Cowen admitted that "the issue of gay people assimilating into mainstream culture was starting to become very prominent.... Do we assimilate? Do we stay in our gay community? Are we separatists?" (Goldberg). Questions such as those came to dominate the writing of the final season. For the series' most popular characters, Brian and Justin, and the resolution of their relationship, the ramifications of this new philosophy would be profound.

Season five finds Brian, having survived cancer and having asked Justin to move in permanently at the end of the preceding season, once again alone, with Justin in Hollywood working on a movie version of Rage. Everyone assumes this is a brief hiatus in their relationship, but Brian reads it as permanent: Justin, a talented artist, deserves better than Pittsburgh, and if Hollywood can offer that opportunity, so be it. But emotionally, Brian is stung by Justin's absence, which causes him to retreat back into his promiscuous ways. Rather than investing in a house in the country ("I hate the fucking country!" Brian declares in the first episode of the final season—words that will come back to bite him later) with the profits of his advertising agency, Kinnetik, as suggested by his accountant/confidant Ted, Brian buys his favorite "playroom": Babylon. When Ted questions the practically of this transaction, Brian climbs up onto the catwalk over the dance floor and declaims:

And what would be practical, Theodore? To get married? And move to the sub-urbs? And become a home-lovin,' child-raisin,' God-fearin' imitation heterosex-ual? And for what? So that I can become another dead soul, going to the mall, and dropping my kids off at school, and having barbecues in the backyard? That's their death, not mine. I'm a cocksucker. I'm queer. And to anyone who takes pity or offense, I say, "Judge yourself." This is where I live. This is who I am.

Just then, a voice-over narrator intones: "And as Rage stands at the precipice of a new world…" As in the very first episode of the series, everything is about to change in the new *Queer as Folk* world, but especially Brian Kinney.

The shelving of his movie sends Justin back to Pittsburgh and Brian. They are once again living together yet now find themselves in a gay community moving toward the mainstream, including marrying and raising families. In the episode "Hard Decisions," Brian, seeing his own queer beliefs marginalized by "imitation heterosexuals," rails against the "doomsday machine" of marriage, an institution he sees as destined to self-destruct, and a view he assumes Justin shares. But while working to stop Proposition 14, a statute that would strip gays and lesbians in Pennsylvania of rights such as civil partnership and adoption, Justin begins to realize how much he really does want "normal" things, or at least the possibility of them. Justin and Michael's latest Rage comic, which features the gay superhero and his boyfriend J.T. getting married on the planet Massachupiter, becomes their best-selling issue: "Everybody loves that J.T. finally got his man," crows Michael. But Justin laments that life with Brian will never imitate art because he has been "suckered into [his] own fantasy," as he explains in the episode "Bored Out of Ya Fucking Mind." As the gay world grows more heteronormative, Brian digs in his heels fiercely, seeing himself as the last bastion of queer manhood, and lashing out at queers who have become "infected" with this new plague. In the episode "Excluding and Abstemiousness," when Michael's husband, "Zen Ben" (as Brian has nicknamed him), lectures Brian that "not everyone regards marriage and monogamy as a death sentence— for some of us, they're simply a part of growing up," Brian retorts, "You mean giving up. Surrendering to the straight world's conception of what it means to be a man." The defiant Brian, who has never defined his manhood according to straight values, has no intention of surrendering this time, even if it estranges him from his best friend, the happily married Michael, as well as his lover, Justin.

"You already know what I want," Justin finally tells Brian in the fifth-season episode "Hope Against Hope." "A husband. A family. A home. All the things that make life worth living," Brian says sarcastically, basically repeating the conversation they had at the end of season two before Justin, looking for the romantic gestures Brian would never provide, left him for the seemingly appealing but deceitful Ethan (played by Fab Filippo). When Justin says he realizes Brian can't give him those things, Brian responds, "Not *can't*. Can't implies that I'm incapable. It's that I *won't*." Once again, Brian loses Justin because he will not budge from his principles, even if those principles devastate him. As he tells Ted, the series' resident twelve-stepper, who encourages Brian to unburden himself in the episode "Honest to Yourself":

> My mother is a frigid bitch. My father was an abusive drunk. They had a hateful marriage, which is probably why I am unwilling or unable to form a long-term, committed relationship of my own. The fact that I drink like a fish, abuse drugs, and have more or less redefined promiscuity doesn't help—much. As a result, I've lost the two people in my life [Justin and Michael] that mean the most to me.

"Don't you feel better?" Ted then chirps. "No. But I'm sure you do," Brian quips.

Before he leaves, Justin bitterly refers to Brian's obsession with Babylon and what it represents, in the episode "Hope against Hope," when he says, "Whatever else happens, by all means keep on dancing." Brian's refusal to be defined by straight culture and heterosexual values leaves him alone and in pain. He further fears the loss of his queer identity as he sees Michael easily becoming one of the faux-heterosexuals represented by Eli and Monty (played by Michael Carley and Edgar George), the *Gay as Blazes*–like "Stepford fags" who are gentrifying an old neighborhood near the university. When he finds out that Justin has moved in with Michael and Ben, who have also bought and renovated a house on "Stepford Avenue," Brian blames them for turning Justin into a "defector" and filling his "blond little head" with images of babies, weddings, and white picket fences. Drunk and grieving, Brian confronts Michael in the episode "Hope against Hope": "Congratulations! You won.... You infected him with your petty bourgeois, mediocre, conformist, assimilationist life.... It's a farce! It's a freak show!" But Michael, who for so long has idolized and rarely challenged Brian, now reads him some hard truths: "He was not perfectly happy! Waiting for years for you to say 'I love you. You're the only one I want.'" "That's not who I am!" Brian blasts. "Don't we all know!" Michael affirms, pointing out that "nothing's more pathetic ... than an over-the-hill club boy," echoing Justin's remark about Babylon. "He left because of *you*—who wouldn't?"

This split seems to signal the actual end of the relationship. Brian focuses on his advertising agency and Babylon, while Justin joins the campaign against Proposition 14, even getting arrested during a protest at his homophobic father's store. But the bombing and destruction of Babylon drives the pair back together, with Brian, terrified at almost losing Justin yet again to a homophobic attack, finally saying the words Justin has been waiting to hear since the first episode: "I love you" (these same words also provide the title of the episode). In the next episode, those three words also lead Brian to reverse himself on every position on marriage he has previously held: "I am, without doubt, the worst candidate for marriage alive. But, conversely, that's also the reason that I'm the best candidate.... Because as strongly as I was opposed to the idea, now that I'm behind it, I am as fervently and passionately committed." When the dubious Justin asks why he has changed his mind, Brian answers, "I finally thought of one good reason to do it.... To prove to the person that I love how much I love him. That I would give him anything, I would do anything, I'd be anything to make him happy." Thus, Brian moves from "do anything, say anything, fuck anything" to vowing monogamy, making plans to sell his loft and what is left of Babylon and buying a ridiculous faux–Tudor mansion with tennis courts, swimming pool, and stables—the house Justin once mentioned as his dream home. "It's [a palace] for my prince," says Brian, as Justin stares at him, and the house, incredulously. But once Justin agrees (dubbing their palace "Bri-tin" in a nod to all the Brian/Justin-shippers in the fandom), they plunge into grandiose wedding plans, including having the ceremony at Fallingwater, the Frank Lloyd Wright house near Pittsburgh, and Justin ordering Golden Gardenias to be flown in from some remote mountains in China because of a legend that once your lover breathes their scent, he will love you forever. If that is what Justin wants, that is what Justin will have, the individual masquerading as Brian Kinney decrees.

As the day of the ceremony approaches and the members of the Liberty Avenue gang have gotten used to the idea—"He must've knocked up Sunshine [her nickname for Justin]," Debbie says when she receives her wedding announcement in the series' second-to-last episode—of a changed Brian, Justin begins to see something different: a Brian Kinney trying desperately to turn himself into someone else. The night before their rehearsal dinner, Justin challenges the man, who now claims that he prefers to cuddle rather than fuck. Thus, Showtime's wish for a show that privileges cuddling over fucking finally claims Brian Kinney—and explodes *Queer as Folk*'s most beloved couple. Brian understands that his attempt to become an "imitation heterosexual" has failed: Justin wants a different kind of relationship but he also wants the old Brian Kinney, and those two people cannot be reconciled. As Ron Cowan commented in 2015, "Justin realized in wanting Brian to get married and settle down, he was turning the tiger he fell in love with into a house cat" (Goldberg). Brian also realizes, in the series' final episode, that Justin has become "the best homosexual" he can be by acknowledging that they can love each other without rituals or sacrifice: "I don't want to live with someone who sacrificed [his] life and called it love to be with me." The irony, of course, is that Brian is the one sacrificing his own happiness in order to retain his queer principles and allow Justin to choose his own path. "Whether we see each other next weekend or next month—never again—it doesn't matter. It's only time," Brian says to Justin before the younger man leaves to pursue his art in New York City. The supposedly unsentimental Brian keeps the rings from their aborted ceremony and they make love one last time, with the image of Justin literally disappearing from under Brian's naked body.

Babylon, a scene of death and destruction that Brian had no desire to rebuild, rises again, at the bidding of Michael, who also wants back the Brian he has long loved, the "Rage" who oversees Gayopolis, the "King of Liberty Avenue." But are we really left with the Brian of the series' premiere episode, the "Face of God," or the changed and chastened Brian of the Golden Gardenias? In its second season, *Queer as Folk* mocks the hypocrisy of the politically correct gay drama *Gay as Blazes* and of conservative assimilationist Andrew Sullivan with the character Howard Bellweather (played by Stewart Arnott), who preaches traditional values while trolling barebacking websites and indulging in non-safe sex, something the promiscuous but honest Brian Kinney would never do. Yet by season five, *Queer as Folk* seems to be validating those same traditional values. When all is said and done, how are we to read the series' ultimate position on the normalizing assimilative position in the pairing up of all the other members of the gang—Michael with Ben, Ted with Blake (played by Dean Armstrong), and Emmett with some guy who shows up out of the blue in the last ten minutes!—versus the boldly anti-heteronormative position in the lone body of Brian Kinney? Is Brian, back in the reconstructed Babylon and dancing vigorously above the crowd, with Justin nowhere in sight and his son in another country, pathetically sad or defiantly triumphant? Is he the personification of "Proud"—the series' final, defining song—or is he making do, biding time, and already an aging gay anachronism?

Perhaps with his proposal to Justin, Brian sees the writing on the wall: that assimilation and the fading of a distinctive queer culture is inevitable, just as legal same-sex marriage is inevitable. Brian may dance, alone and above the fray, but time is running out on his days as the hottest stud on Liberty Avenue—and on Liberty Avenue itself. That reality was brought home not long ago when an article appeared in *OUT Traveler* reporting that Fly, the Toronto dance club that (along with another club, 5ive) portrayed Babylon in the early episodes of *Queer as Folk* and provided the template for it in subsequent seasons, was closing in June 2014, after one last World Pride celebration. It was the "last large dance club in Toronto's gayborhood" (Broverman). The article quotes owner Keir McRae as lamenting that the city was actively discouraging gay clubs within the Church Street Gay Village, even though "'dance clubs have always been a significant part of gay culture'" (Broverman). The article ends by asking the question: "Is assimilation behind the closure of big-city clubs or is it something else?" (Broverman). Fly eventually reopened farther from the Village as Fly 2.0, catering to a more mixed (i.e., less gay, more straight) crowd, so the "thumpa-thumpa" continues, albeit with a different vibe. Ultimately, 5ive and another gay club, Zipperz, also closed, and they were developed into family-friendly condos. I doubt the now forty-five-year-old Brian Kinney is living in one.

Works Cited

Aurthur, Kate. "Speaking Out for Their Folk." *Los Angeles Times*, 24 July 2005. Web. 29 November 2015.

Broverman, Neal. "Toronto Club That Played *Queer as Folk's* Babylon Is Closing." *OUT Traveler*, 29 April 2014. Web. 29 November 2015.

Elber, Lynn. "'Queer as Folk' to Tackle Subject of Gay Marriage." *Los Angeles Times*, 9 July 2004. Web. 29 November 2015.

Goldberg, Lesley. "'Queer as Folk' Reunion: Creators Talk Early Obstacles and a Potential Reboot." *Hollywood Reporter*, 5 June 2015. Web. 29 November 2015.

Robinson, Paul. *Queer Wars: The New Gay Right and Its Critics*. Chicago: University of Chicago Press, 2005. Print.

Rowe, Michael. "The Men Behind QAF." *Advocate*, 15 April 2003: 49. Print.

Sullivan, Andrew. "The End of Gay Culture: Assimilation and Its Meaning." *New Republic*, 23 October 2005. Web. 29 November 2015.

_____. *Virtually Normal: An Argument about Homosexuality*. New York: Vintage, 1995. Print.

Wallenstein, Andrew. "Playing It Straight with Gay Dramas." *Hollywood Reporter*, 8 January 2004. Web. 29 November 2015.

Warner, Michael. *The Trouble with Normal: Sex, Politics, and the Ethics of Queer Life*. Cambridge: Harvard University Press, 2000. Print.

We're Here, We're Queer— and We're Better Than You

The Representational Superiority of Gay Men to Heterosexuals on Queer Eye for the Straight Guy

KYLO-PATRICK R. HART

During summer 2003, Bravo's new reality series *Queer Eye for the Straight Guy* (2003–2007; the title was shortened to *Queer Eye* after season three) became a breakout hit and one of the most talked-about television programs of the year. This latest take on the makeover format features five gay men who swoop into the life of a heterosexual man in distress as he approaches some important crossroads in his life and recognizes the need to acquire style—fast! The goal is not to turn the unkempt straight guy gay but rather to infuse him with wisdom about culinary, fashion, grooming, decorating, and cultural matters that gay men in U.S. society are presumed, stereotypically, to inherently possess.

My hackles went up the moment I first learned that this series was in production. Having studied media representations of gay men in U.S. film and television offerings as an academic researcher for more than a decade at that point—and based on the early publicity materials I encountered—I expected that this reality show would simply offer continuous images of five flamboyant queens as its gay male cast each week, along with all of the stereotypical representational baggage they could bring with them. As a result, I was expecting to hate this show, but I can't. Refreshingly, I was proven wrong. And now I am going to make an assessment that I never envisioned possible: *Queer Eye for the Straight Guy* consistently offers the most positive representation of gay men available to viewers up to that point in U.S. television history.

Without a doubt, the harshest critics of this good-natured reality series will disagree with me. Some have said that it raises concerns about harmful stereotyping (Rutenberg C9) and is taking American viewers "back to a time when derision about homosexuals was the norm" (Siegel). Others have argued that the series endangers both children and traditional values and is "part of the downward progression of TV being led by cable" (Cook). I could not disagree with them more.

In this essay, I demonstrate why I find *Queer Eye for the Straight Guy* to offer one of the most positive representations of gay men in U.S. television history. To do so, I begin by providing a brief overview of representations of gay men on U.S. television over the last four decades of the 20th century. Then, I use that essential historical context to show how *Queer Eye for the Straight Guy* is qualitatively distinct from the related kinds of representations of gay men that preceded it, enabling this reality series to work representational "magic" by consistently communicating, in implicit ways, that gay men are superior—rather than inferior—to heterosexuals.

Brief History of Gay Men on U.S. Television

It has long been argued that representations of gay men on U.S. television matter because they provide ideological guidance to American viewers about how they should think about and respond to gay men and their lived realities. Although potentially affecting all audience members in powerful ways, the influence of such representations is believed to have the most substantial influence on individuals with little or no firsthand opportunity for interacting with and learning about gay men as they go about their everyday lives (Gross 144; Hart 76). This is bad news for gay men generally because far more negative than positive representations of their demographic group have been presented to audience members in recent decades, especially during the last four decades of the 20th century.

As former CNN correspondent Edward Alwood has documented, the first representation of gay men in the United States to a national audience occurred in March 1967 with the airing of a *CBS Reports* documentary titled "The Homosexuals" (69). A wide range of harmful stereotypes about gay men were communicated in this program, including that the average gay man is inherently promiscuous and incapable of forming lasting relationships (Alwood 73). Interview subjects, including a sexually needy sailor and a female impersonator, were alternately featured with their faces hidden in shadows or lying on an analyst's couch, implicitly suggesting that they were either filled with shame, perpetually unhappy, or—to use the word of one closeted gay subject—even "sick" (Alwood 72–73). Experts reinforced such perceptions by maintaining that gay men were individuals who would never find happiness in life (Alwood 72).

That influential representation from the late 1960s set the stage for how gay men were subsequently represented on U.S. television programs during the 1970s: as objects of ridicule (Hart 63). During this era, it was considered taboo for writers and producers to include any content in their scripts that appeared to condone homosexuality or to present gay men in positive ways, for fear that doing so would drive away both viewers and advertisers (Alwood 139). In contrast, jokes and derogatory comments about gay men were encouraged as "appropriate" and "entertaining" forms of content (Alwood 139; Hart 63). As a result, influential episodes of *Marcus Welby, M.D.* (1969–1976) portrayed homosexuality as a serious illness (at a time when the American Psychiatric Association challenged such a view) and gay teachers as likely rapists of defenseless young boys (Alwood 130, 142, 148). The predominant representation of gay men on popular shows such as *Hawaii Five-O* (1968–1980), *Kojak* (1973–1978), and *Police Woman* (1974–1978) was that of the "limp-wristed effeminate drag queen who walked with a swish and talked in a high-pitched voice" (Alwood 140). Derogatory terms for gay men—such as "homo," "fag," "fairy," and "pansy"—were commonly encountered on U.S. talk shows and dramatic series during this era (Hart 63).

During the 1980s, as AIDS emerged as an unexpected health threat in U.S. society and around the world, the most common representations of gay men on U.S. television involved linking them, both explicitly and implicitly, with HIV/AIDS. During the first half of this decade, it was television news programs that socially constructed AIDS as a "gay plague" in the minds of American viewers despite the fact that noteworthy studies had identified heterosexual patients with AIDS from the pandemic's earliest days (Padgug and Oppenheimer 253). During the second half of this decade, entertainment programming contributed substantially to this representational trend. In 1985, NBC aired *An Early Frost* (directed by John Erman), the first made-for-television movie about AIDS, which featured a young male lawyer who visits his family to tell them he is gay and is ill. Shortly thereafter, gay male characters with AIDS began appearing in the plots of several prime-time television shows, including *21 Jump Street* (1987–1991), *Designing Women* (1986–1993), *The Equalizer* (1985–1989), *Houston Knights* (1987–1988), *Midnight Caller* (1988–1991), *Mr. Belvedere* (1985–1990), and *A Year in the Life* (1987–1988), among others (Netzhammer and Shamp 92). As social worker Steve Cadwell has characterized this unfortunate state of affairs, gay men who were already stigmatized as "deviant" during this era became further stigmatized as "lethally contagious" threats to "innocent" heterosexuals in the population at large (237).

Although numerous shows continued to reinforce perceptions of AIDS as a "gay disease" during the 1990s, representations of gay men on U.S. television improved substantially during this decade. A growing number of popular daytime and prime-time programs increasingly began to represent diverse and inclusive gay male characters that reflected the wider range of roles and personality types that gay men possess in U.S. society. For example, in 1990, the dramatic series *thirtysomething* (1987–1991) introduced two recurring gay male professionals who became romantically and sexually involved. In 1992, the daytime soap opera *One Life to Live* (1968–2013) featured a gay male teenager coming to terms with his sexual orientation and exploring his first romantic relationship with another guy, and the prime-time dramatic series *Melrose Place* (1992–1999) introduced the gay character Matt Fielding (played by Doug Savant) as a likable, well-adjusted, and civic-minded member of a group of young adults who reside in the same Los Angeles apartment complex. In the mid-1990s, the situation comedy *Roseanne* (1988–1997) introduced two recurring gay male characters in the form of Roseanne's business partner and his lover, who eventually took part in a commitment ceremony on the show. From 1995 onward, the daytime soap opera *All My Children* (1970–2011) offered groundbreaking storylines about a gay male high school student as well as two gay professionals (a high school history teacher and an orthopedic specialist) who entered into a long-term committed relationship. In 1997, the year that the situation comedy *Ellen* (1994–1998) made history by featuring the first lesbian lead character in a U.S. prime-time television series, regular and recurring gay male characters could be found on numerous prime-time programs, including *Chicago Hope* (1994–2000), *Cybill* (1995–1998), *Frasier* (1993–2004), *Melrose Place*, *Party of Five* (1994–2000), *Profiler* (1996–2000), *Roseanne*, *The Simpsons* (1989–), *Spin City* (1996–2002), and *Unhappily Ever After* (1995–1999). In 1998, NBC's situation comedy *Will & Grace* (1998–2006) introduced viewers to prime-time television's first gay male lead character, Will Truman (played by Eric McCormack), as well as to his flamboyant gay friend, Jack (played by Sean Hayes). These and similar representations contributed to increased social tolerance and wider recognition of the status of gay men in U.S. society during that decade.

What Distinguishes Queer Eye for the Straight Guy *from Other Televised Representations of Gay Men*

Queer Eye for the Straight Guy premiered in the summer of 2003, during a period in which the rhetoric of President George W. Bush about marriage suggested that gay and lesbian relationships were less valid than heterosexual ones and the Vatican warned that both gay marriage and gay adoption were immoral actions. These developments and related others suggest that the status of gay men in U.S. society is always already inferior to that of heterosexual men. The majority of media representations of gay men on U.S. television over the last four decades of the 20th century communicated, and continually reinforced, a similar message both explicitly (e.g., by featuring gay male characters primarily as objects of ridicule in relation to heterosexuals or as lethal health threats to heterosexuals) and implicitly (e.g., by featuring gay male characters in substantially more limited numbers and more limited roles in comparison to their surrounding heterosexual characters). Even *Will & Grace*, the series that was identified repeatedly as providing evidence that gay men had "made it" with regard to social acceptance in U.S. society, has been criticized by many critics (myself included) for offering highly restrictive representations of gay men that lie at extreme opposites on the spectrum of possible such representations: Will remained so low-key about his sexual orientation during the series' early seasons that it was almost inconsequential to the show, whereas Jack was consistently presented as the most highly stereotypical version of a self-centered, promiscuous, mean-spirited, flamboyant queen (Hart 60). As such, it is difficult to regard that situation comedy as a substantial "breakthrough" in televised representations of gay men in U.S. society (with the exception, perhaps, of its later seasons), despite the fact that it continued to attract a sizable viewing audience each season.

Perhaps surprisingly, and in contrast to *Will & Grace* and the variety of other (seemingly) well-intentioned representations of gay men on U.S. television that preceded it, *Queer Eye for the Straight Guy* does indeed serve as a groundbreaking series. More so than any other series offered to U.S. television viewers up to the time of its premiere, it consistently makes trouble for the notion, so commonly communicated in preceding representations, that gay men are inherently inferior to heterosexuals by virtue of their sexual orientation, and it did so for a rapidly expanding viewing audience. Although this hour-long series appeared primarily on the NBC-owned Bravo cable network, it also aired twice during prime time on the NBC broadcast network with impressive ratings in 2003, first with a condensed half-hour episode in July of that year and then again with a full-length episode in August. Early press reports indicated that the unexpected success of this series might lead to its becoming a regular offering on the NBC prime-time schedule in future seasons, but ultimately this did not happen (Shister).

In each episode of *Queer Eye for the Straight Guy*, the "Fab Five"—Ted Allen (specializing in food and wine), Kyan Douglas (grooming), Thom Filicia (interior design), Carson Kressley (fashion), and Jai Rodriguez (culture)—offer guidance in their respective areas of expertise to a hapless heterosexual man in search of style as a special occasion in his life approaches: the first time he will present his art in a gallery, the first time he will throw a surprise party for his wife, the first time he will propose marriage or ask his girlfriend to move in with him, etc. During such trying times, the gang of experts descends on the straight male subject all at once—in a manner they have personally described as "shock and awe" (Sellers B1)—and proceed to update both his personal appearance and that of his home. The straight men are taught how to do everything from picking out their own clothes and dressing themselves appropriately to preparing gourmet meals and shopping for wines that cannot be bought in jugs. They learn to tolerate and even appreciate grooming essentials such as facials, manicures, and nose-hair trimmings. They are introduced to improved living conditions that complement their new-and-improved image. In short, the heterosexual male subjects are trained by the Fab Five to become stylish and metrosexual, rather than stylish and homosexual. "It's not a makeover show," Carson has explained. "It's a make-better show" (qtd. in Sellers B1).

On the surface, *Queer Eye for the Straight Guy* may not appear to offer a more positive representation of gay men than did representations of the past because, admittedly, the series' entire premise embraces a long-standing stereotype about gay men: that they possess a natural flair for style that straight people typically lack. Accordingly, as *USA Today* reported in August 2003, some gay men were "lamenting that the gays-can-only-decorate stereotype [was] again being hauled out of the closet" (Wilson D1). On a related note, although critics who have referred to the Fab Five as "fairy godmothers" (e.g., Macaulay 16) or "fairy godfathers" (e.g., Stanley E3) may be intending to draw attention to the "Cinderella-like" transformations that the straight men go through during each episode, the negative connotations of the word "fairy" when linked to gay men, though perhaps unintentional, cannot go unnoticed. Both of these realities suggest strongly that this series feminizes gay men, even though this is certainly not the case. The widespread perception that it does so, however, contributes to the show's radically subversive potential: it appears to offer only images of gay men that are nonthreatening to heterosexual viewers while, at the same time, it is bombarding those same viewers with representations implicitly suggesting that gay men are actually superior—rather than inferior—to heterosexuals, thereby inverting and undermining the cumulative message that has been disseminated about gay men in U.S. society through television offerings over several decades. Even if additional stereotypes about gay men surface occasionally along the way, the diversity of personalities and ways of being reflected by the individual members of the Fab Five implicitly reminds viewers that all gay men, like all straight men, are individuals, and that no single individual can ever adequately represent the diversity of an entire demographic group. In short, this series provides a powerfully fresh message about the comparative status of gay men in relation to both heterosexual men and heterosexual women in

U.S. society, working its representational "magic" under the guise of being simply a straightforward makeover program.

How Queer Eye for the Straight Guy Works Its Representational "Magic"

Queer Eye for the Straight Guy is not the first reality television series that has featured gay men. During the 1970s, Lance Loud came out before the eyes of television viewers on the first U.S. reality series, PBS's *An American Family* (1973). More recently, gay men have appeared in various seasons of *The Real World* (1992–), *Big Brother* (2000–), and *Survivor* (2000–). What makes the situation different on *Queer Eye for the Straight Guy* is that, for the first time, gay men are in the majority, rather than the minority, on reality TV. This reality, in and of itself, represents a significant breakthrough in the evolution of U.S. television programming. It provides a very different power dynamic within the series, automatically placing the single straight guy at the mercy of the gay Fab Five, who dominate him and control most of his actions during each episode, whether he is physically in their presence or simply carrying out all of the things they have taught him later on. Although it is presumed that the straight guy retains some agency in these encounters, it is remarkable how completely most heterosexual subjects give themselves over to the gay men and adhere to their every instruction, order, or whim, even in situations when they initially appear reluctant to do so. In one episode, for example, the Fab Five persuade a resistant member of their camera crew to engage in "manscaping," the elimination of the freakishly long body hair contained on his chest and back. One of the subject's co-workers describes his friend's hirsute condition by stating that the man's "hairline starts at his butt and works its way up to the front of his forehead." Because the subject whines and protests during the waxing of his back, he is called a "crybaby" to his face by the Fab Five; nevertheless, he allows the procedure to be completed in its entirety. The experts also make the straight guy feel as though he is wimpier than the average woman, for as Kyan points out, "You know what women go through? They get the 'chocha' done, and it's a lot worse than this!" In another episode, the Fab Five effectively convince a long-haired software engineer to cut several inches off his beloved long locks by promising that it will make him "rock 'n' roll shaggy," despite repeated protests from both the man and his girlfriend to leave the hair alone. It is clear that the Fab Five understand and appreciate the power they wield over the straight guys they are attempting to mold. Acknowledging this state of affairs, Carson remarks about one subject, "Ooh, I love how he jumps when I [say] 'jump'!" In a different episode, Carson jokingly asks another of the straight subjects, "Can I call you 'my bitch'?"

Another way that *Queer Eye for the Straight Guy* elevates the representational status of gay men is by constantly using humor to poke fun at, and reveal the ridiculous nature of, gay stereotypes. When one of the straight guys comments that people say that he, himself, looks like Keanu Reeves, Carson quips that people believe Carson looks just like Ellen DeGeneres, revealing how ludicrous it is for individuals to suggest that gay men look just like women. Likewise, when another straight guy wonders what the other members of the Fab Five might be doing to his house, Ted jokes, "They've probably loaded up a power painter and they're spraying the whole place bright pink," effectively undermining another stereotypical notion about gay men with regard to color preferences and femininity. Far more significantly, however, the various members of the Fab Five use humor to poke fun directly at their straight subjects as well. For those who believe that gay guys are "deviant" and straight guys "non-deviant," the Fab Five flip through the various offerings in one subject's collection of print pornography, which includes issues of *Barely Legal* magazine and a brochure pertaining to "she-male" sex videos. While Ted cracks a lobster tail with style and ease at a restaurant table, his heterosexual dining partner struggles incessantly to crack a lobster claw, ultimately giving up and admitting that he looks weak by comparison. Each member of the expert team is also blessed with healthy doses of good-natured wit and sarcasm. Eyeing one subject's belongings, Carson asks, "Do you have bad credit or just bad taste?" Observing the remarkable transformation of another subject, Jai remarks, "He's not the 'guido mumbo' that he was around us." With regard to the shaving techniques of heterosexual men, Kyan notes, "I think it's some straight gene—they don't know how to shave *with* the grain," and "Aside from the blood, he looks really good clean-shaven." Searching for much-needed kitchen accessories, Ted wonders, "If I were a plate, where would I be? Oh, in the sink." And stunned by the decorating choices apparent in some of the straight guys' homes, Thom explains, "The sofa and chair look like you got them free with a fill-up," and "Do you know what minimalism is? Minimal is like 'real clean.' *This* is *bleak*." At times, when the precise words to adequately express their reactions escape them, humorous interjections work equally as effectively: "Ugh! Oof!" Kyan exclaims as he observes all of the filth and clutter in one straight guy's bathroom. The use of humor in these ways reveals that it is just as easy for gay men to make fun of heterosexuals as it has been for heterosexuals, for decades on television, to make fun of gay men. As such, the use of humor in the series further undermines long-standing representational power dynamics pertaining to gay men versus straight ones. Though some may be tempted to claim that such utterances are simply those of stereotypically "catty" gay men, the impact of these comments betrays the validity of such a claim because it is clear that these remarks are made in good-natured (rather than intentionally hurtful) ways and that the Fab Five really seem to care about the individuals they are helping.

The Fab Five also regularly use humor—most commonly in the form of sexual innuendo—as well as the sense of touch to show straight men that there is no reason to be afraid of gay men. By far, Carson is the king of sexual innuendo in this bunch. When one of the heterosexual subjects reveals he likes the look of a clothing article that resembles a pitcher's shirt, Carson inquires, "Are you a pitcher or a catcher?" immediately conjuring up images of gay sex. When another subject explains that he cannot thank the Fab Five enough for all of their help, Carson replies, "Well, *I* can think of a way." When seated next to a handsome hetero hunk, Carson advises, "If at any time today you want to make out with me, just let me know." When wondering why straight guys are not attracted to him, Carson asks, "What has [your girl-friend] got that I don't—besides a working vagina?" Humorous exchanges of sexual innuendo such as these make it clear to the straight subjects, as well as to straight viewers at home, that gay men do not really pose actual threats to their sexuality or well-being. The constant use of touch by the gay experts with their straight subjects sends similar messages. It is not uncommon for members of the Fab Five to lead straight subjects by the hand, massage the necks and shoulders of nervous subjects, or exchange hugs with the straight guys. Carson, again, takes these incidents to greater extremes in order to demonstrate how ridiculous it is for straight men to be fearful of gay ones. For example, approaching one of the straight subjects in a dressing room, Carson insists on being cuddled by the man, who obliges his request. When Carson asks a different subject to give him a little kiss on the cheek, his wish is immediately fulfilled. In yet another situation, Carson asks a straight subject to sit with him on a sofa and imagine that he is making out with him the same way he does with his girlfriend; as the subject cooperates, Carson embraces the man playfully and runs his fingers through the guy's hair. Here again, such exchanges and images are quite significant from a representational standpoint because they regularly show straight men interacting with, and ultimately benefiting from the wisdom of, gay men without demonstrating fear, phobia, or apparent threats to their own sexuality. From time to time, it is refreshing to see the straight subjects really get into the spirit of these harmless incidents. Carson, for example, convinces one subject to rub his stubbly chin against Carson's cheek, to which Carson jokingly exclaims, "Oh, my God, you're gay! You're a homosexual!" The subject, laughing and com-pletely unfazed, responds, "Did you put 'the gay' on me?" In another scenario, a different subject turns the tables on Carson, offering to serve as the fashion expert himself while requiring Carson to try on a skimpy bathing suit. Responding in ways similar to how he, himself, has been treated, the straight guy opens the dressing-room door quickly to catch Carson in the act of undressing, and he kneels willingly at Carson's crotch, offering to him help with the buttons on his pants. "You guys are rubbing off on me," a straight male subject jokes while shopping. "Next thing you know, I'll have a boyfriend, be all set."

Yet another way that the representational status of gay men, in comparison to straight men, is enhanced in *Queer Eye for the Straight Guy* is through the expressions of gratitude and positive comments provided by all of the Fab Five's subjects who, by each episode's end, have "seen the light" and become successfully "converted" into a whole new breed of man. It is not uncommon for the straight subjects to express that they could not have made all of the positive changes in their lives without the help of these five gay experts; many toast the experts and hug each one individually before they depart. "I really just want to thank the Fab Five—five gay guys who hooked me up!" explains one subject, in front of an audience at the nightclub where he is singing his first solo number; another subject's eyes well up with tears as he reflects upon everything the group has done to make the night he will propose to his girlfriend so special. In addition to these positive displays of warmth and appreciation, several of the subjects explicitly express how their views about what is "masculine" or "heterosexual" behavior have changed as a result of their experiences with the Fab Five. When asked by Kyan whether the eye mask, face mask, and manicure he is receiving at a spa are "very homo," one subject explains, "Straight guys just don't think that this is masculine ... but I'm here to tell you guys it's not [homo]." Similarly, another subject states about his first facial, "I always thought this stuff was girl stuff, you know? ... Everybody needs this." Without fail, each episode of *Queer Eye for the Straight Guy* concludes with emotionally moving images that not only confirm the expertise of the Fab Five but also indicate how grateful the heterosexual subjects are for the help they have provided. Positive reactions such as these reveal that there are not nearly as many differences between the appropriate behaviors of gay men and straight men as have stereotypically been assumed in U.S. society for many years, enhancing the representational status of gay men in the process.

Within the world of *Queer Eye for the Straight Guy*, the various techniques just described have proven effective in changing the views of even the most "cautious" straight guy that the Fab Five encountered during the series' first season: a Port Authority policeman from New York City. As soon as he glimpses the Fab Five coming through his front door, the subject, who is clearly uncomfortable being around gay men, exclaims, "[Are you] fucking kidding me?" He tenses up immediately as Carson begins "frisking" him playfully, insisting that Carson keep his hands on the sides of the cop's legs as he runs them up and down. Is Carson getting too frisky while frisking? Not really, but it becomes instantly evident that it will take some work for this subject to realize that gay men do not threaten his sexuality or his identity as a macho straight guy. Accordingly, the various members of the Fab Five begin poking fun at stereotypes of gay men to help put the man at ease, such as when Carson pulls a shirt reading "Barry Sanders 20" out of the subject's closet and, although clearly recognizing it to be a reference to the former Detroit Lions football player, pretends to understand nothing about sports: "I love fried chicken, but Barry Sanders is dead and gone, so who cares?" They also make comments that poke fun at the straight subject directly. "We're gonna play Twister with your [loudly polka-dotted] shower curtain!" Kyan exclaims, before adding, "I found the culture—it's in the bottom of the tooth-brush holder!" "Nothing says love like testicle humor," Ted observes, reacting to a conversation between the subject and his girlfriend. "Wouldn't you cut your own toenail before you let it turn into a weapon?" Thom asks, startled by the man's outward appearance. Playing to the subject's desire to cook and consume only "manly food," Ted renames a vegetable torta "man quiche" so that the straight guy will feel comfortable making and serving it. Instances of sexual innuendo and touching are not far behind. As Kyan and the subject stand side by side wearing only disposable bikini-style trunks, preparing to receive spray-on tans, Kyan asks, "What's 'gay' about this situation?" The sub-ject expresses that he is embarrassed to be standing in "disposable skivvies" next to a "gay guy." Moments later, when Kyan asks the spray artist whether she can make the subject's penis look bigger, the straight guy responds, "Why are you looking at my penis? Come on, please, the belly button up!" Carson follows up his frisking encounter by climbing atop the Twister-inspired shower curtain, with his backside in the air, encouraging the subject to "Get on—seriously—no really!" As he begins to feel more comfortable with, and less threatened by, the gay experts, the subject starts initiating handshakes with all of them as an indicator of his appreciation of their efforts; he also stops cringing when they touch him on the shoulder and even initiates hugs with some of them when their work is done. After the Fab Five depart, the subject tells his girlfriend, "My confidence was low; I just wasn't feeling right, you know? Just all stressed out and stuff. But thanks to you, and to these guys, I feel like I've got a spark in my pants!" Mission accomplished. Even the seemingly most homophobic subject the Fab Five have ever encountered has gained a new acceptance and appreciation of gay men.

Encoding the Fab Five as a Band of (Gay) Superheroes

As if the preceding attributes of *Queer Eye for the Straight Guy* were not impressive enough at helping to enhance representations of gay men on U.S.

television, a final aspect is even *more* impressive in this regard: the way the series encodes the Fab Five as a band of (gay) superheroes who help save the life of a straight guy in need. Accomplishing such a feat apparently is something that their heterosexual male friends are unable to do, and it is apparently something that their heterosexual girlfriends or wives (for those who have them) remain equally unable to accomplish.

In part, the five gay experts appear to possess "superpowers" in their various areas of expertise primarily because the series presents them as being just regular gay guys, rather than leading experts in their fields. While in reality all of these gay men possess substantial credentials and experience in their respective areas (e.g., Kyan received his cosmetology certification from the Aveda Institute New York and has worked as a colorist on various television and magazine projects; Thom has worked at high-end firms including Robert Metzger Interiors and personally founded one of the top design companies in the United States; etc.), such information is available to viewers only through extratextual means, rather than within the various episodes themselves. As a result, it appears that gay men generally possess a range of impressive talents that straight men and straight women seem incapable of fully cultivating, enabling them—just like comic-book superheroes—to swoop in at just the right moment and help transform an ordinary straight guy's life into a glamorous existence. Their apparent motto, as Carson states in an early episode of the series, is "Now that we're here, we're gonna show you the way of the gay!"

When the girlfriend of one subject is in awe of the Fab Five's redecorating accomplishments and asks, "Who knew that all this stuff would go together?" Carson, while viewing the exchange on a television monitor, exclaims proudly, "*We* did!" When the satisfied wife of another subject is bragging about the fantastic work the Fab Five have done to her and her husband's formerly unkempt home, Carson observes, "The other wives are like this: 'Now where do we get some of those gays?'" Even though an apparent goal of the series is to break down the artificial, stereotypical ideological boundaries that have historically separated gay men from straight ones, the structure of each episode of *Queer Eye for the Straight Guy* intentionally calls attention to such distinctions, emphasizing that gay men are indeed distinct from, and perhaps even superior to, heterosexual men and women. For example, the start of every episode, along with a head shot of the week's heterosexual subject, features the words "straight guy" in giant letters. Previews of upcoming scenes in the unfolding episode are labeled "straight ahead." A common toast among the Fab Five is "Cheers, queers!" when they are alone, which has been modified to "Cheers, queers—and straight guy!" when they are in the presence of a subject. As such, the structure of the episodes continues to remind viewers that straight guys and gay guys are classified into separate categories, even as the episodes attempt, at least on the surface, to eradicate such distinctions. Because it is the gay guys who can whip a house into shape in record time, or motivate a love interest to accept a marriage proposal, or accomplish whatever other challenge awaits them, it is the valiant gay men in the series, rather than the straight men or even the straight women, who come out most victorious every time. Furthermore, it is interesting to note that the episodes suggest that it is only gay men who know what it really takes for straight men to be truly happy or to truly please the women they love.

By far, however, the most impressive way that this show encodes the Fab Five as a band of superheroes is that it condenses the activities of several days into what, on-screen, appears to be less than a twenty-four-hour period. While many makeover shows progress too slowly to retain the interest of viewers who have grown accustomed to rapid editing, *Queer Eye for the Straight Guy* defies this trend—all modifications occur at what appears to be a superhuman pace. Information about the series in both the alternative and mainstream press has revealed that the Fab Five spend, on average, four days working with each of their straight subjects (Giltz 41; Sellers B1). The way each episode is shot and edited, however, suggests that all of the experts' actions are completed in the same day. As such, it appears that the Fab Five, as representatives of all their gay brethren, are indeed stylish superheroes capable of repainting entire home interiors in just a few hours and efficiently treating their subjects to spa visits, shopping excursions, exquisite meals, culinary lessons, and related activities all between sunup and sundown. From a representational standpoint, that is at least the equivalent of being able to leap tall buildings in a single bound, and it enhances the perceived status of gay men in the eyes of mere mortals (i.e., heterosexual audience members).

Concluding Remarks

U.S. television contains countless examples of heterosexuals making derogatory jokes and hurtful remarks about gay men in ways that, hegemonically speaking, have contributed to social constructions of gay men as inferior beings to straight men and women. *Queer Eye for the Straight Guy* uses good-natured approaches to reverse those trends, ultimately offering representations of gay men as beings that appear to be superior to heterosexuals. In my opinion, all Americans stood to benefit from exposure to these new kinds of images of gay men when they materialized on-screen in 2003, signaling a watershed moment in U.S. popular culture. Such images were particularly important at a time when the number of gay male characters in U.S. prime-time television had begun to decrease substantially, having fallen to only seven gay characters in 2002 from nearly two dozen in 2001 (Macaulay 16).

Naturally, not all gay men inherently possess the range of impressive skills demonstrated by the Fab Five in each episode. Clearly, not all straight men are as helpless or needy as the subjects they assist. It is hoped that viewers recognize these realities despite the potential power of media representations to influence their perceptions and beliefs. And as far as media representations of gay men on U.S. television go, this is one of the most impressive I have ever seen.

About *Queer Eye for the Straight Guy*, one television critic observed in 2003: "Gone is the joyless obligation to be a role model for your gender-orientation. In its place comes the freedom to be fabulous, swishy, and bitchy again; basically to be gay and superficial. Like ordinary trash TV, gay trash TV is all about embracing one's inner stereotype" (Macaulay 16). That assessment makes me wonder if the critic actually watched even one complete episode of the series. Rather than ascribing to such a pessimistic and seemingly homophobic view, I find myself to be much more persuaded by comments offered by David Collins, executive producer of this noteworthy reality series, who stated:

> The show actually has a narrative structure to it that allows us to kind of come into the guys' world and go through their adventure of the Fab Five taking them and just opening up the doors to different possibilities that perhaps they didn't know were there or were a little intimidated to go down that path alone.... You know, the concept that five gay men are able to kind of look at themselves, make fun of themselves, look at the straight guy, make fun of him, and then turn that around and bring it together, [that's] the heart of the show. It's about the fact that gay guys [and] straight guys may do things a little different in the bedroom, but in the end, they're just men [Siegel].

Along the same lines, Fab Five member Carson Kressley has noted, "We're just six guys hanging out and, in the end, we just wind up being friends. Those stereotypes really kind of fall by the wayside. We end up with a guy who has an increased sense of confidence, looks better, feels better—and I know about hockey now. So, win-win" (Boedeker).

I couldn't have said it better myself.

Acknowledgment

This essay was originally published in *The Journal of Men's Studies* 12, no. 3 (Spring 2004), 241–253. © 2004 by Men's Studies Press, LLC.

Works Cited

Alwood, Edward. *Straight News: Gays, Lesbians, and the News Media.* New York: Columbia University Press, 1996. Print.

Boedeker, Hal. "New Makeover Shows Seek to Help Warring Couples, Straight Guys." *Orlando Sentinel*, 10 July 2003. Web. 8 August 2003.

Cadwell, Steve. "Twice Removed: The Stigma Suffered by Gay Men with AIDS." *Smith College Studies in Social Work* 61.3 (1991): 236–246. Print.

Cook, John. "Cable's Bravo Is Carving Out Gay Turf with Two New Shows." *Chicago Tribune*, 14 July 2003. Web. 8 August 2003.

Giltz, Michael. "*Queer Eye* Confidential." *Advocate*, 2 September 2003: 40–44. Print.

Gross, Larry. "What Is Wrong with This Picture? Lesbian Women and Gay Men on Television." *Queer Words, Queer Images: Communication and the Construction of Homosexuality*. Ed. R. Jeffrey Ringer. New York: New York University Press, 1994. 143–156. Print.

Hart, Kylo-Patrick R. "Representing Gay Men on American Television." *Journal of Men's Studies* 9.1 (2000): 59–79. Print.

Macaulay, Sean. "High Time That Gay Time Is Prime Time." *The Times*, 24 July 2003: 16. Print.

Netzhammer, Emile C., and Scott A. Shamp. "Guilt by Association: Homosexuality and AIDS on Prime-Time Television." *Queer Words, Queer Images: Communication and the Construction of Homosexuality*. Ed. R. Jeffrey Ringer. New York: New York University Press, 1994. 91–106. Print.

Padgug, Robert A., and Gerald M. Oppenheimer. "Riding the Tiger: AIDS and the Gay Community." *AIDS: The Making of a Chronic Disease*. Ed. Elizabeth Fee and Daniel M. Fox. Berkeley: University of California Press, 1992. 245–278. Print.

Rutenberg, Jim. "Reality-TV Idea: Gay Men Groom Straights." *New York Times*, 13 May 2002: C9. Print.

Sellers, John. "Queen for a Day: My Gay Makeover." *New York Times*, 13 July 2003: B1. Print.

Shister, Gail. "NBC Has High Hopes for Bravo's 'Queer Eye.'" *Philadelphia Inquirer*, 11 February 2003. Web. 8 August 2003.

Siegel, Robert, interviewer. "David Collins Discusses the Reality TV Show *Queer Eye for the Straight Guy*." *All Things Considered*. National Public Radio, 15 July 2003. Print. Transcript.

Stanley, Alessandra. "NBC Joins in to Help Hapless Heterosexuals." *New York Times* 24 July 2003: E3. Print.

Wilson, Craig. "Gay Taste? Here's Straight Talk." *USA Today*, 5 August 2003: D1. Print.

From Good to Bad Stories

Examining the Narrative of Pregnancy in The L Word *as a Means to Teach and Destabilize Queerness*

Anna Ciamparella

In the last few years, cable television networks such as HBO and Showtime have shown growing interest in the representation of LGBT subjects. Thus far, most queer programming has focused on the LGBT quest for love and personal fulfillment in a society that, ideally, is becoming less homophobic. Providing greater visibility to LGBT characters means that queer subjects are increasingly becoming "ordinary," so to speak, as they increasingly leave behind those qualities of unusualness and awkwardness with which they were once sketched. Generally, to define a subject as "ordinary" challenges its cultural importance. However, with regard to queer characterizations on the small screen, making LGBT characters "ordinary" signifies giving queerness its due space in mainstream television, a medium that has historically and systematically been dominated by representations of predetermined and gendered sexualities. In recent years, queer television offerings have been decreasing the rigid heterosexual/homosexual dichotomy as their stories reveal the incongruities of this dualism and teach the public to shatter binary oppositions.

As Plato indicates in Book II of his *Republic*, there are stories that can and should be told for the sake of the social well-being, and others that should not be mentioned because they weaken the moral strength of the community. When applied to queer television, this concept allows us to understand the cultural shift that is taking place in the representation of gay characters as their narratives introduce the public—especially the heterosexual one—to the possibility of social cohabitation. Ideally, queer images on cable networks appear to be progressive and groundbreaking; however, as exciting as this may sound, a close reading of these various series reveals subtle cultural tensions that are still far from being resolved. This particular essay focuses on examining the narrative of pregnancy in *The L Word* (2004–2009), a Showtime production that aired over six seasons, in order to indicate the queering success of the program and to unveil, nevertheless, its inconsistencies while speculating on the reasons that led to such discrepancies.

Admittedly, *The L Word* had a promising start. As Margaret McFadden posits, the series generated a positive response from both a general audience and a more specialized public because it is "unapologetically lesbian centered" (3). This series finally made lesbians visible. It not only represents the dynamics of female same-sex couples in all of their nuances but also, most importantly, depicts these relationships as unfolding in a society that does not ostracize their gay potential. At the same time, Pei-Wen Lee and Michaela Meyer are very critical of this visibility, arguing that "despite the gains in visibility and even intimacy, the show offers little to no coping mechanisms for the underlying problems of heterosexism and homophobia other than avoidance" (Lee 235). If that is the case, more recent television artifacts have also adopted the same strategy. In the HBO series *Looking* (2014–2015), for example, heterosexism is similarly avoided, rather than confronted, thereby suggesting, according to the implication of Lee and Meyer's argument, that debunking homophobia on the small screen may be an unfeasible task. Even valuing these considerations, it is impossible to deny that *The L Word* marked a radical shift in the characterization of the queer subject. Furthermore, it is not wholly accurate to claim that the series avoids homophobia: The storyline of Tasha Williams (played by Rose Rollins) indeed is reminiscent of the loathsome "don't ask, don't tell" policy that the Clinton Administration instituted in the military in 1994. Frederik Dhaenens recognizes that "queer resistances on television destroy heteronormative discourse from within by corrupting or undermining it" (521). Even conceiving of that, *The L Word* avoids confrontation with homophobia, the dodging of which may signify resistance to heterosexism as the focus of the series remains the lesbian experience as it is, or can be, in a queer space that does not necessarily grow out of a heterosexual matrix but rather exists *a priori*. The lesbian plot in the series is unrestrained, and not only because it is composed of many erotic scenes. The quasi-pornography undertaken in the series is a rhetorical strategy to reach a large audience, but it is not seminal. What counts most is the "educational system" of the series, which challenges and undoes lesbian stereotypes and gives queerness a fictional cosmos wherein the problems faced by same-sex couples are not exclusively related to how they express, or live, their sexuality. In other words, *The L Word* provides an "educational system" that changes the epistemology of the lesbian individual and the way society relates to it.

From Bad to Good Stories

What viewers saw on television prior to *The L Word* were primarily examples of "bad literature" that virtually obliterated queerness because, even if in these portrayals queer characters were out, their narratives never did them justice. Over the course of the five seasons of the situation comedy series *Ellen* (1994–1998), for example, the sexuality of the main character, Ellen Morgan (played by Ellen DeGeneres), although expressed through the cultural function of masculine clothing, is never completely fulfilled. As Rachel Loewen Walker notes, "Ellen Morgan's *lack* of a relationship left an unspoken silence on the show, and during discussions concerning how to tie up these loose ends, one of the writers suggested that Ellen simply get a puppy in the fourth season" (1, original emphasis). Walker also suggests that a close reading of the series reveals a "build up" of the queer characterization throughout the seasons; clearly, however, Ellen remains sexually *silent*. It is possible to identify other noteworthy instances of "bad literature" preceding *The L Word*, but the example of *Ellen* should suffice for the following two reasons: first, because it is regarded as the first lesbian "coming out" in U.S. television, which coincided with the real-life coming out of Ellen DeGeneres; and second, because other television series produced in the 1990s fall more or less into a narrative pattern that focuses on characters who are either in denial of their sexuality or choose to remain closeted in order to shun homophobic judgment. Such narratives are examples of "bad stories" for they deliver a misleading image of queer individuals, as they suggest that they are people who do not mind hiding their sexual orientation. Obviously, the legal and political battles of the gay rights movement prove that the voluntary and happy closeted queer does not necessarily exist and that past television productions instilled in audience members' minds inaccurate ideas about queer communities. Today's queer television offerings typically offer more realistic images of gay people and reject previous interpretations. As Plato expressed,

> Our first job, apparently, is to oversee the work of the story-writers, and to accept any good story they write, but reject the others. We'll let nurses and mothers tell their children the acceptable ones, and we'll have them devote themselves far more to using these stories to form their children's minds than they do to using their hands to form their bodies. However, we'll have to disallow most of the stories they currently tell [Plato 50].

Discarding previous, unacceptable stories is precisely the pedagogical task of *The L Word* as it represents characters who openly express their sexuality. As Janet McCabe and Kim Akass point out, Ilene Chaiken, executive producer and one of the writers of the series, felt the urge to tell her own stories in order to debunk lesbian stereotypes and "fill a representational void" (xxvi).

But *The L Word* goes beyond mere depictions of lesbian sexuality and reflects another touching issue related to the experience of many lesbians: pregnancy. This narrative is rather crucial in the series. The pilot episode introduces the struggle of Bette Porter (played by Jennifer Beals) and Tina Kennard (played by Laurel Holloman) to form their own family and have their first child. Their storyline, although very dramatic at times, communicates a positive message about parenting possibilities for lesbian couples. By portraying Bette and Tina's attempts at parenthood, the series shows that same-sex couples have the same rights as heterosexuals and simultaneously, by humanizing lesbian pregnancy, teaches the public about the processes that gay women experience as they attempt to successfully fulfill their desire to conceive a baby. In the real world, this process is emotionally painful, difficult, and distressing, just as Bette and Tina's storyline documents on the small screen. According to the decision-making model articulated by Jennifer Chabot and Barbara Ames (which is based on real-life experiences), for a lesbian couple, parenthood resolution is a multistage process that plays out over time. The model includes seven stages distributed in a circular diagram:

(1) Do We Want to Become Parents?
(2) Where Do We Access Information and Support?
(3) How Will We Become Parents?
(4) Who Will Be the Biological Mother?
(5) How Do We Decide on a [Known or Unknown] Donor?
(6) How Do We Incorporate Inclusive Language?
(7) How Do We Negotiate Parenthood within the Larger Heterocentric Context? [Chabot and Ames 350–359].

As stages three and five indicate, lesbian couples must choose between two or more options and, sometimes, they also have to bargain with other alternatives (Chabot and Ames 352–353). The first question that lesbian couples need to answer, then, is whether they want to become parents. With regard to Bette and Tina, this first step is implied because their storyline begins with Tina checking the ovulation test results to make sure that she is ready to be inseminated. The brief shot reveals that Bette and Tina have already made the decision to become parents via donor insemination. The reality that these two women opt for the insemination procedure, rather than adopting a child, demonstrates a noteworthy finding of Chabot and Ames' study: that donor insemination is frequently chosen because it offers "a pregnancy, birth experience, and a desired genetic link" (Chabot and Ames 352). The participants in their research "wanted the experience of giving birth, and they challenged the assumption that because they were lesbians, they should be left out of this experience" (Chabot and Ames 352). Similarly, in *The L Word* it is clear that Bette and Tina, like the real couples participating in Chabot and Ames' research, seek through pregnancy an emotional and biological connection with their child and challenge the heterocentric assumption that lesbians cannot experience motherhood. Like the women studied by Chabot and Ames, these two fictional characters choose among multiple options and even decide to engage in sexual intercourse in order to make the donor insemination as natural as possible for Tina to get pregnant. Bette's attempt to inseminate Tina fails the first time because the donated sperm, according to the doctor who supervises Tina, "wouldn't get anyone pregnant. Those little fellas just don't have what it takes." Nevertheless, Bette and Tina's storyline demonstrates that they wish to conceive their child through an act of love, thereby informing the audience that debunking heteronormative tenets is indeed possible.

As Bette and Tina's tale unfolds, the audience also encounters representations of the other stages included in the decision-making model. Following their initial insemination failure, this same-sex couple faces the dilemma of finding a suitable second donor. They turn to Jean-Paul Chamois (played by Robert Gauvin), an artist that Bette knows, who is ready to sign the donor contract that releases the biological father from any future parental rights. However, the man refuses to use the seminal cup because, as he says, "Oh, no, no, no, we don't do [it] that way; we do [it] as a man and a woman," entirely disregarding the women's request. This demonstrates that choosing a donor is not one of the easier steps, even if a man readily agrees to provide his semen. In the second episode of the series, this quest for a donor continues, but now the drive to become parents becomes so obsessive that Bette and Tina are willing to have a threesome with a young man to "steal" his sperm. When the target male character realizes the women's intent, however, he refuses to have sexual intercourse with Tina without using protection. In the third episode, Tina finally decides to use the sperm of Marcus Allenwood (played by Mark Gibson), which is stored in the California Cryobank. Marcus is an African American man who complicates the couple's decision to have a baby because Tina is not ready to raise a child of color, but later she says, "I don't know what I was thinking, there's no reason on earth that I wouldn't want to make a baby with you using a donor who's black. I think I was really scared." Eventually, she resolves her own anxieties and racial conundrum.

It takes Bette and Tina three episodes to find the right donor, and an entire additional season for Tina to deliver the baby. Of course, the writers of the series complicate their storyline for dramatic effect; however, the drama is a narrative strategy that humanizes the lesbian stories as it simultaneously teaches the audience about life's unpredictability. In real life, when she was playing pregnant Tina, Holloman was expecting and she, too, delivered her child through surgical incision, which occurred on-screen during the final episode of season two. To keep things as realistic as possible, after Bette and

Tina have their baby, the series instructs the public about how lesbians manage to raise their children in a society that often sees parenthood as a right reserved for heterosexual couples. Again, according to the decision-making model proposed by Chabot and Ames, new parents choose between available options and, for their child's sake, mediate among culturally accepted ideals of parenting. Throughout the rest of the series, Bette and Tina try to negotiate an acceptable balance between social expectations and their own concept of a non-traditional family.

That process of mediation begins in the first episode of season three, titled "Labia Majora," in which Bette, who is not the baby's biological mother, files for adoption. At this point, the lesbian couple must choose between risking Bette's rejection as a legal parent (if the two women are unable to show the government official a healthy interaction of their child with a male figure) and allowing a man in the child's life to give their cranky social worker a "good impression." The first time the official visits their house, some of the parenting choices the couple is making puzzle her. The social worker observes and comments on (in her assessment) Tina and Bette's controversial lifestyle. She ironically notes that the content of Bette's collection of paintings is "sexually explicit" and a form of "anti-patriotic propaganda." Moreover, she points out the absence of a male presence in the home, regarding the current family dynamics as a hindrance to the child's emotional growth. "How is Angelica going to know what a man is?" the social worker asks. Tina expresses that their child will be around many men as she grows up, but her answer does not satisfy the woman. This conversation in Bette's house, while showing the complexity of the social worker character, leaves the lesbian couple with the dilemma of what is best for Angelica (played by Olivia Windbiel) and how much their "lesbian life" will affect the child's future ability to cope with social expectations. At this moment, Bette and Tina begin to negotiate with the "real world," and they find themselves in Chabot and Ames' final stage of decision-making as they "negotiate parenthood within the larger heterocentric context" (359).

Bette and Tina's drama can easily be envisioned as the fictional representation of Chabot and Ames' study, which concludes, "Lesbian couples planning for parenthood have many decisions to negotiate in order to begin and implement their journey" (355). By watching *The L Word*, the audience learns about the difficulties and the steps involved in a certain queer couple's decision-making. Examining these difficulties helps to humanize the lesbian experience of parenthood in both the fictional and real worlds. Bette and Tina's storyline thereby neutralizes (at least some of) the influence that previous queer representations have had on its audience members. As Plato puts it,

We should neutralize the poets' influence on mothers, which makes them scare their children with terrible stories about how some gods tend to prowl around during the hours of darkness in a wide variety of unfamiliar human guises, so that we stop the mothers blaspheming against the gods, and at the same time stop them making their children too timid [54].

When applied to *The L Word,* the Platonic idea of neutralization implies that we need to disregard the bad queer stories we have seen so far; those, indeed, were tales that made us "timid" because they showed an unrealistic side of queerness. What we had prior to *The L Word,* in a sense, were "horror stories" that prowled our minds. In contrast, Bette and Tina, through the narrative of pregnancy, show the inaccuracy of previous queer representations. The two women's tale, then, is best adapted for our "moral improvement," and the audience likely feels greater sympathy for gay-rights politics as a result of the viewing experience. In other words, Tina's successful pregnancy represents a "good story" and achieves a useful pedagogical function.

When a Good Story Turns Bad Again

The L Word's pedagogical intent is a subject that Jennifer Reed analyzes in her exploration of Max's story, as well. Max Sweeney (played by Daniela Sea), aka Moira, is an FTM transgender male who is introduced in the series at the beginning of its third season. Once in Los Angeles, Max first starts to cross-dress and then initiates his physical transition. As such, his character teaches the audience about the realities associated with transitioning through genders. According to Reed, even when Max's story is not overtly pedagogical, "The very experience of watching gender and sexuality as processes teaches a deeper social and political—even ethical—understanding of sexuality and gender as complex categories of identities that are not the same experience for everybody" (171). This implies that *The L Word* not only makes lesbians visible but is also inclusive of many sexual identities that sometimes, as in Max's case, can be (re)negotiated and (re)interpreted. On an emotional level, the lesson that the series delivers pertains to the difficult and continuous personal struggle that many trans people face every day.

A restaurant scene that Reed examines is emblematic of Max's constant social turmoil as his otherness comes through fully: he is "other" not only because he is a man living in a female body but also because he is from a small Midwestern town whose name the lesbian friends cannot even remember. Alice (played by Leisha Hailey) calls the town Spokane, but Shane (played by Katherine Moennig), correcting her, says that the town is actually Skokie. Alice replies, "Whatever. They're both in the Midwest, right?" (Reed 172), revealing that Alice is not at all interested in knowing about geographical differences, let alone about the indeterminacy of gender identity. To her, the Midwest is an indistinct agglomeration of villages without political or social identity because, as city-oriented as she is, the world begins and ends in Los Angeles. As such, Max's emotional turmoil does not really concern Alice because she herself has never experienced any identity issue. Alice's insensitivity indicates that Max has to take on many challenges in order to fit in as part of his new circle of friends. As if being both transgender and a "foreigner" were not enough, in *The L Word*'s final season, he also becomes pregnant, making his story the most misshapen of the series. As a result, Max undergoes at least two significant transitions in *The L Word*: from butch to transgender, and from transgender to pregnant woman. Whereas the first transition is necessary in order to construct the male identity that Max has been seeking for years, the second challenges the logic of his entire storyline. It is unlikely that a woman injecting testosterones in her body could become pregnant without completely stopping her transition, an intention to which Max never alludes.

In this regard, the series' writers seem to lack basic medical knowledge that would enable them to create a more credible story. This is perhaps all the more surprising because, about the same time as the final season was being produced, news of the FTM Thomas Trace Beatie's pregnancy circulated throughout the world. It is hard to believe that this real-life episode did not affect the series' plot and that, instead, Max's pregnancy is just an unfortunate, illogical invention that undoes the "good story" of successful pregnancy and parenthood delivered through Bette's and Tina's characters. In 2007, Beatie, a male transgender who decided to stop his transition in order to bear children because his wife at the time (the two filed for divorce in 2012) was infertile, came to be known to a worldwide audience as "The Pregnant Man." In a November 2008 interview broadcast on the ABC television network, following the birth of his first child, Beatie shared his story with broadcast journalist Barbara Walters ("Journey"). The rhetoric that the media used at the time defined Beatie's experience as the first male pregnancy ever documented; however, a nurse interviewed in the same special by Walters stated that she helped many transgender men to give birth ("Journey"). Beatie, she says, is not the first male to get pregnant, a statement that Timothy Murphy confirms in his article on the ethics of helping transgender individuals have children (47). But the difference between Beatie (who, to date, is a father of three children and has four pregnancies on his medical record) and these other men is that the latter preferred to remain anonymous. Nevertheless, the correspondence between Beatie and Max's character is evident, and, even if their similarities are just a coincidence, through *The L Word*, the audience learns that male pregnancy can be a possibility.

Male pregnancy breaks the cultural and ethical norms that only a female body can carry a baby, a principle that the right to reproductive liberty is already challenging. According to Robert Sparrow, "Since the 1980s, a number of medical researchers have suggested that in the future it might be possible for men to become pregnant" (275). If viable, the male body would carry an extrauterine pregnancy. The blastocyst (the structure that contains an inner cell mass which will form the embryo) would implant into the abdominal cavity such that a placenta could form and the baby could be delivered via a C-section (276). Extrauterine pregnancies are difficult in women and often result in hemorrhages and other health problems, but if most of the risks could be prevented (as perhaps advanced prenatal technologies indicate) through constant medical monitoring, a male pregnancy could be possible. Sparrow suggests that, in order to make this kind of pregnancy viable, the risks do not have to be reduced entirely to zero, as there are women, for instance, who sometimes carry their pregnancies despite possible health complications: "The level of risk involved in male pregnancy need only be reduced to the level at which one would be inclined to respect a woman's autonomous consent to medical procedures intended to facilitate a risky pregnancy" (277). In other words, even if dangerous, male pregnancy could be feasible if the risk can be reduced to an ethically acceptable threshold.

Medical researchers had been considering the possibility of male pregnancy long before the subject was represented on television. Examining the gender-related challenges that their studies document, even the awkward transgender pregnancy in *The L Word* appears to be somewhat natural because Max's biological body maintains the natural capacity to gestate. At the same time, this transgender pregnancy, in contrast to the pregnancy of Tina, strikes viewers as odd because it is wholly unwanted and unexpected. On a narrative level, viewers have a hard time reconciling the gap between Max's consistent characterization as a male and his unexpected pregnancy because it does not appear to make any sense. However, Max's pregnancy is shocking not necessarily because the plotline is incongruent. If that were simply the case, viewers should promise themselves never to watch television again and instead opt to become "members of the TV Diaspora," as TV critic Marvin Kitman calls "viewers who [give] up on the medium because it is dull, repetitive, prosaic, bland, banal, boring tripe" (38). But if we can cushion for a moment the urge for an aesthetic judgment, we may focus on the queer value of the intricacy of Max's pregnancy. The transgender gestation is outrageous because it is sublime, and the picture of a bearded pregnant individual can barely be contained in our imagination insofar as we are not accustomed to this sort of male depiction. According to Immanuel Kant and his analysis of the sublime, "In presenting the sublime in nature the mind feels *agitated*.... This agitation (above all at its inception) can be compared with a vibration, i.e., with a rapid alteration of repulsion from, and attraction to, one and the same object" (526, original emphasis). Generally, when one experiences the sublime, unless he or she is in a safe place (and being in a safe place is certainly the typical viewer's case because, most likely, he or she is watching Max's story from the comfort of his or her own living room), one feels the urge to avoid it. At the same time, however, because of the mind's capacity to perceive the grandeur contained in the sublime, this later becomes attractive. That is why, for example, viewers do not flee the room while watching the final season of *The L Word* but rather endure the viewing experience. By enduring, they achieve a state in which they are acquainted with the image of the pregnant male as it finally becomes an acceptable expression of the male body. As irrational as it can be, the narrative of Max's pregnancy helps the audience to at least ponder the possibility of male gravidity.

Agitation, repulsion, and attraction are not only sensorial and emotional states that Max stimulates in the audience; his fictional friends also perceive his sublimity, but they are not quite sure how to manage it. Indeed, nobody in the lesbian group knows how to help Max in his process to become a mother. This is particularly evident in the baby-shower scene of the sixth-season episode "Lactose Intolerant," during which the man is transformed into a clown, the atmosphere is surreal, and the lesbian friends engage in several different conversations in which the transgender experience remains absurdly marginal. Max is depicted as feeling uncomfortable, emotionally and physically exhausted. When his friends play a game to guess the size of his belly, nobody seems able to estimate it correctly; only Shane, the quasi-butch who, due to her sexuality and lifestyle, may understand a little better Max's maleness, guesses it right. However, when it is time to measure Max's belly, even Shane acts as if she does not want to play this nonsensical game. Max's sublimity overwhelms the group; his friends seem to want to turn away from him yet apparently endure the shower out of a sense of politeness. Only Tina tries to comfort the new "mom-to-be": "Hey, you know what, Max? Don't be scared. Really," she says. "I mean, don't.... When the baby is born, and you hold that baby in your arms, you're going to know exactly what to do. I promise you." Max replies with a faint "okay," barely holding back his tears. Then the attention turns to Shane smoking marijuana in the kitchen, unconcerned that the pot smell can make Max sick. The quasi-indifference of the group is a reaction to Max's sublimity, as his friends "perceive the inadequacy of the imagination—unbounded though it is as far as progressing is concerned—for taking in and using, for the estimation of magnitude, a basic measure that is suitable for this with minimal expenditure on the part of the understanding" (Kant 524). In other words, they cannot break through Max's sublimity by using their imaginations. In a way, they are unable to conceive of Max as a pregnant person, to find a reasonable "measure" to gauge male pregnancy, and to contain its conceptual idea in their minds. By preferring to talk to each other while excluding Max from their random conversations, they avoid a direct interaction with this sublime being. Rather than sympathize with Max's pregnancy, they shy away from it because his situation is rationally uncontainable. Their "mental attunement"—namely, their relating to male pregnancy—makes them judge Max's situation as that which is "absolutely large." This sublimity, a sense of horror and awkwardness, resides more in their own minds than in the natural object that Max represents.

Max is a natural object in the sense that he conceives naturally because, "down there," he is biologically female, but the beard he still sports in the baby-shower scene creates a mimetic friction greater than that which can be rationalized with "reason's ideas." Max's friends find themselves inadequate to cope with this pregnancy, and even when Tina attempts to console Max, she talks in terms of motherhood, never in terms of fatherhood. In her mind, giving birth is automatically an act of feminization, and when Max finds a breastfeeding pump among the other shower gifts but claims that he will not breastfeed, Tina peremptorily tells him that breastfeeding is "what's best for the baby. All the doctors say so, and it's a wonderful bonding experience. I had such a good time with Angie." Next, Jenny (played by Mia Kirshner) intervenes, reinforcing the awkwardness of the moment, when she states, "I understand that you identify as a man, but I think it's important, as a parent, that you can't be selfish for the child." This statement indicates the lesbian avoidance of male transgenderism because it equates pregnancy with a biological state that only a woman can perform. "It's my fucking choice if I breastfeed or not. Okay?" Max replies, perceiving that he cannot escape from the cultural standards embedded in his friends' minds. Alice's speech that follows (which is delivered more to reproach Jenny's recent despicable behavior than to praise Max), about how the world can be harsh but Max's intimate knowledge of what both sexes go through will help him to be uniquely knowledgeable and strong for his child, makes things even worse. Upon hearing Alice's words, Max almost passes out, and his friends now react hysterically—proposing to give him Diazepam, Lexapro, Valium, or Xanax to calm him down—and start looking around frantically for their purses. The fact that some of them actually carry these drugs is emblematic of two things: (1) their own ongoing anxieties that they attempt to cure with benzodiazepines (the controlled medications they identify all belong to this specific class of drugs); and (2) they believe that Max requires pharmaceutical treatment in order to recompose himself. Still envisioning him as a woman rather than a man, Max's lesbian friends confuse his reaction to the clumsiness of the baby shower with one or more anxiety disorders, which, as Carmen McLean et al. have demonstrated, affect women more than men (1027). The friends' reaction subtly reinforces their expectation for Max to be, and to perform, the gender he does not identify with.

By offering Max those drugs, the women demasculinize his identity because their efforts to "calm him down" signify reinstating him in his abject womanhood, placing him back in his pregnant, gendered body. As such, they are attempting to bring Max back to an emotional and biological state he does not wish to experience because, in his heart and mind, he is not a woman. Throughout his pregnancy experience, Max finds it necessary to shout out that he is, in fact, a *he*. He constantly has to remind Jenny that he is a *man*. In the baby-shower scene specifically, Max takes offense as Jenny, yelling at the hysterical friends who offer Max the various drugs, says, "Okay, people! People, she's pregnant! You can't give a pregnant lady drugs." To this, Max immediately responds, "*He. He's* pregnant. *He's* pregnant, okay?" (emphasis added). Max is conscious of his gender identity, and there are no drugs to undo his transition. As awkward as it is, the scene reveals Max's resistance to identify himself as a woman, which makes the gestation a difficult and painful experience; on the other hand, the lesbian friends, resisting male pregnancy with their gendered discourses and hysterical reactions, remake Max as a female, pregnant transgender. His pregnancy is difficult precisely because the friends cannot unbind their minds and accept the fact that *he* is pregnant. They are not able to "elevate their minds" to Max's sublimity simply because they dodge it rather than *embrace* it, as viewers typically expect in successfully queer stories.

Max's character deserves consideration not because, as many have noted, he is the only transgender individual in the series. *The L Word* is certainly not the first production in the history of cinema and/or television to represent gender-identity transition, as the GLAAD website clearly demonstrates (Kane). Nor is this the first time that Hollywood has tackled the novel subject of male pregnancy (for example, in the 1994 film *Junior* [directed by Ivan Reitman], Arnold Schwarzenegger plays Alex Hesse, a geneticist who, in partnership with Larry Arbogast [played by Danny DeVito], experiments on his own body with a fertility drug that allows him to become pregnant). Rather, the narrative of Max's pregnancy is worthy of consideration because it makes the series' audience aware of the complexities associated with transgender identities. Max is a woman who self-identifies as a man and who, until a certain point in the narrative, is sexually attracted to women but then, during the process of transitioning, finds himself sexually attracted to other men primarily because such same-sex relationships make him "feel [like] a man," as he himself puts it. Of course, he forgets altogether that "down there" he is still biologically female and can get pregnant. This complex yet fluid sexuality, coupled with the unexpected pregnancy, is what makes Max's character sublime. Such dense characterization is conceptually difficult to come to grips with, and not even his "next-of-kin queer friends" can understand it. As such, the series certainly has the potential to liberate transgender people from being represented as individuals who are constantly troubled, but overall it fails in this regard because the transgender identity will eventually be remade. If the series were to make a sincere effort to resolve the tension between his friends' feminist ideals and his own trans position, Max's character could deliver a more effective transgender storyline. Unfortunately, that does not happen in *The L Word*. Clearly, dealing with transgenderism is not an easy task; even when one analyzes it from a theoretical perspective, it provides a variety of dilemmas. Transgenderism and transgender theory pose theoretical and practical dilemmas that, according to Patricia Elliot, are far from being over. Citing Viviane Namaste and her discussion about how neither queer theory nor the social sciences have been able to make transgender people visible, Elliot states that "our inability to resolve [the tensions] rather than our erasure of the conflict constitute[s] the critical possibilities of feminist scholarship" (149). Thus, the current inability to adequately understand transgenderism and to effectively represent "trans bodies [in order] to promote their own [queer and feminist] views about gender identity" (Elliot 10) can provide an effective starting point for further critical inquiry. The theoretical "rifts," as Elliot calls them, help to create a map of "the differences and divisions between and among trans, queer, and non-trans feminist theorists" (149). We assume that by looking at these divisions as a cartography of the queer community, we can identify and explain the theoretical cracks and/or shifts that give viability to gender identities. As rudimentary (and academically uniformed) as it sometimes is, *The L Word* is able to depict the cultural cracks in the LGBT discourse but fails to resolve them. What emerges from Max's storyline is the division of the LGBT community, a division that can also be read in more recent television productions such as HBO's Emmy-winning movie *The Normal Heart* (2014, directed by Ryan Murphy), in which Ned Weeks (played by Mark Ruffalo) strives to make New York City's gay community aware of the tragic effects of AIDS. With regard to transgender people, the LGBT community and LGBT theorists are divided because, as Elliot notes, trans experiences pose a challenge to the established gender order (8–9). As a result, trans experiences are challenging because, in a way, they further complicate queer discourse by unsettling queer theoretical frames, for once one defines himself or herself as a gendered individual, he or she falls within the normative categorizations that queerness should rather strive to destabilize.

The Echo of a Failure

For the various reasons just identified, *The L Word*'s treatment of Max's pregnancy fails to deliver a good story and contradicts its intention to teach about sexual identities and the LGBT community. It is hard to believe that a trans person becomes pregnant unintentionally. As Beatie's real-life story suggests, a transgender pregnancy is typically a very conscious, planned choice. In Max's storyline, the good narrative of pregnancy becomes a monstrous tale that, by imprisoning the transgender individual within an identity that he refuses, once again thwarts the representation of the LGBT community. In the series, Max is a threat to the fictional queer community and to his friends who, not knowing what to do with him, try to undo his identity. His gestation, however, remains unresolved. Viewers do not know whether Max will keep the baby and/or whether he will continue to pursue his transition. Perhaps, given that Bette and Tina are attempting to have a second child and because Max, in a moment of desperation during the baby shower, asks them to adopt his baby, viewers can speculate that the couple will adopt his child; however, because the series ends before Max gives birth, they will never know. As a transgender individual, Max represents a threat to his lesbian friends because he destabilizes their own gender order. Contrary to Bette and Tina's storyline, Max's pregnancy is exploited to describe the queer subject as one that can be constantly de-formed to suit the canons of heteronormativity. As a pregnant individual, Max has to recover those female characteristics that fit into ready gender categorization. His pregnancy gives him the absurd chance to (re-)remake himself as a woman, but what is most interesting in the series is that his LGBT community questions Max's identity, as his friends attempt to (re-)remake him as a woman who will raise his newborn according to those standards that are culturally accepted as "exclusively female." The fictional lesbians undo Max's transgender identity, complicating his cultural position within the LGBT community. For once, heteronormativity is not competing with queerness from outside, but rather it is inherent to the performativity of gender in the fictitious lesbian space. To think of performativity in relation to a lesbian gender role is strikingly odd, but Max's narrative of pregnancy suggests that it is a possibility as he destabilizes the "queer order" in the reality of the series; it is difficult to examine his story without taking into consideration the gendered response to lesbian performance. This narrative shift confuses the portrayal of the LGBT community on U.S. television because, in *The L Word*, queerness appears to be almost self-destructive as it starts to represent female gender roles that remind viewers of a compulsory heteronormativity, a concept to which a successful queer TV production would not typically be expected to allude.

As *The L Word* creates a fictional space for female same-sex couples, it annihilates transgender identity as a self that can be reshaped according to specific situations. In the series' final season, the theme of pregnancy takes an unanticipated turn that contradicts the more realistic portrayal of lesbian life that viewers have come to see in *The L Word*. Through the narrative of pregnancy, the series promotes a progressive view of same-sex groups, but the same narrative, unfortunately, tends to destabilize queerness in favor of representing more socially accepted roles of womanhood. By recasting irresolvable gender roles in Max's life, the heterosexual/homosexual dichotomy endures in the final season. *The L Word* therefore teaches its viewers that these social constructs are still effective and embedded in any community, regardless of people's sexuality. The narrative of this Showtime production is inconsistent not so much because it fails to craft a sound story for Max's character but rather because its contradictions reveal that which queer audience members (and others) never want to see, especially in the midst of political fights for gay equality. It reveals the flaws inherent within the LGBT community, and, while it tries to do justice to a specific group of people, it leaves out others who remain in an "in-between position" that overwhelms their social status. Max's story, as it was presented in the third season of *The L Word*, was a perfect instance of queerness as Lee Edelman identifies it—as that which "can never define an identity [but that] can only ever disturb one" (17). That is because, at the beginning of his storyline, disregarding any possible normalization, Max does not establish an unchangeable sexual identity, and he is attracted to both women and men as long as they can make him feel "like a man."

Ideally, this is what queerness implies, and this is how Max can continue to queer the fictional space in the series. But when, through pregnancy, he loses this indeterminate, privileged queer status in order to establish an identity to which he is subjected (but does not want), he ceases to be queer and simultaneously loses his queer potential. In other words, once Max, who is the queerest of the queer, loses his sexual indeterminacy, this triggers a domino effect of sorts that normalizes and reinstates the female gender as a category that ineluctably has to define the lesbians in the series. Accordingly, this is a bad story that, as Plato would say, no poet should ever write because it is as confusing as it is intimidating. Now that audience members are ready for lesbian visibility, they are implicitly told that they should not be ready for trans experiences because these either potentially do not exist or can exist only according to certain gendered paradigms. In *The L Word*, "queer" can stop being queer in order to belong to a symbolic reality within which queer individuals become subjects only because they invest themselves in doing so. Investing in their own pregnancies as the primary means to become mothers, the characters in *The L Word* undermine queerness—that is the real inconsistency of a television series that pretends to be queer. In Max's tale, pregnancy and parenthood are not mere representations of human rights but rather become lurking means to undo queerness from within: a very bad story indeed.

Works Cited

Akass, Kim, and Janet McCabe. *Reading The L Word: Outing Contemporary Television.* London: I.B. Tauris, 2006. Print.

Chabot, Jennifer M., and Barbara D. Ames. "It Wasn't 'Let's Get Pregnant and Go Do It': Decision Making in Lesbian Couples Planning Motherhood via Donor Insemination." *Family Relations* 53.4 (2004): 348–356. Print.

Dhaenens, Frederik. "Articulations of Queer Resistance on the Small Screen." *Continuum: Journal of Media & Cultural Studies* 28.4 (2014): 520–531. Print.

Edelman, Lee. *No Future: Queer Theory and the Death Drive.* Durham: Duke University Press, 2004. Print.

Elliot, Patricia. *Debates in Transgender, Queer, and Feminist Theory: Contested Sites.* Burlington, VT: Ashgate, 2010. Print.

"Journey of a Pregnant Man: A Barbara Walters Special." ABC News, 14 November 2008. Television.

Kane, Martin. "Transgender Characters That Changed Film and Television." *GLAAD*, 12 November 2013. Web. 9 December 2015. http://www.glaad.org/blog/trans gender-characters-changed-film-and-television-transwk.

Kant, Immanuel. "Critique of Judgment." *The Norton Anthology of Theory and Criticism.* Ed. Vincent B. Leitch. New York: Norton, 2001. 499–535. Print.

Kitman, Marvin. "Still Not Ready for Prime Time." *New Leader* 93.3–4 (2010): 37–38. Print.

Lee, Pei-Wen, and Michaela D. E. Meyer. "'We All Have Feelings for Our Girlfriends': Progressive (?) Representations of Lesbian Lives on *The L Word.*" *Sexuality and Culture* 14.3 (2010): 234–250. Print.

McFadden, Margaret T. *The L Word.* Detroit: Wayne State University Press, 2014. Print.

McLean, Carmen P., Anu Asnaani, Brett T. Litz, and Stefan G. Hofmann. "Gender Differences in Anxiety Disorders: Prevalence, Course of Illness, Comorbidity, and Burden of Illness." *Journal of Psychiatric Research* 45.8 (2011): 1027–1035. Print.

Murphy, Timothy F. "The Ethics of Helping Transgender Men And Women Have Children." *Perspectives in Biology and Medicine* 53.1 (2010): 46–60. Print.

Plato. "From Book II." *The Norton Anthology of Theory and Criticism.* Ed. Vincent B. Leitch. New York: Norton, 2001. 49–56. Print.

Reed, Jennifer. "Reading Gender Politics on *The L Word*: The Moira/Max Transitions." *Journal of Popular Film and Television* 37.4 (2009): 169–178. Print.

Sparrow, Robert. "Is It 'Every Man's Right to Have Babies If He Wants Them'? Male Pregnancy and the Limits of Reproductive Liberty." *Kennedy Institute of Ethics Journal* 18.3 (2008): 275–299. Print.

Walker, Rachel Loewen. "Politically Queer: *Ellen* and the Changing Face of American Television, 1997 to 2007." *Queers in American Popular Culture.* Ed. Jim Elledge. Santa Barbara, CA: Praeger, 2010. 1–24. Print.

The Stylized Image of the White Lesbian
A Model Minority

Renee DeLong

> While it has been acknowledged that race is not simply additive to or derivative of sexual difference, few white feminists have attempted to ... describe the powerful effect that race has on the construction and representation of gender and sexuality.
> —Evelynn Hammonds [302].

Bodies (i.e., texts, authors, or celebrity personas) that are marked in one category and unmarked in others are rarely discussed in their wholeness but rather in pieces: race here, gender there, and sexuality over there. In the quote above, Hammonds points out the inherent privilege of this dissociation, perpetuated and sustained through language, which simplifies the lived experiences of multiple oppressions. As Audre Lorde expresses, "The oppression of women knows no ethnic nor racial boundaries, true, but that does not mean it is identical within those differences.... For then beyond sisterhood is still racism" (70). Disconnecting the white writer from her text and reflecting it back to her through a racialized lens is work that has often been taken up by women of color. The title of the 1980s anthology *This Bridge Called My Back: Writings by Radical Women of Color*, edited by Cherríe Moraga and Gloria Anzaldua, reminds readers exactly who becomes trampled by (white) feminist scholarship.

This essay examines the raced and classed lesbian bodies that have been produced through television. The images of Rachel Maddow, Suze Orman, and Ellen DeGeneres participate in a stylized white lesbian representation: fit, stylish, coiffed, smart, and wealthy. White heterosexuals consume and converse

93

with these images through the lens of liberal politics. Much of the exception-alist mythology that produces white lesbian celebrities is subtly framed by the racial and sexual othering (and erasure) of people of color, often cisgender heterosexual men. The black male and the Latino male provide images whose participation in narratives of masculinity measures the acceptability of white lesbians. As court cases and state legislation have advanced same-sex mar-riage, these "celesbians" have made LGBTQ people more palatable to main-stream audiences. However, at the same time, such images have overshadowed the classed and raced elements of marriage law, and they continue to separate LGBTQ activism from race, class, and immigration concerns.

Rachel Maddow: Sex Symbol and Sage

The Rachel Maddow Show (2008–) on MSNBC is a space for the female political analyst to be seen as both masculine and feminine. As Winnie McCroy notes in her Village Voice article "Rachel Maddow, the New Sexy," "The new butch is not only not afraid to be pretty, but she's equally comfort-able with men and straight women."

Maddow made the move from radio (an invisible medium) to television in September 2008. Her appearances on television require a daily makeover, as Maddow notes that her preferred wardrobe is "'like a first grader'" but her on-camera garb is "'lady clothes'" (qtd. in Traister 24). The resulting drag act, which allows her to appear not only grown-up but also marks her class status, makes her image palatable to mainstream viewers.

Maddow's persona calls to mind that of a clever but firm high school teacher. Her Ph.D. in political science was gently mocked in the "Ask Dr. Maddow" segment of her radio show, and her "Moment of Geek" segment occurs weekly on MSNBC. As Alessandra Stanley states about the differences between Maddow and the "unruly, often squabbling schoolboys" on cable news, "Her program adds a good-humored female face…. Ms. Maddow's deep, modulated voice is reassuringly calm after so much shrill emotionalism and catfights among the channel's aging, white male divas" (Stanley). Stanley disrupts gender stereotypes to examine Maddow's brand of (young, queer, white) female energy: her deep, calm voice contrasts with the high-pitched rows among the male hosts. Even the motto of her show, "Mind over Chatter," seems to position Maddow against the assumptions about the vapid female and male talking heads on TV. As Rebecca Traister points out in her article "Mad for Rachel Maddow," "Maddow is one of the few left-liberal women to bust open the world of TV punditry" (22). In other words, these critics inter-pret Maddow's presence as the catalyst that makes television into a freewheel-ing genderqueer space.

Maddow's glamorous butch image attracts heterosexuals to her show: women *and* men. Traister posits that Maddow is universally loved: "The 'gay for Rachel' meme appears to transcend gender and sexuality. Women, men, straight and not straight: they're all gay for her" (23). In the article "Butch Fatale," Daphne Merkin notes that "every weekday night … [Maddow] makes love to her audience" (Merkin). *New York* magazine's "Daily Intelligencer" column of July 17, 2008, lists six reasons why the publication's editors are "gay for Rachel Maddow" ("Why We're"). Two of the points pertain to Maddow's quirky job history, three highlight Maddow poking fun at her role as an über-lesbian and sex symbol, and one admires her educational credentials. The column ends with "Okay, we still don't want to kiss her or anything. But still: swoon" ("Why We're").

The swooning critics grasp for words as they attempt to describe their awe and desire. However, "sexy" often translates as "white," "cheery," and "approachable." In "The Rachel Papers," Jonanna Widner speculates on how many analyses of Maddow's show remark about how kind she is: "her natural ease, her politeness, and her refusal to engage in the pile-ons so beloved by the dudes of cable news…. But much of the media's treatment of her niceness borders on fetishization" (39). As a sex symbol, Maddow's female masculinity becomes less complicated to her overwrought heterosexual viewers. Straight men and straight women alike can admire the flickerings of femininity along with the echoes of masculinity.

The heterosexual couple's crush on Maddow, referenced by McCroy in "Rachel Maddow, the New Sexy," sounds like a dalliance with intellectual desire in a heterocentric and visually obsessed culture focused on physical desire. Perhaps the language for intellectual desire becomes overwrought simply because the writer must rely on the simplistic language of sexual desire. However, the desired object need not have any desires. It is much simpler if her image exists as a cipher to be filled with the needs of the desiring public. McCroy calls Maddow "a bona fide butch sex symbol, desired by lesbians, straight women, *and* men." She also quotes Maddow describing herself as "'a big lesbian who looks like a man…. My goal is to do the physical appearance stuff in such a way that it is not comment-worthy'" (McCroy, "Rachel").

Straight cisgender white men on television get a free pass on their appearance, as long as they generally reproduce the norm, and Maddow points to this privilege while attempting to tap into it. In contrast, the images of women of all races and sexualities on television are open to comment by viewers. The common image of the "anchorbabe" (qtd. in McCroy, "Rachel"), to use Maddow's own term, is only noteworthy in its failed reproduction, while Maddow's on-screen image is consistently called "authentic," as Judy Berman asserted in Salon.com (qtd. in McCroy, "Rachel"). Butch authenticity, therefore, occupies a queer space beyond the "anchorbabe" and her suited male counterpart.

Before-and-after photos may be subtly different; however, the on-screen image does indeed feminize Maddow's boyish edges. Prior to her television makeover, *The Advocate* published a photo of Maddow in its July 15, 2008, issue, accompanying the article "Air America's Sweetheart" by Mette Bach. In this shot, Maddow wears little to no makeup, her short hair fits her head tightly, and she sports no glasses or jewelry. Maddow's finely knit gray sweater frames her face with a high, round neck. This image of Maddow marks her as a soft butch lesbian. In a later screen shot reprinted in the March/April 2009 issue of the *Columbia Journalism Review*, accompanying "The Sarcastic Times" by Alissa Quart, Maddow wears lip gloss, her professionally sculpted eyebrows accent the slightest bit of eye makeup, and her longer and softer haircut wraps around her ears. Her bangs flip up and over with the help of hair gel. She does not wear jewelry with the gray pinstripe suit jacket and black round-necked sweater. This "television version" of Maddow reproduces enough female markings to keep her from being mistaken for a boy, and her tailored suit marks her as smart, professional, and businesslike. Missing in both photos are her trademark heavy black glasses; Maddow says they reflect too much and cannot be worn on television (Jeffery 72). This version of "lady drag" allows the straight audience to see Maddow's queerness throughout the performance. As Merkin describes the butch–femme dance in Maddow's on-screen persona, "her brown eyes [are] given depth with flattering eye shadow, her short (but not too short) haircut [is] artfully coiffed. With her Poindexter glasses, Jil Sander pantsuits, and Converse sneakers … she's willing to prettify her image sufficiently to endear her to male viewers" (Merkin). Merkin's term "prettify" suggests that Maddow uses enough female markers to attract heterosexual male viewers. Although the men on MSNBC also wear dark suits, their eyebrows are a bit messier and their lips shine less. Maddow herself deflects questions about her makeover with quips such as "I wear just as much makeup as the other guys on MSNBC" (qtd. in McCroy, "Conversation"). In this era of high-definition television, and with new formulations of makeup to hide imperfections, media personalities must carefully craft their appearances. In "The Maddow Knows," Clara Jeffery asks about her change in appearance and Maddow notes, "It wasn't at anybody else's encouraging. I wanted my appearance to not be the only thing people would pay attention to. So essentially I was seeking genericness" (73).

The "genericness" Maddow performs connects her to her male colleagues while participating in "female masculinity," a term coined by Judith Halberstam. Although the dark suit jacket without jewelry reproduces masculinity, the eye makeup echoes femininity. Having her name on a news program also links Maddow to a conventional yet iconoclastic performance of masculinity. If "masculinity in this society inevitably conjures up notions of power and legitimacy and privilege [and] often symbolically refers to the power of the state and to uneven distributions of wealth" (Halberstam 2), then (left-wing or right-wing) cable news sets the stage for digestible performances of masculinity. Accordingly, Maddow's "generic" presentation can be read as a performance of bombastic masculinity.

The notion of genericness also contains racial privilege: Maddow's whiteness allows her to blend in with the "other" white guys in dark suits whose opinions are worth hearing and debating. In January 2015, nineteen news shows were listed on the MSNBC website, and there were six anchors of color: Jose Diaz-Balart, Tamron Hall, Melissa Harris-Perry, Joy Reid, Al Sharpton, and Alex Wagner. A few additional journalists of color appear in ensemble casts, while white men anchor the majority of these broadcasts.

In her *Mother Jones* interview with Clara Jeffery, Maddow jokes, "I'm sort of in 'Dude Looks Like a Lady' territory anyway" (73). Although Alissa Quart leaves her comment on Maddow's appearance until the end of her article, she refers to Maddow as "Chaplinesque, with her dark cap of hair and expressive black eyebrows set against pale skin" (14). Before Maddow was granted a television program of her own, she often appeared on Keith Olbermann's show, which earned her the reputation for being a "ballsy gremlin" (Traister 22), a description that links Maddow's boyishness, cleverness, and visual image. Traister argues that the "tomboy Maddow" creates a new space from which to critique politicians and contemporary issues, even though cable news as a whole continues to stabilize white middle-class masculinity (22).

Daytime talk shows on broadcast networks reproduce a version of white middle-class femininity that clashes with Maddow's butch masculinity. During Maddow's March 5, 2009, appearance on the daily talk show *The View* (1997–), four of the show's five female co-hosts refrain from identifying with Maddow while highlighting her idiosyncrasies. Each co-host marks her own personality or image through her wardrobe. Actor Whoopi Goldberg wears tennis shoes and a loose gray smock with black pants, comedian Joy Behar sports a cerulean cardigan over a low-cut black tank top, actor Sherri Shepherd is dressed in a black V-neck wrap dress, designer Elisabeth Hasselbeck also wears a black dress but with a high neck and long, chunky gold necklaces, and journalist Barbara Walters' classic red blazer tops a white button-down shirt with a thick gold choker. At this table, with her heavy black glasses and lack of jewelry, Maddow's black, finely knit sweater with a high round neck marks her image as the most masculine.

The hosts ask questions that mark Maddow as queer. After requesting that she stand and show off her "big lesbian" height (her own description), they ask her how she got a TV show, to which she answers, "I don't know!" and laughs. Then, they show a photograph of Maddow and her same-sex partner and ask: "How did you meet your partner?" "Do you get any hate mail because you're gay?" "How did your conservative parents react when you 'came out' to them?" "Were you a tomboy?" These questions about personal relationships and family roles repeat the narratives of middle-class hetero-femininity that are performed by the program. When these narratives are smoothly retold, the political and racial differences between the five co-hosts are spackled over with laughter and cheery conversation. In a genre that privileges the performance of female bonding, disruptions spotlight the performances of femininity.

Maddow confesses that she had long blonde hair as a child, and Goldberg breaks in to say that she did, too. At this moment, all of the women at the table break into laughter and must fleetingly acknowledge how race is silently woven through this performance of femininity. Goldberg and Shepherd both are African American, and Behar, Hasselbeck, Walters, and Maddow are racially white. The absurd notion of Goldberg with blonde hair stops the discussion and acknowledges Maddow's whiteness while it connects the female masculinity of both women. Walters points to Goldberg and quips, "She's about to come out of the closet!" and Goldberg acknowledges, "That door's been open for years." This exchange points to Goldberg's race while revisiting rumors that her casual masculine femininity calls her heterosexuality into question. This rupture indicates how dependent the performance of femininity is on whiteness and heterosexuality. When the "big lesbian" comes to the women's talk show, race emerges as the sexual orientation of the guest is being discussed, and several narratives unravel simultaneously. While the joke revolves around the potential links between Goldberg and Maddow, the two women at the table with the most masculine physical presentations, what also stands out in this rupture is the stereotypical femininity of the petite Hasselbeck (with her long blonde hair), who perches to the left of Maddow. When Maddow comes to *The View*, Goldberg gains an ally.

Gay and lesbian media sources use the narratives of authenticity and sagacity to enfold Maddow. In the December 2, 2008, issue of *The Advocate*, a newsmagazine for LGBT readers, editor Jon Barrett explains the importance of the role of lesbians when he writes, "When we Americans decided it was again time for a dose of good old-fashioned authenticity ... we instead turned to lesbians ... who not only are open about their sexual orientation but aren't afraid to rip the Band-Aid off the scab of disillusionment" (5). This discourse minoritizes "the (white) lesbian" while giving her a role in a masculinist heterosexual empire. The narrative follows this chain of logic: "the lesbians" are not easily swayed by the mainstream hype that catches the rest of us. Lesbians possess their own brand of knowledge, their own community, and a unique access to the truth because they are not swayed by trends or fashion. We call on lesbians to tell us the truth when *we* are completely lost. Those lesbians serve as oracles and soothsayers for a damaged or lost world, and they have direct access to female intuition (a leftover notion from 1970s feminism). When this narrative is repeated in *The Advocate*, gay men are placed with the mainstream heterosexual population while lesbians and other queer women are shunted to the fringes. This separation happens even while "the (white) lesbian" is worshipped for her candor. While Maddow and Suze Orman gain media attention through the use of this narrative, they also become disposable commodities in the process.

Barrett's editorial in a gay magazine yokes authenticity and the figure of the (white) lesbian to a deeper, more painful truth that the gay white middle-class audience needs to hear. When the wild party is over, the sensible lesbians will help gay men find the way home. This condescending connection keeps Maddow's sexuality and gender foregrounded while her racial and class status remain unspoken and unanalyzed.

Suze Orman: Preacher and Therapist

Bloggers do not write mash notes to Suze Orman, star of *The Suze Orman Show* (2002–2015) on CNBC, author of nine best-selling self-help finance books, and creator and star of seven PBS specials on personal finance. Orman's financial advice has become more valuable to middle-class Americans since the economic collapse of 2008, but her image is often described as distasteful or even grotesque. Orman told a *New York Times* reporter that she is a lesbian in February 2007, after she had already become a best-selling author and television celebrity (Kregloe). Her fiftyish California-girl image contains markings of femininity, masculinity, and middle-class values within a field of unmarked whiteness. A photograph of her short, wavy blonde hair, direct blue eyes, and bright grin appears five times on the homepage of her website (www.suzeorman.com) and on the cover of each book.

In a *New York Times* article titled "Off the Shelf: The Ubiquitous Suze Orman," Harry Hurt introduces Orman as follows: "Among the substances that need hazmat warning labels are the liquid that bronzes Suze Orman's hair, the paste that whitens her teeth for her publicity photographs, and her latest financial advice manual" (Hurt). Hurt's humor suggests that, because Orman's grooming products are making her artificially beautiful, her financial advice must not be trustworthy. In the above passage, the anxiety about her manipulated image suggests that Orman may be a huckster—and although sexual desirability and the manipulation of one's image are often linked, Hurt instead links Orman's transformation to her marketability. This uneasiness suggests a discomfort with the seen and unseen ways by which Orman performs (an aging) femininity. Halberstam notes, "When and where female masculinity conjoins with possibly queer identities, it is far less likely to meet with approval" (28). By the time Hurt's article appeared, Orman's sexual orientation had already been revealed to the press (although he does not include this tidbit about his interviewee). In addition to Orman's performance of femininity, and with an aging body, she preaches within a traditionally male field: economics.

The titles of Orman's books connect spirituality and money to individual growth and financial independence; they include *The Courage to Be Rich: Creating a Life of Material and Spiritual Abundance* (1999), *The Road to Wealth: A Comprehensive Guide to Your Money* (2001), and *Women and Money: Owning the Power to Control Your Destiny* (2007). One of Orman's lessons is that all women (even married ones) need to pay off their debts and take control of their own finances so that they do not have to rely financially on others. Although this message does not challenge the mythology of the American Dream or question capitalism, extended interviews with Orman often contain an anxious subtext related to Orman's image and motivations.

People frequently call Orman's CNBC show with such personal and varied questions as how best to spend an inheritance, how to talk to children about money, how to justify buying a new designer purse, and whether a daughter's dance lessons are too expensive. During the calls, Orman asks specific questions about living wills, trustees, the ages of children, and sometimes the caller's income. The answers to these questions appear on the split screen as the caller continues to explain his or her situation. Orman sometimes calls female callers "momma" or "girlfriend" and tells callers to repeat her favorite words as she answers questions: "I was wrong; I made a mistake." Another of her mantras appears on her website: "People first, then money, then things." During the brief counseling sessions, Orman remains upbeat and pushes viewers to take responsibility and set up contingency plans. According to Susan Dominus, "She has figured out a way to channel an innate charisma and a televangelist's intensity into an otherwise bland message of fiscal responsibility" (Dominus). As Martha Burk explains in "Suze Orman's Bottom Line," "She's fifty percent pop psychologist, fifty percent rock star, and one hundred percent about financial empowerment for women" (34). However innocuous this mission might sound, critics nevertheless target her television image.

In Sheelah Kolhatkar's "Suze Orman: Queen of the Crisis," Orman's monstrous image emerges as she counsels people on camera. Kolhatkar writes, "Orman's ubiquitous presence has become a sort of unofficial economic barometer: the worse things get, the harder she is to avoid. Her style seems almost intentionally annoying: she screams on camera, her blue eyes practically bugging out of her head" (Kolhatkar). Orman's power grows as people become more nervous about their finances and she stalks the viewer from medium to medium. The hysterical and omnipresent huckster reaches out to a stunned audience that cannot escape her antics. Kolhatkar criticizes Orman for saturating the marketplace with her image—the very definition of celebrity. However, descriptions of Orman vary in different publications. Orman's image in *Ms.* magazine, a feminist publication, is more complimentary than descriptions published in *Time* magazine or the *New York Times.*

Orman's image meshes masculinity, femininity, and class privilege—which links to the continuing promise of following her advice. In the opening photo accompanying Susan Dominus' article in *New York Times Magazine,* "Suze Orman Is Having a Moment," Orman lounges on a gray sofa, wearing a pink robe with white cuffs. Reading a thick investment report and holding a white cup of coffee, she turns to smile at the camera. A tall vase of white roses rests on the end table, as the breeze blows a floor-length curtain around the edge of the table. Because she took her own investment advice, Orman enjoys her coffee and is in her bathrobe all morning—unlike others, who scurry off to toil for someone else each morning. Meshing symbols of relaxation, studiousness, and femininity allows class privilege to exist just within the viewer's reach and whiteness to remain unspoken. As this dream sequence seems crafted specifically for a female-identified viewer, the image suggests that if the reader follows Orman's advice, she could also go into business for herself and feel this relaxed about her own 401K. The accompanying caption sharpens the edge of the image: "At home near Fort Lauderdale. Like many evangelists, Orman was once a captive of her wants" (Dominus). This caption frames the journey toward class privilege as a simple twelve-step program that any self-disciplined woman can take.

Dominus calls Orman an "evangelist," and Damon Darlin describes her as a "telegenic personal finance guru" (Darlin). This connection between finance and spirituality resonates in Orman's book titles *The Nine Steps to Financial Freedom: Practical and Spiritual Steps So You Can Stop Worrying* (1997) and the aforementioned *The Courage to Be Rich: Creating a Life of Material and Spiritual Abundance.* Orman connects self-help rhetoric and spiritual rhetoric to increase readers' sense of self-efficacy. Connecting financial wealth to spiritual clarity also distances Orman's teachings from unearned and unexamined racial privilege and the generational aspects of social class. In this framework, Orman emerges as a holy leader, beyond the trappings of privileges and oppressions. In contrast, a violent image for the economy emerges in *Time* magazine in 2009, when Kolhatkar describes Orman as "a medic tending injured soldiers on a battlefield" (Kolhatkar). At a moment when the United States was fighting expensive wars in both Afghanistan and Iraq, this battle-zone metaphor instilled Orman with the expertise to save American lives. In the economic war zone, many of Orman's patients are fighting for their country's economy and losing everything. This startling metaphor, inflected with tropes of masculinity, also connects the American Dream to jingoism and militarism.

In *Ms.* magazine, Orman explains herself to economists and financial experts who critique her connection between spirituality and money: "You have certain indicators of consumer confidence levels—what do you think [they are? They are] emotional indicators that you base the stock market on. [However,] because a woman writes a book about emotions and money, you want to attack it" (Burk 38). Because the masculinist narrative of finance employs clinical assumptions about money and the stock market, Orman's female-identified personal, emotional approach to finance threatens. Narratives of masculinity value stoicism and long-range investments, while narratives of femininity emphasize spending money and immediate happiness. Orman's approach links saving and financial control to female power, a formula that meshes noteworthy aspects of both masculine and feminine narratives.

Although Orman has her critics, her visibility has risen exponentially since 2007. In the *Wall Street Journal* article "Crisis Makes Suze Orman a Star," Suzanne Vranica and Stephanie Kang attempt to measure Orman's influence. "'Her star has really risen,' says Sal Taibi, president of the New York office of Lowe, the Interpublic Group ad firm that created the 'Got Milk?' ads. 'She went from a cult personality to a really mass celebrity very quickly'" (qtd. in Vranica and Kang). Advertising executives quoted in the article note that her "likeability scores" went up considerably from 2007 to 2008, when Orman earned twenty-five thousand dollars for a "Got Milk?" print advertisement and regularly commanded seventy-two thousand dollars per speaking engagement (Vranica and Kang). Vranica and Kang explain that Orman refuses to endorse banking companies, as they tend to encourage people to overspend and undersave (Vranica and Kang). This valuable visage does allow Orman to attract viewers, however. Ratings for her television program increased twenty-two percent between May 2008 and May 2009 (Dominus).

In Carmen Wong Ulrich's article "Seven Money Principles for Black Women" in the June 2007 issue of *Essence* magazine, Orman's message is altered in several ways. This article is accompanied by three photographs of young and thin black women wearing expensive clothing and displaying their relationship to money. In the first photo, an African American woman in a blue halter dress sits on a white chaise, throws cash over her head, and laughs. The second photo features a different African American woman with her hair in loose braids, pursing her lips critically and holding a black pump in front of a shoe display. In the final photo, the woman in the blue halter dress is featured once again; this time, she leans back on the white chaise and fans herself with a bundle of money. All three of these images create a narrative of professional black women who have spent some money on clothing and makeup yet also understand that saving their money is tied to happiness. Unlike in the articles featured in publications geared to white audiences, a photograph of Orman appears halfway through Ulrich's article in a small shot of her book cover. As such, *Essence* uses the largest photographs to mirror back to its readers a vision of their own actual or potential relationship to money. The sixth point of advice in the article—"Watch how your honey handles money"—is similarly tailored to *Essence*'s target audience, reminding the black female reader that, if she makes more money than the man in her life, she needs to watch out, because he could become a burden to her with his shaky financial history. In this particular publication, the black heterosexual female is constructed with access to class privilege that could be compromised by a boyfriend or husband. This rupture in heterosexual normativity is precipitated less by the presence of the white lesbian in the black women's publication than it is a symptom of the cross-pollination/interdependence among the narratives of class mobility, whiteness, heterosexuality, and femininity.

In contrast to the article in *Essence*, the articles in *New York Times Magazine*, *Time*, and the *Wall Street Journal* silently employ white privilege to describe the unfettered journey toward class privilege. This assumption becomes more noticeable in the article "Smart Money: In a Time of Economic Calamity, One Voice Rises above the Panic" by Neal Broverman, which appeared in the December 2, 2008, issue *The Advocate*, a publication for LGBTQ readers. Broverman begins the article by undercutting the presumed financial stability that comes with same-sex marriage within the unstable international economy. He assumes that these newlywed same-sex couples are middle to upper class because they own property and have some money in the stock market. In contrast, the single, working-class LGBTQ individual who rents an apartment and lives from paycheck to paycheck would have a much smaller need for Orman's retirement-fund and mortgage advice. The narrowing of *The Advocate*'s target audience continues with the quote that Broverman chooses from Orman's speech at the Human Rights Campaign's national dinner: For "all of us to truly change what's going on in this world you have got to be financially powerful. You cannot be in debt; you cannot have financial bondage if you want to set yourselves free" (qtd. in Broverman 11). Orman's advocacy is limited to the richest queers, a target market that has gleaned a great deal of attention over the last decade and one *The Advocate* courts in order to keep its print magazine alive. However, this focus overshadows the reality that the total percentage of LGBTQ households that are working class or below is higher than that of heterosexual households.

After analyzing the results of the 2000 Census, the 2002 National Survey of Family Growth, and the 2003 and 2005 California Health Interview Surveys, researchers at the University of California, Los Angeles' Williams

Institute found that same-sex households were more likely to live in poverty than opposite-sex households (Cisneros and Sakimura). Racial privilege was also linked to class mobility, and, once the data were broken out, the researchers concluded that African American and Latino/Latina people living in same-sex households are more likely to live in poverty than white people in same-sex households (Cisneros and Sakimura). One finding of the report pointed out that "African Americans in same-sex couples have poverty rates that are significantly higher than black people in different-sex married couples and are roughly three times higher than those of white people in same-sex couples" (Cisneros and Sakimura). This separation in poverty rates between African American gays and lesbians and white gays and lesbians partially accounts for the images of white same-sex couples and their desirability as consumers. However, the Williams Institute report indicates that same-sex female couples are much more likely to live below the poverty line: "The poverty rates of lesbian/bisexual women are higher than those of heterosexual women (and the difference is statistically significant at the 10% level), with one quarter of lesbian/bisexual women living in poverty versus only one-fifth of heterosexual women" (Albelda et al. 6). Furthermore, the myth of the wealthy gay man evaporates when the Williams Institute's researchers crunch the data. According to this report, "Gay men are as likely to be poor as are heterosexual men in the United States as a whole, and are more likely to be poor than are heterosexual men with the same characteristics" (Albelda et al. 15). Even the sacrosanct narrative of the rich (white) gay man wavers as researchers closely examine the data.

Although Orman may not be seen as a sex symbol, she is nevertheless idolized as an independent lesbian and savvy businesswoman. As a result, the construction of her image participates in and perpetuates the pervasive notion that all LGBTQ people are, or can become, wealthy.

Ellen DeGeneres: Pioneer and Talk Show Host

Ellen DeGeneres' career has also benefited from the changing attitudes toward the (white) "butch" lesbian, but her on-screen persona is markedly different from Maddow's on *The Rachel Maddow Show* and Orman's on *The Suze Orman Show*. Maddow's program centers on political discourse and has a decidedly liberal bent, and Orman's program dishes out bracing financial advice. In contrast, *Ellen: The Ellen DeGeneres Show* (2003–) centers on "lifestyle" issues and rarely ventures into politics. As the program's website explains, "Through her show, [Ellen] brings her humor, personal warmth, insight, and talent for tackling topical issues into viewers' lives with her distinctive style touching every aspect of the show" ("About"). This website also emphasizes how much fun the show is while reminding online readers and television viewers that they can win products and watch celebrities compete in games.

In 2001, DeGeneres hosted the Primetime Emmy Awards show, "receiving several standing ovations and widespread critical acclaim for her work in a post–9/11 atmosphere" (Fees 30). That ceremony marked her reentry into mainstream culture at a moment when U.S. nationalism was being used as a response to the attacks on the Twin Towers in New York City. After 9/11, the cultural capital of whiteness in the United States took on an additional importance, one in which DeGeneres' whiteness trumped her sexuality. For as Steve Garner explains in his book *Whiteness: An Introduction*, "When people are talking about hierarchies of entitlement and justice, they set up a scenario in which nationality generates entitlement, and when it comes down to it, … whiteness is a kind of flag" (151). At a moment in history when American flags were flying on many homes and taxicabs, DeGeneres reintroduced herself to the nation with several jokes, including, "What would bug the Taliban more than seeing a gay woman in a suit surrounded by Jews?" In other words, the viewer who cheers for DeGeneres also hopes to simultaneously irritate the Taliban, and DeGeneres' status on the awards show symbolizes diversity and tolerance in the United States.

In 2003, DeGeneres voiced the part of Dory, an "absent-minded fish," in the Disney/Pixar animated film *Finding Nemo* (directed by Andrew Stanton and Lee Unkrich) (Fees 30). This "absent presence" in a children's movie reintroduced her to the families who watched the film in theaters and on DVD in a nonthreatening, disembodied way. In conjunction with the film, DeGeneres appeared on several talk shows and presented the public with her new persona. That same year, *Ellen: The Ellen DeGeneres Show* debuted in a daytime slot, a program that still enjoys high ratings years later. In her latest incarnations, DeGeneres has become a CoverGirl model for its Simply Ageless makeup line, a judge on *American Idol* (2002–), and host of the 2014 Academy Awards ceremony. As such, there are at least five "Ellens" here—a character, a TV host, a comedian, an actress, and a model. It is perhaps unsurprising, therefore, that DeGeneres has joked about her chameleon-like qualities in various interviews.

Barbara Smith points out, in her preface to "Where's the Revolution?" (as reprinted in her book *The Truth That Never Hurts: Writings on Race, Gender, and Freedom*), that DeGeneres does not advocate the overthrow of heterosexism, and not one of her personas has done so, either (175). She further notes that, in an April 14, 1997, interview with a reporter for *Time* magazine, she was asked if she is angry that other actors have not come out publicly, and DeGeneres responded that all members of the gay community are individuals and she does not judge their choices (Smith 175). The appeal to the freedom of the individual over the needs of the community puts DeGeneres in line with the American Dream. It further presumes that she came out in order to help her earlier television situation-comedy series, *Ellen* (1994–1998), a miscalculation at the time. DeGeneres also foreshadows her next career move: "Maybe I'll find something even bigger to do later on. Maybe I'll become black" (qtd. in Smith 178).

In two senses, then—as a woman and as a lesbian—DeGeneres is already seen as "other." Even though, in the aforementioned 1997 *Time* interview, DeGeneres indicated that she is anxious that she will not get work after her daring (and commercial) outing(s), in 2015, her face time has increased exponentially. Her blonde hair, Greek surname, and pale skin mark her as white in the United States, and by joking that this was also a chosen identity, DeGeneres flexes her white privilege. After all, in the face of all that uproar from the religious right about her former sitcom, DeGeneres still has her whiteness, and, as she predicted, this gave her another rebirth in daytime TV.

The Ellen DeGeneres Show markets itself to stay-at-home moms: white, suburban, and straight. Its guests include the stars of current movies and television series, and DeGeneres often plays herself as the fool in order to make her guests and her audience comfortable: dancing to her desk, asking obvious questions, and staging ridiculous competitions between audience members. Her daytime persona hinges on her need for fun, so she sometimes pretends not to understand jokes, and her sexuality is only a minor part of that persona. In "Resisting, Reiterating, and Dancing Through: The Swinging Closet Doors of Ellen DeGeneres' Televised Personalities," Candace Moore notes that "DeGeneres avoids the topic of her own homosexuality and actively closes down conversations in which the very word or concept comes up" (17). This strategy effectively enables her to continue to attract viewers and acclaim for the show.

Moore contends that the daily ritual of DeGeneres' dancing at the beginning of her talk show reminds the audience of her queerness. She states, "Ellen's coming-out dance is similarly repeated in the first fifteen minutes of every show, unanchoring its meaning, while effectively performing the extraordinary in the everyday…. Literally dancing out into the audience, she provides an effective performative pun" (22). This ritual may be so buried in the text of the everyday, however, that DeGeneres' sexuality can be read as having nothing to do with the dancing. In one sense, the viewer expects Ellen to dance for the audience, and she performs on cue in this way every weekday. The discourse of the daytime talk show is shaped by heteronormativity and capitalist values, and these forces overshadow any latent queerness attached to the performer.

Viewers of the program know that DeGeneres is gay, but she sometimes embodies a heterosexual female persona as she questions the guests. In an interview with Jake Gyllenhaal during the show's 400th episode (on November 10, 2005), DeGeneres asks him to take off his shirt yet notes that he does not need to do it for her (Moore 27). In this way, DeGeneres acts as an intermediary for the straight female members of her audience, channeling their desires into her questions and downplaying any homosexual desires some of the non-heterosexual ones might have. In the above example, any crush that the women may have on the host can be reoriented toward the blushing Gyllenhaal. Moore characterizes DeGeneres' behavior during the Gyllenhaal interview as a "faked crush" that she camps up for effect (27). This particular Ellen persona does not quite become straight, though. Instead, she performs a semblance of the straight woman's desire and, in the process, stabilizes the heterosexual narrative.

As Moore explains, the interview ends quickly with an awkward gesture toward Gyllenhaal's movie *Brokeback Mountain* (2005, directed by Ang Lee), which centers on a love affair between two men (Moore 27). The queer content of this movie seeps into the cracks of the interview, but the spoken dialogue focuses primarily on *Jarhead* (2005, directed by Sam Mendes), Gyllenhaal's other movie about heterosexual Marines. Because straight women's desires are central to the success of this daytime talk show, DeGeneres intentionally bridges the space between the straight women watching the show.

When DeGeneres interviews actor Mario Lopez on October 21, 2009, another layer of power and otherness emerges in their banter. Lopez comes on the show to promote both his new children's picture book, *Mud Tacos,* and his appearance on the television series *Nip/Tuck* (2003–2010). First, DeGeneres shows the straight female audience a beefcake shot of Lopez running out of the ocean with his wetsuit unzipped, and they squeal and clap as he blushes and talks about his first triathlon. Then, DeGeneres cuts to a shot from *Nip/Tuck* of Lopez in a tight black leather corset and garters with fishnet stockings. Lopez sucks in a breath and, over the titters of the audience, exclaims, "How did you get that? I don't think you're supposed to show that one! It's okay, he's doing that for the woman he loves." DeGeneres uses this intriguing photograph to pique viewers' interest in the *Nip/Tuck* series while simultaneously queering the straight Latino actor. Seeing a photo of Lopez in a corset echoes the retouched photos of Tony (Okungbowa), the D.J., on the show's website, which depicted him in sexually compromising vignettes. In some ways, therefore, both Okungbowa and Lopez must end up negotiating their masculinity in the presence of DeGeneres' white female masculinity. At the end of Lopez's appearance, DeGeneres talks him out of his shirt and into the dunk tank, for the sake of charity. Clothed, he would have raised ten thousand dollars, but topless he is worth twenty thousand dollars, a negotiation that he calls "shady."

While DeGeneres works within liberal capitalism in order to solidify her position as a celebrity, "women of color feminism attempted to dislodge interpretations of racial domination from the normative grip of liberal capitalism" (Ferguson 115). In addition, queering racialized masculinity wields white privilege and centers (straight) female desires. White heteronormativity and homonormativity, therefore, provide the framework for *The Ellen DeGeneres Show.*

Is Queer Television Ever for Queer Viewers?

These various images of white lesbianism deliberately appeal to heterosexual white audiences, not queer or queer of color audiences. In *Disidentifications: Queers of Color and the Performance of Politics*, José Esteban Muñoz theorizes that a queer of color viewer taking in a performance of race or sexuality must adopt a "both/and stance" toward the figure (Muñoz; DeLong 151). While being intrigued or excited by the character, he or she must also "act straight" (and, presumably, repelled) for the preservation of his or her safety in a heterosexual setting (DeLong 151). For example, comedian Marga Gomez recalls the lesbian on television who first attracted and horrified her— while her mother measured her reaction (DeLong 151).

In "Epistemology of the Console," Lynne Joyrich questions why LGBTQ activists use visibility to challenge the mainstream culture. She writes, "While relying so heavily on discourses of enlightened visibility is certainly understandable in this post–Enlightenment society of the image, this nonetheless means that queer political and cultural opposition becomes framed in the same terms as the dominant ones that we'd like to challenge" (16). Joyrich's connection between Enlightenment thought and the metaphors of knowledge and visibility aptly lays out the territory. On television, the "visibility equals knowledge" trope constitutes both the medium and its narration about itself. The problem is not only that the programs being made do not reflect the experiences of many viewers but also that the white queer viewers and the queer viewers of color all desire a sense of intimacy with queer figures— while at the same time always knowing that mainstream media sources ensure that this desire cannot be fulfilled.

The image of the model minority lesbian was never constructed to satisfy queers. Much like the lesbian teen pining for the homecoming queen, the queer female viewer reaches again and again for the unattainable and inauthentic "celesbian" on the screen.

WORKS CITED

"About the Show." *Ellen: The Ellen DeGeneres Show*, n.d. Web. 14 October 2009. http://www.ellentv.com.

Albelda, Randy, M.V. Lee Badgett, Alyssa Schneebaum, and Gary J. Gates. "Poverty in the Lesbian, Gay, and Bisexual Community." Williams Institute, UCLA School of Law, March 2009. Web. 2 October 2009. http://williamsinstitute.law.ucla.edu/wp-content/uploads/Albelda-Badgett-Schneebaum-Gates-LGB-Poverty-Report-March-2009.pdf.

Bach, Mette. "Air America's Sweetheart." *Advocate*, 15 July 2008: 13. Print.

Barrett, Jon. "The Moment of Truth." *Advocate*, 2 December 2008: 5. Print.

Broverman, Neal. "Smart Money: In a Time of Economic Calamity, One Voice Rises Above the Panic." *Advocate*, 2 December 2008: 11. Print.

Burk, Martha. "Suze Orman's Bottom Line." *Ms.*, Fall 2008: 34–38. Print.

Cisneros, Lisa, and Cathy Sakimura. "Legal Advocates Challenging Stereotypes and Increasing Access to Justice for LGBT Communities." *Legal Services of Northern California*, 18 August 2009. Web. 13 October 2009. http://equity.lsnc.net/2009/08/legal-advocates-challenging-stereotypes-and-increasing-access-to-justice-for-lgbt-communities/.

Darlin, Damon. "A Guru Offers Help on Credit Scores, but No Longer Makes Any Promises." *New York Times*, 7 May 2007. Web. 4 December 2015.

DeLong, Renee. "Missing Bridges: The Invisible (and Hypervisible) Lesbian of Color in Theory, Publishing, and Media." Diss., University of Minnesota, 2013. Print.

Dominus, Susan. "Suze Orman Is Having a Moment." *New York Times Magazine*, 14 May 2009. Web. 8 March 2011.

Fees, Jarre. "Tracking Ellen's Career Highlights." *Television Week*, 28 January 2008: 30. Print.

Ferguson, Roderick A. *Aberrations in Black: Toward a Queer of Color Critique*. Minneapolis: University of Minnesota Press, 2003. Print.

Garner, Steve. *Whiteness: An Introduction*. London: Routledge, 2007. Print.

Halberstam, Judith. *Female Masculinity*. Durham: Duke University Press, 1998. Print.

Hammonds, Evelynn. "Black (W)holes and the Geometry of Black Female Sexuality." *Black Studies Reader*. Ed. Jacqueline Bobo, Cynthia Hudley, and Claudine Michel. New York: Routledge, 2004. 301–314. Print.

Hurt, Harry, III. "Off the Shelf: The Ubiquitous Suze Orman." *New York Times*, 18 March 2007. Web. 8 March 2011.

Jeffery, Clara. "The Maddow Knows." *Mother Jones*, January/February 2009: 72–73. Print.

Joyrich, Lynne. "Epistemology of the Console." *Queer TV: Theories, Histories, Politics*. Ed. Glyn Davis and Gary Needham. New York: Routledge, 2009. 15–47. Print.

Kolhatkar, Sheelah. "Suze Orman: Queen of the Crisis." *Time*, 5 March 2009. Web. 3 March 2011.

Kregloe, Karman. "Suze Orman Comes Out." *After Ellen*, 25 February 2007. Web. 4 December 2015. http://www.afterellen.com/tv/5276-suze-orman-comes-out.

Lopez, Mario, and Marissa Lopez Wong. *Mud Tacos*. New York: Celebra, 2009. Print.

Lorde, Audre. *Sister Outsider: Essays and Speeches*. Berkeley: Crossing Press, 2007. Print.

McCroy, Winnie. "A Conversation with Rachel Maddow, Reluctant Sex Symbol." *Village Voice*, 24 June 2009. Web. 1 December 2015.

_____. "Rachel Maddow, the New Sexy." *Village Voice*, 24 June 2009. Web. 2 October 2009.

Merkin, Daphne. "Butch Fatale." *New York Times Magazine*, 19 February 2009. Web. 2 October 2009.

Moore, Candace. "Resisting, Reiterating, and Dancing Through: The Swinging Closet Doors of Ellen DeGeneres' Televised Personalities." *Televising Queer Women: A Reader*. Ed. Rebecca Beirne. New York: Palgrave Macmillan, 2008. 17–31. Print.

Moraga, Cherríe, and Gloria Anzaldua, eds. *This Bridge Called My Back: Writings by Radical Women of Color*. Watertown, MA: Persephone Press, 1981. Print.

Muñoz, José Esteban. *Disidentifications: Queers of Color and the Performance of Politics*. Minneapolis: University of Minnesota Press, 1999. Print.

Orman, Suze. *The Courage to Be Rich: Creating a Life of Material and Spiritual Abundance*. New York: Riverhead Books, 1999. Print.

_____. *The Nine Steps to Financial Freedom: Practical and Spiritual Steps So You Can Stop Worrying*. New York: Crown, 1997. Print.

_____. *The Road to Wealth: A Comprehensive Guide to Your Money*. New York: Riverhead Books, 2001. Print.

_____. *Women and Money: Owning the Power to Control Your Destiny*. New York: Spiegel and Grau, 2007. Print.

Quart, Alissa. "The Sarcastic Times." *Columbia Journalism Review*, March/April 2009: 12–14. Print.

Smith, Barbara. *The Truth That Never Hurts: Writings on Race, Gender, and Freedom*. New Brunswick: Rutgers University Press, 1998. Print.

Stanley, Alessandra. "A Fresh Female Face Amid Cable Schoolboys." *New York Times*, 24 September 2008. Web. 29 November 2015.

Traister, Rebecca. "Mad for Rachel Maddow." *The Nation*, 18–25 August 2008: 22–24. Print.

Ulrich, Carmen Wong. "Seven Money Principles for Black Women." *Essence*, June 2007: 95–96+. Print.

Vranica, Suzanne, and Stephanie Kang. "Crisis Makes Suze Orman a Star." *Wall Street Journal*, 17 October 2008. Web. 8 March 2011.

"Why We're Gay for Rachel Maddow." NYmagwww. *New York*, 17 July 2008. Web. 12 December 2009. http://nymag.com/daily/intelligencer/2008/07/were_gay_for_ rachel_maddow.html#.

Widner, Jonanna. "The Rachel Papers: What a Hot, Smart Lesbian Pundit Means for an Uneasy America." *Bitch: Feminist Response to Pop Culture*, Spring 2009: 37– 39. Print.

Digital Drag
Queer Potentiality in the Age
of Digital Television

Looi van Kessel

During the seven seasons that have been broadcast so far, Logo TV's popular television series *RuPaul's Drag Race* (2009–) has made drag performance more visible than ever before. The group of contestants consists of young queens who dream of a breakthrough and older, more seasoned queens who want to get recognition for the years of work they have put into their drag personas. Each participant competes for a jeweled crown, a generous sum of money, and, of course, the title of "next drag superstar" in this reality game show. Over the course of its run to date, the series has grown tremendously in popularity among television audiences in the United States and abroad. The program's ratings have steadily been on the rise, making it the most-watched program in Logo TV's program catalog (Gorman). In addition to its successful ratings, the series has also proven to be popular on social media. The number of followers that the series enjoys on popular social websites such as Facebook, Instagram, and Twitter surpasses those of most queer-themed television offerings, and its online popularity is in many cases rivaled only by the popular series *The L Word* (2004–2009).

The series' popularity and its championing of drag performance have garnered ample exposure for its contestants. The many different styles that the participating queens—or "drag racers"—have sported over the past seasons attest to the series' appreciation of many different types of drag. As such, many commentators applaud *RuPaul's Drag Race* for allowing drag performance to be appreciated as an art form by a mainstream audience. However, not everybody agrees with the accolades that befall the show. In a critical reflection on the first season of *RuPaul's Drag Race*, which aired during the spring of 2009, Eir-Anne Edgar accuses the series of maintaining a traditional perspective on drag culture: the genre of female impersonation, or female illusion. She argues that, even though the series has committed itself to representing a varied array of drag performance, it privileges a drag genre of total transformation from male into female without problematizing perceived gender boundaries like other, more avant-garde and androgynous drag styles do. After critically examining the elimination process of season one, Edgar asserts, "We see that the Queens of *Drag Race*, while appearing distinct from one another, are eliminated or normalized through discourses of natural beauty and stereotypical depictions of womanhood" (137). The series' proclivity toward non-complex gender representations, as shown by two of the finalists and the eventual winner of the first season, counters queer activists' and theorists' acknowledgement of the complexity and constructedness of gender. Edgar argues, along the lines of Judith Butler and Jack Halberstam, that drag performance can lay bare the slippages of gender identification and is "ultimately successful (and most subversive) at the very moment that a type of doubled-ness occurs, a layering of the performances of everyday gender and drag gender" (141).

Edgar's claims that *RuPaul's Drag Race* conforms to a stereotypical and normalized drag should be nuanced. While it might be true that the early winners in the series were queens who emanated a traditional feminine gender representation, later seasons have also known winners who complicate gender representation through their particular style of drag. The theatrics of Bianca Del Rio, Jinkx Monsoon, and Sharon Needles foreground the gender slippage that Edgar deems essential to successful drag. Their take on drag performance does not concern itself with attaining the perfect semblance of a woman. Instead, they exaggerate and ironize attributes that are regularly associated with femininity. In a similar vein, Raja became known for her signature androgynous look that challenges normalizing representations of femininity as she, for example, performed her drag without the aid of prosthetic breasts during her appearance on the show. Drag, for Raja, is based on a theatricality that foregrounds the constructedness of gender, race, and class. Other contestants, too, have increasingly problematized the boundaries of gender construction through their drag performance. The "genderfuck" that for Edgar typifies first-season contestant Ongina has also been present in the styles of contestants such as Milan, who impersonated a suited-up Janelle Monáe-as-drag-king in season four, and Milk, who wore a beard as a part of her outfit during season six. The increasing popularity of such gender-bending visuals is also reflected in how the series has developed over the years. While Milk's bearded drag sparked some controversy at first, season seven had its contestants don a beard as a part of their outfit on the main stage.

In all fairness, it can be argued that *RuPaul's Drag Race* still maintains a certain normative and stereotypical view on drag performance and queer lives. This becomes most obvious during the behind-the-scenes, or "untucked," segments. Here, the contestants are shown relaxing in between their performance on the runway and the eventual judgment and elimination round. During these moments, the queens are often portrayed as mean and bitchy, which for many mainstream viewers is certainly entertaining yet simultaneously perpetuates certain stereotypes of queer lifestyles. Similarly, during judgment, many contestants continue to be called out for flaws in their female illusion. Low voices, beards showing through the thick layers of makeup, and a lack of padding (i.e., making hips more pronounced with the use of foam pads) are invariably denounced as masculine and an improper way of "doing drag." Based on such instances, one could argue that the series indeed subscribes to a type of drag that is recognizable for a general audience, a genre of drag that is more concerned with the mystification of gender performance and a semblance of femininity than with the foregrounding of gender constructions.

For Edgar, this traditional take on drag performance is partly the consequence of the reality game show format of *RuPaul's Drag Race*. This format, or "scenario" as Diana Taylor would call it (28), is a formalized manner of transmitting certain cultural memories and knowledge. As Nick Couldry explains when he discusses reality game shows as media rituals, "Media rituals are formalized actions organized around key media-related categories and boundaries whose performances suggest a connection with wider, media-related values" (85). The particular scenario of a game show, in which one contestant needs to perform better than his or her fellow contestants, calls for a normalizing of actions and gestures that are recognizable to a wider audience accustomed to a limited number of narratives and outcomes associated with game shows that follow a similar scenario. *RuPaul's Drag Race*, too, adheres to a game show scenario, which requires a sequence of standardized images and narratives in order for audiences to be able to relate to the characters and actions that are shown on-screen. Through this standardization of images and narratives, the series also perpetuates a certain notion of drag culture that is intelligible to a mainstream audience. The game show scenario, which includes a host of mini-games and qualitative judgments, further celebrates this standardized image of drag as contestants are continuously scrutinized for attributes and skills that are popularly associated with drag performance, such as "reading," lip-synching, and voguing.

Despite the criticism that *RuPaul's Drag Race* has received from some commentators, I argue that there is more to the series than merely a normalizing presentation of what drag performance entails. In recent years, we have witnessed a great surge in digital media convergence that has destabilized the processes of representation and cultural meaning-making at their very foundations. Ever since Henry Jenkins predicted that new media convergence will dramatically transform the cultural production of traditional media outlets, digital media have become increasingly important transmitters of cultural codes and values encrypted in an incessant flow of images, sounds, news, and opinions (13). The ways by which the comparatively older medium of television has engaged with digital media platforms have warranted a change in how the medium relates to its viewership and vice versa. *RuPaul's Drag Race*, too, relies heavily on digital media by promoting itself via several social networking websites and digital broadcasting. The producers of the series make use of digital media to improve its online visibility, but, as I will point out, the show has also been subject to debates pertaining to identity politics and representation within queer and transsexual communities. I argue that it is precisely because of these changed dimensions of television broadcasting that racial, sexual, and gendered minorities have been given access to new forms of social and political activism.

Subjectivation Will Be Televised

Edgar's contention that *RuPaul's Drag Race* fails to successfully represent a variety of drag genres due to the restrictions of the reality game show format to which it adheres touches upon a broader debate among feminists and queers pertaining to the need for representation in mainstream media. It is often argued that visibility of racial, sexual, or gender minorities in popular and mass media will result in a wider acceptance of these groups. The strategy of visibility has historically been an important aspect of gay liberation politics, and it remains a strategy that queer activists invoke in order to achieve their political aims (Hanhardt 83). However, television theorist Amy Villarejo refutes the assumption that mainstream broadcasting companies have the responsibility to represent these minority constituencies in an inclusive manner. Tracing queer representation on cable television from the 1950s to the mid–1990s in her book *Ethereal Queer: Television, Historicity, Desire*, Villarejo presents an opposing view on queer televisual presence and the transformative potential that gay rights activists ascribe to politics of representation. She argues that the assumptions that "television reflects its viewers; that television *ought* to do so; that it has an *obligation* toward diversity of representation; or that diverse representation leads to political change" instead lead to "inflated claims" and a conflation of "revolutionary or emancipatory political struggle with the appearance of queer marginalia" (3, original emphasis). Villarejo claims that television producers have no responsibility to provide diverse sexual representations. Nevertheless, her study engages deeply with the representation of queer desire in mainstream network and public television as a result of socioeconomic changes in U.S. society and technological developments of the *apparatus* itself.

Villarejo's overarching project of historicizing televised images of queer persons centers on the intersection of different debates about the role of mainstream television in the logic of late capitalism, the structures of public and private time, and the production of queer subjectivities. Following Theodor Adorno's seminal essay "How to Look at Television," Villarejo maintains that the specific temporality of television (or television time) both reflects and constitutes the social time of its viewers. In other words, television time is not only structured around the private time of its viewers but in turn also reshapes and reinforces the same private time that it reproduces in its programming. Thus, television constitutes its spectators temporally as subjects (Villarejo 46). Television time is always interwoven with discursive practices of subjectivation, which work according to the logic of the normalization of class, gender, race, and sexuality. As such, in the 1950s television programming was based on a predominantly white, middle-class female audience, whose private time was confined to domestic activities. By reproducing the daily rhythms of suburban housewives in their daytime programming, broadcast companies regulated and reinforced racial, sexual, gendered, and class-based subjectivity production (Villarejo 64).

The discursive category of television time is centered on a reification of various other social categories that converge into the televised image. Its coding of private lives into mass culture is the result of an intricate interplay of (gendered and racialized) private time, broadcast programming, and the technological dimensions of the apparatus itself. Developments in television technology shape and transform the programming of broadcasting companies. Villarejo reflects on the difference between the mid-century television technology that Adorno had access to when writing his essay, which was "centralized, limited to network channels, picked up through the ether via an antenna on a home set" (34), and the more contemporary "digital spectrum on offer in the household and in public spaces through the five-hundred-channel world" transmitted through a "plasma, liquid crystal display (LCD), or light-emitting diode (LED) screen" (35). Changes in the structure of television time, whether they result from a changed socioeconomic situation of its spectatorship or technological developments, then also demand different forms of representation (Villarejo 65). Villarejo notes that, in response to socioeconomic changes in both the public and private time of American lives during the 1960s and 1970s, television programming shifted toward a more progressive representation of sexual lives (83). However, harking back to Adorno's notion of the culture industry, Villarejo argues that these shifts in televisual representation of queers do not necessarily pave the way for societal inclusion but rather produce queer subjectivities that are accommodated to the norms and beliefs of society at large (42). Just as the game show scenario demands a certain mode of representation that is recognizable to its viewership, other television scenarios also require queer characters to be made intelligible to an audience that needs to relate to what is represented on-screen.

As television technology changes, it transforms the way that its spectatorship is represented and, in effect, also subjectivated. If we want to argue that a series such as *RuPaul's Drag Race* serves as an example not only of how queer representations have changed in 21st-century television but also of how such representations have increasingly become more political and intertwined with social activism, we must look at the dimensions and properties that have changed in the transition from network and cable television to digital television. These include an increasing convergence with other digital and new media platforms, broadcasting devices, and viewing environments. While mid–20th-century television, as Villarejo has already pointed out, was transmitted during restricted time slots, making available only a limited number of programs on a few channels that showed their offerings in sequential order, digital television is marked by an almost infinite number of programming choices and networks, all with their own socioeconomic, gendered, sexual, and racial constituencies (and/or any combinations and intersections thereof). The most radical change in the contemporary television experience, however, would undoubtedly be the simultaneity and instantaneity through which televised images become available to the public. Online broadcasting services have caused a sea change in the position that television has in the lives of many persons and households. From being a domestic and shared activity (e.g., the image of an entire family sitting around their television set to watch the news or any other specific program springs to mind), watching television has changed into a highly individualized and irregular pastime. Once aired through online outlets or added to online streaming databases, episodes of shows, movies, and related sorts of televisual offerings remain available for individuals to watch whenever they so desire. The convergence of the television set with other media platforms and portable devices no longer confines the act of watching television to the living room. Now, one can watch television whenever and wherever an Internet connection and an appropriate device are available. This reality radically transforms the experience of time and space that has traditionally been associated with television time, and it simultaneously also alters the way in which cultural knowledge is produced through the activity of watching television.

Queer Potentiality on Digital Television

In order to understand the changed nature of cultural knowledge-production in televisual representation, we need to re-evaluate David Harvey's seminal critique of the experience of time-space compression in the postmodern condition. Harvey's assertion that the increasing diminution of temporal and spatial distances through technological advancements has caused an economic and political logic of ephemerality and volatility in which the Fordist production of capital has been replaced by the commodification of images still rings true (285). If anything, his analysis seems even more relevant in the age of digital media convergence, as images are produced and consumed at ever-increasing speeds, and the collapse of one Internet bubble is quickly forgotten when the next digital media conglomerate makes a spectacular attempt at playing the stock market. However, Harvey could not foresee other challenges and tensions that the development of the Internet would bring, which have had a significant impact on political practices and meaning-making. Andreas Huyssen attempts to bridge the gap between the cultural logic of time-space compression and the increased information flow of the digital media landscape by looking critically at the production and shaping of memory through digital media practices. He argues that the commodification of images and cultural knowledge through various digital media platforms is detrimental to the production and functioning of cultural memory (Huyssen 31). Although U.S. and European societies alike seem to be obsessed with memory and the act of commemoration, the documenting and storing of the atrocities of the 20th century in vast digital archives lead instead to a collective forgetting, a cultural and collective lapse of memory. Digital television, one could argue, induces a similar forgetting as it decontextualizes and dehistoricizes the televised image into a perpetual present. Digital television's convergence with the Internet and other new media platforms has resulted in an on-demand economy that legitimizes itself through its instantaneity. Whatever is produced, whenever and under what conditions, becomes obscured, as viewers can consume anything they want, at any given time, on any device at their disposal. The instantaneous and interchangeable formats of the consumed products (often merely another image attached to the same scenario, which, following Harvey's analysis, is then sold as a wholly new and authentic media event) also put the longevity of cultural memory in peril. The distinction between productive and disposable memory that Huyssen proposes in his essay becomes blurred in the maelstrom of images that are made available for a vast audience (38). The volatility and ephemerality of Internet and digital media images—which manifest themselves in recent media crazes such as the taking of group "selfies" after the manner of Ellen DeGeneres, or having a bucket of ice water thrown over you for a then-in-vogue good cause—attest to the shrinkage of cultural memory and the ever-growing importance of the commodified image. The audience's active engagement with these short-lived images, by replicating them in great numbers, makes it easy to conflate their cultural production with the work of what Huyssen calls productive memory. Instead, such images displace people's investment in the cause or historical moment that they purport to support into a societal obsession with self-imaging as a means to remedy the fear of forgetting or, better still, the fear of being forgotten.

Nevertheless, there might be a place for productive memory in the age of digital media, even if such memory seems to be destined for oblivion. What Harvey and Huyssen both fail to address is that the ephemerality and volatility of images also allow for counter-hegemonic knowledge to manifest itself and reach a large audience. In an excellent critique of Harvey's analysis of time-space compression, Jack Halberstam argues that his preoccupation with the material conditions and economic logic of cultural production puts under erasure the categories of race, ethnicity, gender, and sexuality, among others (*In a Queer* 9–10). These identifications, Halberstam maintains, do not necessarily adhere to the logic of commodification that is central to Harvey's analysis. Instead, minority groups often transmit cultural knowledge and social memory through different means and usages of images, which, in a Marxist analysis such as Harvey's, could only be understood as a process of commodification. Through counter-hegemonic practices and image production, social activists manage to reach an increasing audience. Their affinity with the digital media landscape, in which a major portion of social activism is acted out, makes it essential to look at the potential of digital media for creating social awareness and political leverage.

José Esteban Muñoz takes up Halberstam's call for a deeper appreciation of queer experiences of time and space when he proposes the notion of queer potentiality. He expands upon this notion by arguing that "queerness is essentially about the rejection of a here and now and an insistence on potentiality or concrete possibility for another world" (1), which means that he makes a plea for a rigorous analysis of cultural production from a perspective of utopianism. Queer cultural production, he argues, is marked by the "not-yet-conscious": the potentiality to organize the world in ways that include queer lives and experiences without reverting to the banal optimism that utopianism is often associated with (3). It is tempting to project this thinking about queer potentiality on the representations of drag performance and queer culture in *RuPaul's Drag Race*. However, the series' focus on the wholesomeness of queer experiences and its strategies of substituting personal and traumatic events with the promise of transformation, choice, and popularity demand a critical scrutiny of what kind of queerness is produced in this scenario.

Over the course of each season, contestants on *RuPaul's Drag Race* share some of the hardships of their private and family lives. They talk about their experiences coming out as a gay or bisexual person, as a drag queen, or as transgender. During these moments, RuPaul invariably responds with one of her well-known mantras, such as "If you can't love yourself, how the hell are you gonna love somebody else?" or "We as gay people get to choose our family and the people we're around." During other moments, the contestants are confronted with videotaped messages in which their parents or other relatives try to reconcile differences in the past after acknowledging that they, through *RuPaul's Drag Race*, have finally learned to accept the individual's queerness. The message that is communicated during these moments seems straightforward: If you are courageous enough to express your queer lifestyle on television, those whom you hold dear will also learn to accept you for who you are.

In addition to such life lessons, the series promises a narrative in which the power of transformation helps queer persons to overcome hardships. The contestants, after having transformed into their drag personas, are applauded for their "Courage, Uniqueness, Nerve, and Talent" (C.U.N.T., if you will). Here, viewers see a promise of acceptance of queer lifestyles resulting from the aesthetic transformations that the contestants undergo. Such celebrations of the television-spectacle-as-affirmative-action echo Muñoz's claim that aesthetic sensibilities can and should insist on queer potentialities and a "collective political becoming" (189). Yet common loci of the reality game show format that *RuPaul's Drag Race* employs—such as transformation, reconciliation, and also elimination—might channel such political becoming into a normalizing standard of what queerness should entail. Through the format of the game show, the aesthetic expressions and queer identifications of its contestants are validated in a way that, as Edgar pointed out, is intelligible to a mainstream audience that needs to be able to identify with the identifications portrayed on the show.

The series extends these narratives of acceptance and transformation to the program's audience on a regular basis. RuPaul's motivational messages are often directed at the series' viewers, who are also invited to build a strong community around the images and stories of these drag performances. Fans are urged to watch the episodes together in queer-friendly establishments, and homemade fan videos that celebrate the contestants or recapitulate the episodes are actively promoted via the various online media to which the series has access. This community building via digital media, however, also creates a platform in which the show's producers must engage in a dialogue with the community at large. The widespread accessibility of social media has given many voices the opportunity to start a dialogue about the series' redemptive messages as well as its vision of queerness, both of which are placed under increasingly heavy scrutiny. One can recognize in this interaction between television audience and producers, during which audience members actively and politically engage with televisual representation, the surfacing of a different style of activism among queers. While dominant media images are contested, other experiences of sexuality and gender identifications are in turn privileged in the many confessions and testimonies that attest to the discursive violence the contested media images perpetuate. Of interest, then, is the question of whether the dialogue that manifests itself in digital media platforms indeed opens up the queer potentiality that Muñoz calls for or, instead, represents a different turn in queer political becoming.

"Responsitrannity"

During the spring of 2014, while the sixth season of *RuPaul's Drag Race* was in full course, the complexities of digital media convergence and the vulnerability of traditional media platforms that engage with new media suddenly became very palpable. Halfway through the season, a controversy about a mini-game segment on the show sparked an online debate that also addressed other increasingly controversial elements of the series, and which eventually extended into larger debates about representation and identity politics in the LGBTQ community. More than anything, this controversy—which has jokingly been dubbed "trannygate" by some commentators—foregrounds a tension within the LGBTQ community that coincides with recent transformations in network and digital television programming due to its entanglement with new media platforms.

The particular incident centers on the issue of misusing and appropriating derogatory terms that are seen as acts of defiance by some members of the LGBTQ community yet interpreted as slurs by others. The fourth episode of season six featured a mini-game that was teasingly dubbed "Female or She-Male." The *Drag Race* contestants were to examine various close-ups of (often surgically enhanced) body parts of celebrities—either cis women or drag queens—who were related to the show and then guess whether each individual pictured was "biologically" a woman or "psychologically" a woman (with the necessary "reads" that make up an important component of the repertoire of drag performance). As soon as this episode aired, a wave of critical reactions were voiced on the Internet. Trans activists and critical thinkers, headed by former *RuPaul's Drag Race* contestants and trans activists Carmen Carrera and Monica Beverly Hillz, expressed their discontent with the transphobic connotation of this particular episode (Nichols). As with most discussions that take place predominantly on the Internet, the number of opinion pieces, blog posts, and online news articles pertaining to this controversy is vast and difficult to survey in its totality. Thus, the texts that I discuss in this section are limited out of necessity to a small portion of the overall discussion on this topic.

In light of the problematic history of dehumanization that the slur "she-male" connotes for transgender communities, it likely comes as little surprise that many bloggers voiced their displeasure over the conflation of the categories of cis-male drag queens and trans women that the usage of the term implies in this situation (D'Angelo). The episode uncovered a perceived transphobia within the gay community itself, as commentators felt that the experiences of trans persons were claimed and misappropriated by cis-gender gay males. The eagerness with which cis-gender bisexual and gay persons seem to claim pronouns and designations of the opposite gender frequently frustrates those who struggle with their transgender identification (Edidi). As Shane Phelan argues, this process marginalizes trans persons within the LGBTQ community while it simultaneously occludes the difference between homosexual and transgender identification and structures the political aims of these different groups under the organizing category of queerness (118). The different experiences of transgender individuals are occasionally assimilated into similar identity politics of sexually nonconforming people. Still, the political desires and aims of trans people are often far removed from those who identify themselves as being sexually different yet conform to the socially dominant position of cis-gender identification (Phelan 130–131).

Another argument expressed frequently during the public outcry following the broadcasting of the "Female or She-male" segment was that *RuPaul's Drag Race*, which many believe should be geared toward increasing the visibility and acceptance of the drag and queer communities, instead contributed to the normalization of derogatory terms pertaining to transgender persons (Roberts). The series, it was argued, sent the message to its mainstream audience that it was okay to use pejorative terminology, especially if done only in jest. By extension, the series' usage of terms that are injurious to a certain part of the minority group that it claims to represent divests that group from its self-representational potential. Many commentators claimed that, rather than advocating acceptance for the transsexual community, the series actually helped to normalize a heteronormative dehumanization (or "othering") of certain sexual and gender identifications (Edidi). Perusing the debates that dominated popular LGBTQ websites and blogs, one notices a specific tenet that resembles strategies of identity politics in the argumentation of many activists: by claiming to represent sexual minorities, the series commits itself to represent them respectfully and inclusively in the way that the minority groups want themselves to be represented, not in the way the show thinks they should be represented. In other words, if the series could not adhere to the image by which trans persons wanted themselves to be represented, it would lose its legitimacy for representing that community.

Adding insult to injury (at least for some bloggers), RuPaul Charles decided to enter the digital arena and add to the discussion by voicing his opinion about the controversy. In a podcast interview with comedian Marc Maron, he responded to the charges of slander by saying he felt that using words like "tranny," "she-male," or "lady-boy" were not insults but, instead, acts of defiance (Charles). The transvestite and drag communities, he said, have fought hard for visibility and acceptance in society and, in the process, have adopted and appropriated slurs to resist the injurious power that such acts of naming can have. As a result, attempts at censoring the defiant usage of such words by the minority community could be regarded as censoring the history of political and social activism accompanied by the reappropriated use of derogatory terms. RuPaul proceeded to argue that those who feel injured by certain derogatory terms do not feel comfortable with their own sexual or gender identification and base their self-image too substantially on how others respond to that identification. Rather than identifying themselves as proud genderqueer or nonconforming persons, they use such identity politics to "strengthen their identities as victims" (Charles). *RuPaul's Drag Race*, he concluded, does not have any responsibility to trans people or others from the LGBTQ community who feel injured by the usage of certain terms on the show.

Despite RuPaul's defiant response to the controversy, Logo TV nevertheless decided to pull the episode from its website and remove the offending segment from both future broadcasts and the episode's online version. As a growing number of non-trans and non-activist persons joined the debate, the producers of the series had no choice but to acknowledge their responsibility to represent this segment of the LGBTQ community in a manner that, if nothing else, at least refrains from being offensive and pejorative. Thus, segments from other episodes of the series were also heavily scrutinized, along with some of RuPaul's popular song titles (including "Responsitrannity" and "Tranny Chaser"). Eventually, the public outcry led the series' producers to eliminate the well-known phrase "Girl, you've got she-mail" from the show. In the seventh season of *RuPaul's Drag Race*, which aired in the spring of 2015, this phrase, which previously had introduced the announcement of a new main challenge, was replaced with another of RuPaul's catch phrases (this one in African American Vernacular English): "She done already done had herses."

"If you can't love yourself..."

The tensions between various political claims in the queer community, here centered on those who take offense at the use of certain terms and those who use these same terms as badges of pride, are emphatically foregrounded in the "Female or She-male" controversy. While one group accuses the other of being transphobic, others accuse the offended persons of censoring what many regard to be an important part of their activist history. As such, it becomes evident that what is generally considered to be a coherent social and political community based on alliances between and among different sexual and gender identifications is actually a loose collection of sometimes deeply entrenched opposing positions. Responding to a similar incident, Jack Halberstam has provided thoughtful cautionary insights about the perils of hypersensitive reactions to reappropriated slurs. Halberstam argues that the obsessive policing of others' language, and particularly the language of those from within the community, is servient to the neoliberal project of covering up its repressive and exploitative processes ("You Are"). By uncritically policing derogatory terms while disregarding the histories, contexts, and intentions behind their usage, Halberstam writes, activists work toward a "re-emergence of a rhetoric of harm and trauma that casts all social difference in terms of hurt feelings and divides up politically allied subjects into hierarchies of woundedness" ("You Are"). Rather than focusing on the strategies of neoliberal policy makers and multinational companies to curb sexual and gender identification, these activists are entrenched in identitarian debates about whether certain terms can be injurious to parts of their community even when these slurs are voiced in a playful or ironic fashion by other members of that very same group ("You Are").

Looking back at the debates that surfaced on the Internet following the airing of the "Female or She-male" mini-game and the producers' eventual decisions to remove the segment from future airings and to refrain from using sensitive terms in future episodes, it becomes clear that the intertwining with new media platforms may potentially result in a profound transformation of mainstream television programming. At the same time, this convergence of old and new media platforms has also greatly affected the ways by which queer activists vocalize their concerns and political agendas. While Villarejo maintains that network and mainstream broadcasting companies are not responsible for representing the diversity of their viewership, the move from cable television to digital broadcasting has made it virtually impossible for production companies to ignore public outcries. Social activists, too, have moved to digital media platforms wherein they can amass and mobilize a wider readership more quickly than ever before. We are, then, confronted with several questions that reflect on queer lives and activism in the age of digital television: Can we indeed speak of a radical shift in the relation between television programming and its viewership? Are the positions of Halberstam and Villarejo being countered by processes of new forms of queer activism? And how should queer theory engage with the sometimes identitarian strategies of activists who, rather than taking to the streets, make use of the same outlets as production companies in order to police mainstream representation of racial, sexual, and gendered minority groups?

As I have already noted, Villarejo's historicizing of queer televisual representation limits itself to cable television. By doing so, her analysis is unable to account for more contemporary movements of queer activism that seek to transform dominant narratives and misrepresentation in mainstream media and, with increasing frequency, are successful at doing so. This reality provokes the question of whether it is indeed possible to hold media producers accountable for their programming and the (lack of) inclusiveness in their representations of minority groups. Media convergence also means a greater accessibility to media production for fans, which not only affects the production of fan culture tremendously but also leads to the effect that commercial television producers increasingly incorporate fan-made material in their own programming. Villarejo herself points toward the potentiality of new media convergence when fans of older queer media offerings take it upon themselves to re-edit fragments of their favorites into homages on social websites. After watching a fan's re-edit of the film *Losing Chase* (1996, directed by Kevin Bacon), Villarejo admits to having radically reinterpreted its contents. Rather than continuing to read the film as being about loss, she now reads its representation of intimacy from the perspective of relationality and love:

> Before YouTube, in fact, I saw *Losing Chase* as an ode to loss, as a way of grieving lost forms of intimacy, creativity, and expression and dying visions of equity, intimacy, and connection that were articulated in the cultural feminist and lesbian-feminist practices of the previous two decades (the 1970s and 1980s). But "deltarosel," who mashed *Losing Chase* and Whitney Houston, reads the film as a baldly declarative lesbian love story: "I Have Nothing" begins, "Share my life / take me for what I am." And she does, they do [157].

This reimagining of a queer movie enabled by digital media technologies is, of course, a different mode of engaging with politics of sexuality and representation than the type of online activism I discussed above. The transformation that the film undergoes through a fan's loving re-editing of its scenes is a different form of producing cultural knowledge than a public outcry of queer activists on the Internet. Rather than demanding the representation of a certain set of feelings and beliefs in television programming, Villarejo's example presents an alternative strategy of political becoming. Fans of televised images make use of new digital technologies to add layers of interpretations and interconnections to images they are affected by. These additions make for a community that shares a worldview and identification based on those televised images. The controversy that followed the airing of the *RuPaul's Drag Race* segment "Female or She-male," on the other hand, reveals a community that shares a worldview and identification they feel is misrepresented by televised images. This latter group prefers to see such misrepresentation changed rather than reappropriating and (lovingly) transforming such representations into something they can identify with. Notwithstanding the difference between the two strategies in engaging with digital media, these two forms of cultural production do point toward a similar transformation of meaning-making in 21st-century television. Television in the digital age, we can argue, has become increasingly intertwined with the identity politics of its viewers, and, by extension, television-making has become affected by the political agendas of the social groups that feel (mis)represented by these specific programs.

Most poignantly, the controversy over the *RuPaul's Drag Race* segment lays bare the tensions and complex affiliations of what we perceive as the LGBTQ community. Often perceived as a social group with similar political aims, the debate following the "Female or She-male" segment exposed an entrenched difference between the various sexual and gender identifications that make up this group. Initial responses to the transphobic sentiment of the segment were countered by other parts of the community that felt there was no place for trans activism in a series primarily (but not exclusively) about cisgender drag queens. The controversy that grew out of this sixth-season episode of *RuPaul's Drag Race* might be seen as indicative of a new direction in which television production seems to be pushed. That is to say, we have seen that the dimensions and dynamics of television production and watching in the 21st century have changed dramatically due to increasing convergence with other digital media. Watching television is no longer organized around the traditional nuclear family, as on-demand digital television has enabled audiences to watch their programs of choice at any given time and in any given place. Changes in the time and place of television watching have also led to changes in the expectations that viewers have of certain shows. The widespread array and availability of television shows on digital media go hand in hand with an increasing demand for responsible representation. The challenge for queer theorists lies in the question of whether these strategies move toward a queer potentiality that Muñoz has called for or instead play into an identity politics that foregrounds trenchant differences within the community and the political aims that are at stake. Here it might be wise to keep in mind a previously mentioned catch phrase from RuPaul: "If you can't love yourself, how the hell are you gonna love somebody else?"

Arguing that the logic of these broadcasting corporations is one of late capitalism, theorists such as Amy Villarejo and Jack Halberstam refute the claims that commercial broadcasting networks should be held accountable for equal and inclusive representation. They caution against a surge in identity politics that is focused on the policing of language use within the LGBTQ community itself rather than taking aim at heteronormative societal structures and institutionalized disenfranchisement. Still, the case of the "Female or She-male" segment on *RuPaul's Drag Race* undeniably points toward a transformation of the social economy of representation and online political activism, to which television programmers have to respond. This changed social economy means that television production is becoming more sensitive to identitarian claims expressed in social media and other online platforms. If, as Muñoz argues, aesthetic representation can enable a queer political becoming, the task at hand is to critically examine how this sea change in the politics of televisual representation, caused by convergence with digital media platforms, will be able to open up into queer potentiality for a new generation of the LGBTQ community.

Works Cited

Adorno, Theodor W. "How to Look at Television." *The Quarterly of Film, Radio, and Television* 8.3 (1954): 213–235. Print.

Charles, RuPaul. "Episode 498—RuPaul Charles." Interview by Marc Maron. *WTF with Marc Maron*, 19 May 2014. Podcast.

Couldry, Nick. "Teaching Us to Fake It: The Ritualized Norms of Television's 'Reality' Games." *Reality TV: Remaking Television Culture*. Ed. Susan Murray and Laurie Ouellette. New York: New York University Press, 2004. 82–99. Print.

D'Angelo, Rafi. "*RuPaul's Drag Race* Crosses the Line with 'Female or She-male.'" *Slate*, 19 March 2014. Web. 5 December 2014.

Edgar, Eir-Anne. "'Xtravaganza!' Drag Representation and Articulation in *RuPaul's Drag Race*." *Studies in Popular Culture* 34.1 (2011): 133–146. Print.

Edidi, Dane. "RuPaul and Transphobia within the Cisgender Gay Community." *Communities Digital News*, 17 April 2014. Web. 5 December 2014. http://www.comm diginews.com/life/edidi-rupaul-and-transphobia-within-the-cisgender-gay-community–15186/.

Gorman, Bill. "Logo's Season Debut of 'RuPaul's Drag Race' on Monday Night Scores as the Highest-Rated Premiere in Network History." *TV by the Numbers*. Zap 2 It, 29 January 2013. Web. 5 December 2014.

Halberstam, [Judith] Jack. *In a Queer Time and Place: Transgender Bodies, Subcultural Lives*. New York: New York University Press, 2005. Print.

_____. "You Are Triggering Me! The Neo-Liberal Rhetoric of Harm, Danger, and Trauma." *Bullybloggers*. Wordpress, 5 July 2014. Web. 7 December 2014. https:// bullybloggers. wordpress.com/2014/07/05/you-are-triggering-me-the-neo-lib eral-rhetoric-of-harm-danger-and-trauma/.

Hanhardt, Christina B. *Safe Space: Gay Neighborhood History and the Politics of Violence*. Durham: Duke University Press, 2013. Print.

Harvey, David. *The Condition of Postmodernity: An Enquiry into the Origins of Cultural Change*. Malden, MA: Blackwell, 1992. Print.

Huyssen, Andreas. "Present Pasts: Media, Politics, Amnesia." *Public Culture* 12.1 (2000): 21–38. Print.

Jenkins, Henry. *Convergence Culture: Where Old and New Media Collide*. New York: New York University Press, 2006. Print.

Muñoz, José Esteban. *Cruising Utopia: The Then and There of Queer Futurity*. New York: New York University Press, 2009. Print.

Nichols, James. "Carmen Carrera and Monica Beverly Hillz Address 'Drag Race' Transphobia Allegations." *Huffington Post*, 1 April 2014. Web. 6 December 2014.

Phelan, Shane. *Sexual Strangers: Gays, Lesbians, and Dilemmas of Citizenship*. Philadelphia: Temple University Press, 2001. Print.

Roberts, Monica. "Why I Can't Stand RuPaul." *Transgriot.* Blogspot, 30 January 2013. Web. 5 December 2014. http://transgriot.blogspot.com/2013/01/why-i-cant-stand-rupaul.html.

Taylor, Diana. *The Archive and the Repertoire: Performing Cultural Memory in the Americas.* Durham: Duke University Press. 2003. Print.

Villarejo, Amy. *Ethereal Queer: Television, Historicity, Desire.* Durham: Duke University Press, 2014. Print.

Gay Fathers in *Modern Family* and *The New Normal*
Class, Consumption, Sexuality and Parenting

JULIA ERHART

Over the course of the first decade of the 21st century, a new queer trope became prominent in U.S. popular culture. While gay (and, to a lesser extent, lesbian and bisexual) characters had been a feature on network and cable television during the 1990s, many of these characters were single or sidekick figures acting in adult-only environments, without partners and children of their own. Over the past decade, the popular network dramas *Desperate Housewives* (2004–2012) and *Brothers & Sisters* (2006–2011) brought gay parenting into the mainstream in their series' seventh and fifth seasons while on pay television, quality or niche series such as *Queer as Folk* (2000–2005), *The L Word* (2004–2009), and *Nurse Jackie* (2009–2015) introduced lesbian and, in *Queer as Folk*'s case, gay male parents right from the start. The ability of pay TV to cater more pointedly to narrow audiences—i.e., to foreground gay *and* lesbian parents, and to do so earlier and more centrally than network series do—is unsurprising from a commercial standpoint; it furthermore explains why *The Fosters* (2013–), the only series to date to center on a *lesbian*-headed family, materialized on ABC Family rather than on ABC.

Although *The Fosters* breaks new ground in its portrayal of lesbian parents, its impact, based on viewer ratings and high-profile awards, does not come anywhere close to that of the sitcom behemoth *Modern Family* (2009–). As is well known, *Modern Family*, an unprecedented blockbuster success, has received top accolades each year it has aired from prestigious industry bodies including the Academy of Television Arts and Sciences, the Television Critics Association, the Hollywood Foreign Press Association, the Producers Guild, the Screen Actors Guild, the Writers Guild, Critics' Choice, and Peabody. Emmys awarded to this series include outstanding comedy series (2010, 2011, 2012, 2013, and 2014); outstanding directing for a comedy series (2011 for "Halloween," 2012 for "Baby on Board," 2013 for "Arrested," and 2014 for "Las Vegas"); outstanding writing for a comedy series (2010 for "The Pilot" and 2011 for "Caught in the Act"); outstanding supporting actor in a comedy series (Eric Stonestreet in 2010 and 2012; Ty Burrell in 2011 and 2014); and out-standing supporting actress in a comedy series (Julie Bowen in 2011 and 2012). The series has also been recognized by significant cultural institutions outside the media industry, including GLAAD, GLSEN (Gay, Lesbian, and Straight Education Network), and the NAACP (National Association for the Advance-ment of Colored People).

The series' self-positioning as "liberal" and "relevant" and its construc-tion of gay fathers have been pivotal to its success. Referring both to ABC's *Modern Family* and to NBC's commercially less successful *The New Normal* (2012–2013), in this essay I examine how this new queer type in these two television series extends, transforms, and at times shrinks gay television roles with regard to matters of class, consumption, and sexuality. Of particular importance are the ways by which *Modern Family* has reworked these themes in order to leverage its characters for popularity with a range of audiences.

Gay Men, Affluence and Taste—Oh My!

While working-class and/or financially struggling families have recently reappeared in television comedies such as *The Middle* (2009–), *Raising Hope* (2010–2014), and *2 Broke Girls* (2011–), most of the aforementioned queer-parent series depict lesbian and gay parents more narrowly: as successful middle-class professionals serving in ownership or upper-management roles as arts administrators, obstetricians, restaurant owners, school principals, television producers, and (in a number of shows) lawyers. Positioned as family cornerstones, lesbian and gay parents have an association with financial and social capital that contrasts sharply with the experiences of disenfranchised heterosexual kin in the stories. In *Brothers & Sisters, The Fosters, The L Word,* and *The New Normal,* queer parents negotiate at various times with sperm donors, birth parents, birth relatives, and/or surrogates in disadvantaged cir-cumstances. Throughout these series, the queer parents are presented as the more stable and, it is suggested, more enlightened family members. These oppositions are constitutive and entrenched, as in *The Fosters,* in which the birth mother of the twins is portrayed as a drug addict, or in *Brothers & Sis-ters,* in which the surrogate is represented as unstable. As Lisa Henderson might put it, television's depiction of queer parenting is co-structured by social class, which in the various series I have mentioned is professional and privileged (8).

Regarding the class positioning of gay men in television more broadly, the last two and a half decades have solidified the equation between consumption and gay men, portraying them as the purveyors of taste, refinement, and style. Toby Miller tells the story of the rise of queer capital that begins in the 1990s with the discovery of the "pink dollar" by corporations such as Ikea, Levi Strauss, Subaru, and Volkswagen (115). Recognized as a niche market for perhaps the first time, gay audiences began to see themselves as pedagogical lifestyle experts to their style-challenged straight male counterparts, in advertisements and in television series including *Frasier* (1993–2004) and *Will & Grace* (1998–2006). Reaching its epitome in *Queer Eye for the Straight Guy* (2003–2007), the "professionalization of queerness as a form of management consultancy" (T. Miller 112) to remake straight men into product-purchasing metrosexuals provided new opportunities for derision of the (often) working-class, style-challenged male, sometimes in collusion with straight female counterparts (Clarkson 235). As Andrew Ross explains, in this period the gay male became "the 'new model intellectual' of consumer capitalism, at the forefront of the business of shaping and defining taste, choice, and style for mainstream markets" (61).

The appearance of gay men within the sitcom worlds of *Modern Family* and *The New Normal* potentially extends such managerial concerns to the realms of queer parenting and family. In addition to intensifying relations between queer maleness and commodity fetishism, the late 20th century also saw an increased commodification of childhood and child raising; this development likewise frequently undergirds the premise on which jokes in the two series are based. While in earlier generations (and in poorer countries) children served as economic actors who were expected to contribute to the family's livelihood, childhood has more recently come to constitute a precious phase wherein children need safeguarding via mechanisms such as protective travel equipment and carefully monitored food (Zelizer).

Gay fathers Bryan Collins (played by Andrew Rannells) and David Sawyer (played by Justin Bartha) enact such developments practically to the letter. They are *The New Normal*'s über-consumers, whether they are shopping for children's clothing or color schemes for a new nursery. While surrogate Goldie Clemmons (played by Georgia King) and her daughter, Shania (played by Bebe Wood), are effectively homeless, Bryan and David spend time lovingly redecorating in preparation for their new child. In this series, emotional conflict and political clashes that otherwise struggle to find expression are given shape in retail environments. For example, in the episode titled "The XY Factor," Bryan's fears of exclusion from the experience of fatherhood are expressed via conflict over the nursery's color scheme; in the episode "Baby

Clothes," shopping is the salve that cures David's brush with a bigot. The ability of film (and, by extension, related media forms) to express emotion via elements of mise en scène such as color, costuming, and set design was noted by Thomas Elsaesser as early as 1972; however, the link between such expression and a commodified gay male aesthetic was hardly anticipated at that time. In the new gay-parent world of *The New Normal*, the heightening of commodity fetishism that is part of the gay aesthetic is extended into new purchasing realms of baby and family, thereby giving new life to well-worn processes of visual expression and familiar tropes of sitcom humor. As Bryan presents his rationale for becoming a parent, he exclaims, "I want us to have baby clothes!" He then murmurs, as an afterthought, "... and a baby to wear them."

While *Modern Family* is aware of, and indeed creates humor from, the links among gay men, parenting, and consumption, it places an ironic distance between this theme and its central characters. Prone to theatricality and emotion, Cam (played by Eric Stonestreet) appears as the series' most stereotypically camp character, yet his non-metropolitan/rural origins have been emphasized in numerous episodes over the years. In the first-season episode "Come Fly with Me," he aligns himself with the discount superstore Costco: "I'm big, I'm not fancy, and I dare you to not like me." While the broken-down staircase and cobweb-filled cellar which feature in the Dunphy house would not appear in the gay men's abode, the discomfort of Cam and Mitch (played by Jesse Tyler Ferguson) with the excessive styles of their gay friends is showcased on many occasions, reminding viewers of the difference between these family men and the style-obsessed minor cast members Pepper (played by Nathan Lane) and Longinus (played by Kevin Daniels), or between them and individuals appearing in earlier queer-themed series such as *Queer Eye*. In the series' pilot episode, for example, Mitch voices his dislike of the over-the-top wall mural in daughter Lily's bedroom that features him and Cam as two angels, in a way that would reassure viewers troubled by camp extravagance. In the fifth-season episode "The Help," Mitch and Cam are differentiated from their friend Pepper, whose suggestions for Mitch and Cam's wedding are presented as cheesy and kitsch. The episode insinuates that Pepper, played by an actor who is physically older than both Mitch and Cam, is an old-fashioned "queen-y" character, out of step with modern iterations of more discrete and tasteful gayness. In the fourth-season episode "Bringing Up Baby," Mitch explicitly acknowledges the immoderation of the gay community in general, stating, "Gay guys having kids.... It's relatively new. So our community has not yet learned how to modulate baby gifts.... When Stephen and Stephan had little Rocco, our friend Longinus sent over the whole cast of *Yo Gabba Gabba!* [2007–]."

Running throughout the whole of *Modern Family*, rhetorical moves of this sort are crucial for the series to both seem hip and manage its campiness without appearing biased or homophobic in doing so. In scenes described above and others featuring LGBTQ community (such as the sixth-season episode "Patriot Games," about Mitch's and Cam's discomfort with community boycott of a restaurant), distinctions are drawn between "right" and "wrong" forms of gay cultural practice and clearly communicated to viewers. Yet because these distinctions are determined by the insider community members Cam and (especially) Mitch, audience members are granted permission to laugh at such gaffes and/or find fault with queer "excess" in much the same way as a reaction shot in a conventional three-camera sitcom works in order to cue audience attention to the fact that a social code has been broken. Mitch's words in the last example identified in the preceding paragraph clearly position him as a queer cultural translator (i.e., one who explains queer culture to outsiders); his use of the phrase "*our* community" locates him as an insider. The dual positioning of the main character in this scene in turn provides audience members with opportunities to be included or distanced, as required. The result is a sophisticated and nuanced address to multiple audiences, which keeps gay-averse viewers continuing to watch without simultaneously offending gay-friendly ones.

Liberal Self-Positioning and Queer Representation

Since the early success of *The Office* (2005–2013), much has been made of the formal changes that the situation comedy has undergone. A consistent theme throughout sitcom studies is the genre's reputed openness to themes of difference and diversity. The story of the genre's development has often been told as one of social progress and increasing tolerance. Critics have expressed optimism for the sitcom's ability to impact the social and cultural terrain and address significant ideas and issues in a positive way. In an early study, for example, Darrell Hamamoto claimed that the sitcom featured a higher number of African Americans and other minorities than any television genre other than sports (138). Since then, chronological analyses have tracked the ostensible progress of the genre from the 1950s to the present and its gradual peopling with women and minorities and, more recently, lesbians and gay men (Butsch; Kutulas). Both *The New Normal* and *Modern Family* share a number of features in their purported advancement of a liberal, democratic vision of society that embraces difference in its vision of family. The fact that the words "new" and "modern" appear in the titles of the respective series indicates the shared premise that each will offer new and, it is implied, improved social configurations. The buttressing by both series of a mainstream liberal agenda is further emphasized through plotlines (e.g., in *The New Normal*, the fact that Goldie leaves Ohio for the blue state of California in the pilot and the series' overtly partisan episode "Obama Mama"), scripting (e.g., the layering of bigotry on top of all-around unlikableness in the figure of Goldie's husband, who demands that his lover utter "The United States is the most powerful country on Earth" as he is having sex with her), and paratextual materials, such as interview comments, actor activities, and fan interaction.

Interview comments by actors Andrew Rannells and Eric Stonestreet indicate their respective series' investments in representing themselves as progressive. In a 2012 interview with National Public Radio, for example, Rannells expressed hope that *The New Normal* would "convince more people that gay people can make great parents" ("Andrew"), while Stonestreet stated that "we [the *Modern Family* cast] acknowledge and appreciate the opportunity to educate people" (Voss). In particular, Jesse Tyler Ferguson, the actor who plays Mitchell on *Modern Family*, has been a visible campaigner for social acceptance via his "Tie the Knot" campaign and other high-profile undertakings, such as his hosting of a gay marriage ceremony on board an Air New Zealand flight in August 2013. *Modern Family*'s activities surrounding the 2010 grassroots Facebook campaign "Let Cam & Mitchell Kiss on *Modern Family*" positioned the series as responsive to its fan base. Attracting attention across the blogosphere, the Facebook campaign represented audience demands for *Modern Family* to reflect the lives and activities of 'ordinary' gay people and produce an episode showing the two men kissing. Producers downplayed the overall power of the campaign and emphasized the autonomy of the series in planning for such an episode long before fans lobbied for it. Nevertheless, ultimately an episode (season two's "The Kiss") did air dealing with this matter, revealing the producers' awareness of the need to appear responsive to pro-gay fans.

Despite *Modern Family*'s efforts to self-position as gay-friendly, the aptness of that series and the sitcom more generally to telling LGB stories is unresolved. Writing in positive terms about situation comedy, scholars have noted the sitcom's ability to invite audiences to take up queer reading positions (Doty); the ability of individual series such as *Will & Grace* to assert a different vision of family from those legitimated via normative legal and genetic means and to "broaden [our] understandings of how love works" (Quimby 728); and the availability of queer pleasures, especially in pre–1990s shows (M. Miller). Queer television scholars also agree that the number of LGB characters is on the rise and they are appearing earlier in the arcs of various series (Arthurs; Kessler; Shugart). However, the sitcom's suitability to telling LGB stories is less certain than interviews and other paratextual activities would lead us to believe. For every scholar who has lauded situation comedy's contributions to social change, an approximately equal number have taken issue with the sitcom's ability to tell LGB stories in a nuanced or well-rounded way. Factors that have attracted attention include the essentialist visions of queer identity offered in various coming-out episodes (Peterson); limitations of lesbian supporting characters (Kessler); and the incompatibility of the sitcom format with certain LGB characters altogether (Cragin). Many have noted sitcoms' reinforcement of heterosexism (Battles and Hilton-Morrow), renormalization of heterosexuality (Shugart), and ability to provide for homophobic attitudes in spite of the odd LGBT character (Provencher).

The most prevalent recurring theme in queer criticism of the sitcom is that gay and lesbian characters are denied the romantic and sexual bonds that heterosexual characters enjoy. Analyses of series including *Ellen* (1994–1998), *Friends* (1994–2004), *Mad About You* (1992–1999), and *Will & Grace* identify how gay coupling is consistently downplayed in favor of heterosexual arrangements, with the gay characters serving as secondary characters in order to facilitate heterosexual courting and coupling (Bateman; Conway; Hantzis and Lehr; Kessler; Peterson; Provencher). As Denis Provencher summarizes, commercial prime time has a penchant for portraying its gay characters as desexed and uncoupled second-class citizens who must participate in heteronormative settings in order to achieve a sense of normalcy and belonging (188).

In both *The New Normal* and *Modern Family*, complex couple issues pertaining to sex, sexuality, eroticism, and attraction (including fidelity, jealousy, rivalry with ex-partners, and sexual insecurity) remain largely the province of heterosexuals, who experience the lion's share of the problems—and pleasures. Early episodes of *Modern Family*, for example, deal with rivalries between Jay (played by Ed O'Neill) and Gloria's ex-husband, Javier (played by Benjamin Bratt); rivalries between Gloria (played by Sofía Vergara) and Jay's ex-wife, DeDe (played by Shelley Long); consumption of pornography by Phil (played by Ty Burrell); and the jealousy Claire (played by Julie Bowen) experiences toward Phil's ex-girlfriend. Over the years, the series has made much of Phil's attraction to "inappropriate" women (e.g., Gloria, women who are newly divorced, etc.) in contrast to the gay characters, whose sexuality conforms to normative attitudes around monogamy and "correct" coupling. In later seasons, Phil behaves questionably with his female clients and with the mother of Luke's (played by Nolan Gould) date, Frank Dunphy (Phil's father, played by Fred Willard) picks up a prostitute, and Claire reveals an approach to romance that Mitch calls "ghoulish." In contrast, in the first three seasons of the series, neither Mitch nor Cam has a sexual past of any consequence. When Mitch's ex-boyfriend Teddy (played by Larry Sullivan) finally appears in the fourth-season episode "My Hero," the threat hinges not on Teddy's sexual attractiveness (as compared to Cam's) but rather on the fact that Teddy is more popular with family members than Cam feels he is. The few times that Mitch and Cam do show interest in other men, it is presented as a nonthreatening, shared interest, such as when, in the first-season episode "Up All Night," *both* men find the male firefighters attractive, in contrast to Claire, who spends the entire episode hiding from Phil her attraction to the same men. The fifth-season premiere episode "Suddenly, Last Summer," which gives the heterosexual couples the opportunity to assist Mitch and Cam with their marriage proposals, simultaneously provides opportunities for those couples to retell, in romantic ways, their own proposal stories.

The same points can be made about *The New Normal*, despite the fact the series was cancelled after its first season. An introductory scene with Bryan and David constructs them as the "family-friendly" characters. They are seen in a bar, expressing how tired they are and proclaiming their preference for a stay-at-home lifestyle. Theirs is (as previously mentioned) deemed the more suitable home, into which Goldie and Shania quickly move. Their attitudes toward love and sex contrast sharply with those of Goldie's grandmother, Jane (played by Ellen Barkin), who is impulsive and prone to one-night stands.

I have already indicated the volume of scholarly research that documents television's de-eroticization of lesbian and gay characters; it is important to emphasize that neither *Modern Family* nor *The New Normal* are new in this regard. What *is* novel is the familial role that is invoked to naturalize this phenomenon: in both series, there is the need to care for children, which the gay couples willingly do without complaint. Also innovative is the effect of the gay couples' adoption of these new parenting roles, which in both cases is to free up the heterosexual couples for further erotic/sexual activities. In both series, the comedy and, indeed, the narrative logic proceed by means of a division of labor whereby the straight people trade in matters of sexuality and the gay couples minister to children. (Steven Doran has cited *Modern Family*'s award-winning, first-season episode "My Funky Valentine," in which the two heterosexual couples prepare for a sexy date night, as evidence of this [99–100]). What has *not* been noted, however, is the rationale for why the *gay* date does not also take place, which is the fact that Mitch and Cam are caring for Manny (played by Rico Rodriguez) and Lily (played by Aubrey Anderson-Emmons). The series' sidestepping of the specter of a romantic *gay* Valentine's Day is made natural by the fact of Cam and Mitch being parents; in other words, gay parenting is the alibi that protects the series against the charge that it is de-eroticizing its gay characters.

Although both series find new ways to de-eroticize their gay characters, the heterosexual characters are ultimately re-sexualized to the point of being queered themselves. Many of *Modern Family*'s heterosexual characters behave in non-normative ways for their age, marital status, and/or position in the family. For example, Phil (caught with pornography, attracted to Gloria and other "inappropriate" women as mentioned earlier) has trouble bringing his sexuality into line with what is expected from him as the head of the family. Manny is the show's cub, a premature "kid-ult" who falls for women much older than him, while Cam's mother succeeds in breaking taboos pertaining to both intergenerational and interfamilial attraction (in the second-season episode "Mother Tucker," for example, she has trouble keeping her hands off of her son's boyfriend). All of these characters flaunt versions of masculinity, femininity, and straightness that are queerer than meets the eye. The second-season episode "Caught in the Act" demonstrates this especially well. In this episode, Gloria accidentally sends a rude e-mail message to Claire (claiming that Claire is a "bossy control freak" who hates Gloria's cupcakes) while, in a separate scene, the Dunphy children accidentally walk in on their parents having sex (Mitch and Cam remain in a wholly separate story thread on a play date with Lily). Gloria tries to telephone Claire to rectify the situation of the rude e-mail; however, Claire is too traumatized by the event involving the children to take Gloria's call. A classic comedy of misunderstandings ensues, as Gloria mistakes Claire's reluctance for anger, and Claire mistakes Gloria's attempt to make amends about the e-mail message as an attempt to share stories about being interrupted while having sex. When eventually the two women speak, the conversation is full of double entendres and misunderstandings:

> Gloria (trying to apologize about the rude e-mail message): Claire, it was an accident.
> Claire (assuming she is referring to the children's interruption): That doesn't make it any better.
> Gloria: I know how you feel! It happened to me before with another woman. And that time, I was the one getting it … and it hurt. I'm sorry it had to come out like this, but you have to admit, you're only happy when you're the one cracking the whip.
> Claire: What?
> Gloria: Go on, we all know how you ride Phil. Maybe you just … let go a little, taste my cupcakes. I will join you!
> Claire (embarrassed): No, no, no…. I am so confused right now.
> Phil: I think I'm gonna pass out.

The humor in this scene derives from the misunderstandings and double entendres that occur in the conversation between the two women, about what Gloria (on the one hand) thinks are baked goods and about what Claire (on the other) thinks is a sexual encounter. The humor lies in the confusion of baking terminology with sexual language, exemplifying perhaps one of the most familiar tenets of humor theory, which is that jokes bring to light repressed topics that cannot normally be spoken about. In this instance, the "repressed" begins as the event of a husband and wife having sex but quickly slides (over the course of the conversation) into a reference to a lesbian encounter that Gloria had in the past, and then into a proposal of a future sexual encounter between Claire and Gloria. Given that this episode won the Emmy Award in 2011 for outstanding writing, the exchange is interesting and industrially significant. Lesbians who appear in the series normally stand for a kind of narrow, retrograde political correctness or irritability more generally (see, for example, the episodes "Unplugged" [season two], "Schooled" [season four], and "Fulgencio" [season four]). Here, lesbianism is the "unspoken" at the heart of the joke that winds up being on Gloria. In this episode, as elsewhere in *Modern Family*, gay people and sex cannot be linked in actuality, they can only be associated via the fantasies—in this case, the queer fantasies—of the series' straight characters.

Cracks in the Parenting Vision: Queer Dads and Parenting Fakes

In addition to recycling well-worn tropes of gay male sexlessness, *Modern Family* constructs Mitch's and Cam's parenting world as more decorous and less complex than that of Phil and Claire or Jay and Gloria, particularly in its early seasons. Issues that arise in the heterosexual-headed families include matters of adolescent sexuality (e.g., Haley [played by Sarah Hyland] having a boyfriend; Manny's interest in older women), adults' respect for children's privacy, adult and "tweenage" consumption of pornography, parental trust of children and vice versa, and matters of strictness and punishment. In contrast, during the first and second seasons, Mitch and Cam occupy themselves largely with the practicalities of early childhood, such as the challenges of finding a pediatrician, showing up at a play group for the first time, infant development, and enrolling in schools. In the early seasons of the series, similarities between heterosexual parents and their children are established (e.g., Haley's and Claire's shared interest in boys; Luke's resemblance to Phil), in contrast to relations that are delineated between Mitch and Cam and Lily. Whereas the heterosexual parents reflect on their own childhoods in order to guide them in the task of parenting, Mitch and Cam cannot so easily mobilize their own origin stories in the service of raising Lily.

This divvying up of parenting know-how is evidenced concretely in the second-season episode "Dance Dance Revelation." Phil, Jay, Manny, and Luke go to a shopping mall in search of clothes for a school dance, while together Gloria and Claire prepare the school hall for the event. While Phil, Jay, and the boys are shopping, several seemingly insignificant events ensue that ultimately provide grounds for an argument between Phil and Jay about the definition of manliness and its significance for the boys. Disagreeing about how and whether to "stand one's ground," Phil finally acquiesces to Jay's definition by standing up to a department store employee who, against his wishes, has squirted Phil with cologne (Phil runs after the hapless store employee and squirts him with the cologne). In the school hall, competitive feelings between Gloria and Claire escalate; meanwhile, Mitch and Cam weather Lily's first biting incident in a fully discrete scene. On the one hand, while the heterosexuals are associated with nearly all of the petty, negative, adult activity in the episode (the bickering and competition), they have access to rituals of courtship (e.g., preparing for a dance) and intragenerational knowledge (e.g., debating masculine ideals, passing down information from parents to children, acting as role models for the boys) which the gay characters do not. Physically outside of the spaces where the heterosexual-family activities take place, Mitch and Cam are geographically and socially detached from the bulk of the narrative events—which makes it all the more interesting that Mitchell's words conclude the episode. Accompanying an image of the two boys (Manny and Luke) standing side by side while their respective fathers do up their ties, Mitch's voice-over concludes:

> We like to think we're so smart; we have all the answers. And we want to pass all that on to our children. But if you scratch beneath the surface, you don't have to scratch very deep to find the kid you were, which is why it's kind of crazy that now we're raising kids of our own. I guess this is the real circle of life. Your parents faked their way through it. You fake your way through it. Hopefully, you don't raise a serial killer.

In their seamless linking of past and present and mobilization of the two in the service of the future, Mitch's words identify the prevalent cultural investment in that future as normative and as emblematized most typically in the social valuing of children. In the logic of the sequence, the purpose of one's own existence—"the kid you were"—ensures the perpetuation of a genetic and cultural lineage whose continuation *children*—the "kids of our own"— would appear to guarantee. This is the meaning at the heart of Mitch's utterance, at the center of countless stories in U.S. popular culture told by and for fathers to and about their sons, and at the locus of what Lee Edelman terms the heteronormative politics of "reproductive futurism" (2). In addition to Edelman, Elizabeth Freeman, Dustin Bradley Goltz, and Judith Halberstam have written about the linking of hetero-, repro-, and indeed temporal normativities within utterances such as Mitch's. Edelman in particular has noted the moral valuing that tends to place children at the center of cultural activity; in his formulations, commonplace notions such as time, future, success, and productivity are both heteronormative and culturally constructed.

Although Mitch's role in the scene is collaborative rather than critical (the series conceals its own parenting normativity, as it were), he is (as previously stated) physically external to and unseen in the scene, as is his daughter. The "fake" that Mitch alludes to is not, in his case, the parenting (which he and Cam do capably) but rather the inclusiveness of parenting discourse— "having all the answers" and the act of "passing on"—which does not, in this scene, visually include either the gay parents or their adoptive female child but rather only the boys and their heterosexual fathers.

In later seasons of the series, cracks begin to appear in the heteronormative visions initially depicted, as in the season-four episode "The Future Dunphys," when Phil catches a glimpse of the social outcasts his children could potentially become. As Lily grows up, storylines involving her, Mitch, and Cam begin to explore more complex issues, such as what traits she might stand to inherit from her fathers (see, for example, the fourth-season episode "Fulgencio" and the sixth-season episodes "Closet? You'll Love It!" and "Crying Out Loud") and how gayness is culturally transmitted ("The Future Dunphys"). As Lily becomes older and more vocal, audiences see her more consistently generating humor, making catty gestures about her fathers' ceaseless chatter (see, for instance, the fifth-season episode "The Help" and the sixth-season episodes "Closet? You'll Love It!" and "Integrity"), clever remarks about Phil's poor singing (season five's "A Fair to Remember"), witty asides at Claire's and Haley's expense (season six's "Grill, Interrupted"), and droll observations about her own status as an adoptee (season five's "Suddenly, Last Summer" and season six's "Strangers in the Night"). In the fifth-season episode "Farm Strong," Lily comments on the racial differences between her and her fathers: when Mitch questions why the available colors for his and Cam's wedding palette are both white, Lily quips, "That's what my friend Keisha asks about you and Daddy." As an adopted Vietnamese girl being raised by two gay white men, the relationship between Lily and her dads is developing into a compelling aspect of the series. This relationship cannot help but put pressure on prevalent heteronormative sitcom themes such as father-son bonding, mother-daughter intimacy/rivalry, and intergenerational family resemblances (physical and otherwise). The results of this pressure could be interesting to watch, depending on future decisions regarding the scripting of the Lily's character and relations among family members.

Conclusion

This essay has discussed the class positioning of the gay fathers in *Modern Family* and *The New Normal*, arguing that the former's distancing of the central characters from earlier gay stereotypes enables a range of audiences to remain engaged. I have examined the self-positioning of both series as "liberal" and "gay-friendly" and claimed that such positioning contributes to

Modern Family's success. It has been identified that *Modern Family*'s gay fathers are relatively sexless and their "parenting" is leveraged as a fresh alibi for what is otherwise a well-worn television stereotype. I have established how queerness is nonetheless present in *Modern Family* in the non-normative fantasies and behaviors of a number of the series' non-gay characters. Finally, I have addressed the construction of parenting in the blockbuster series, demonstrating how in its early seasons gay parenting was shown as isolated and sui generis in origin, in contrast to heteronormative parenting. While the family composed of Lily, Mitch, and Cam does break some conventions of traditional family sitcom forms, it is uncertain how (or if) this will be further developed in the seasons yet to come.

Works Cited

"Andrew Rannells: Gay and Serious in 'New Normal.'" *National Public Radio*. 10 September 2012. Web. 28 August 2015. http://www.npr.org/2012/09/10/160879686/andrew-rannells-gay-and-serious-in-new-normal.

Arthurs, Jane. *Television and Sexuality: Regulation and the Politics of Taste*. New York: Open University Press, 2004. Print.

Bateman, Robert Benjamin. "What Do Gay Men Desire? Peering Behind the Queer Eye." *The New Queer Aesthetic on Television: Essays on Recent Programming*. Ed. James R. Keller and Leslie Stratyner. Jefferson, NC: McFarland, 2006. 9–19. Print.

Battles, Kathleen, and Wendy Hilton-Morrow. "Gay Characters in Conventional Spaces: *Will & Grace* and the Situation Comedy Genre." *Critical Studies in Media Communication* 19.1 (2002): 87–105. Print.

Butsch, Richard. "Five Decades and Three Hundred Sitcoms about Class and Gender." *Thinking Outside the Box: A Contemporary Television Genre Reader*. Ed. Gary R. Edgerton and Brian G. Rose. Lexington: University Press of Kentucky, 2005. 111–135. Print.

Clarkson, Jay. "Contesting Masculinity's Makeover: *Queer Eye*, Consumer Masculinity, and 'Straight-Acting' Gays." *Journal of Communication Inquiry* 29.3 (2005): 235–255.

Conway, Richard J. "A Trip to the Queer Circus: Reimagined Masculinities in *Will & Grace*." *The New Queer Aesthetic on Television: Essays on Recent Programming*. Ed. James R. Keller and Leslie Stratyner. Jefferson, NC: McFarland, 2006. 75–84. Print.

Cragin, Becca. "Lesbians and Serial TV: *Ellen* Finds Her Inner Adult." *The New Queer Aesthetic on Television: Essays on Recent Programming*. Ed. James R. Keller and Leslie Stratyner. Jefferson, NC: McFarland, 2006. 193–208. Print.

Doran, Steven Edward. "Housebroken: Homodomesticity and the Normalization of Queerness in *Modern Family*." *Queer Love in Film and Television: Critical Essays*. Ed. Pamela Demory and Christopher Pullen. New York: Palgrave Macmillan, 2013. 95–104. Print.

Doty, Alexander. "I Love *Laverne and Shirley*: Lesbian Narratives, Queer Pleasures, and Television Sitcoms." *Critiquing the Sitcom: A Reader*. Ed. Joanne Morreale. Syracuse: Syracuse University Press, 2003. 187–208. Print.

Edelman, Lee. *No Future: Queer Theory and the Death Drive*. Durham: Duke University Press, 2004. Print.

Elsaesser, Thomas. "Tales of Sound and Fury: Observations on the Family Melodrama." *Monogram* 4 (1972): 2–15. Print.

Freeman, Elizabeth. *Time Binds: Queer Temporalities, Queer Histories.* Durham: Duke University Press, 2010. Print.

Goltz, Dustin Bradley. *Queer Temporalities in Gay Male Representation: Tragedy, Normativity, and Futurity.* New York: Routledge, 2010. Print.

Halberstam, Judith. *The Queer Art of Failure.* Durham: Duke University Press, 2011. Print.

Hamamoto, Darrell. *Nervous Laughter: Television Situation Comedy and Liberal Democratic Ideology.* New York: Praeger, 1989. Print.

Hantzis, Darlene M., and Valerie Lehr. "Whose Desire? Lesbian (Non)Sexuality and Television's Perpetuation of Hetero/Sexism." *Queer Words, Queer Images: Communication and the Construction of Homosexuality.* Ed. R. Jeffrey Ringer. New York: New York University Press, 1994. 107–121. Print.

Henderson, Lisa. *Love and Money: Queers, Class, and Cultural Production.* New York: New York University Press, 2013. Print.

Kessler, Kelly. "Politics of the Sitcom Formula: *Friends, Mad About You,* and the Sapphic Second Banana." *The New Queer Aesthetic on Television: Essays on Recent Programming.* Ed. James R. Keller and Leslie Stratyner. Jefferson, NC: McFarland, 2006. 130–146. Print.

_____. "They Should Suffer Like the Rest of Us: Queer Equality in Narrative Mediocrity." *Cinema Journal* 50.2 (2011): 139–144. Print.

Kutulas, Judy. "Who Rules the Roost? Sitcom Family Dynamics from the Cleavers to the Osbournes." *The Sitcom Reader: America Viewed and Skewed.* Ed. Mary M. Dalton and Laura R. Linder. Albany: State University of New York Press, 2005. 49–60. Print.

Miller, Margo. "Masculinity and Male Intimacy in Nineties Sitcoms: *Seinfeld* and the Ironic Dismissal." *The New Queer Aesthetic on Television: Essays on Recent Programming.* Ed. James R. Keller and Leslie Stratyner. Jefferson, NC: McFarland, 2006. 147–159. Print.

Miller, Toby. "A Metrosexual Eye on *Queer Guy.*" *GLQ: A Journal of Lesbian and Gay Studies* 11.1 (2005): 112–117. Print.

Peterson, Valerie V. "*Ellen*: Coming Out and Disappearing." *The Sitcom Reader: America Viewed and Skewed.* Ed. Mary M. Dalton and Laura R. Linder. Albany: State University of New York Press, 2005. 165–176. Print.

Provencher, Denis M. "Sealed with a Kiss: Heteronormative Narrative Strategies in NBC's *Will & Grace.*" *The Sitcom Reader: America Viewed and Skewed.* Ed. Mary M. Dalton and Laura R. Linder. Albany: State University of New York Press, 2005. 177–189. Print.

Quimby, Karin. "*Will & Grace*: Negotiating (Gay) Marriage on Prime-Time Television." *Journal of Popular Culture* 38.4 (2005): 713–731. Print.

Ross, Andrew. "Uses of Camp." *Camp Grounds: Style and Homosexuality.* Ed. David Bergman. Amherst: University of Massachusetts Press, 1993. 54–77. Print.

Shugart, Helene A. "Reinventing Privilege: The New (Gay) Man in Contemporary Popular Media." *Critical Studies in Media Communication* 20.1 (2003): 67–91. Print.

Voss, Brandon. "Eric Stonestreet: *Modern Family*'s Moon Man." *Advocate,* 10 February 2010. Web. 10 June 2015.

Zelizer, Viviana. *Pricing the Priceless Child: The Changing Social Value of Children.* Princeton: Princeton University Press, 1994. Print.

Brothers in Arms
Spartacus, *Historical Television and the Celebration of Queer Masculinity*

Thomas J. West III

When it premiered in 2010, the Starz series *Spartacus* (2010–2013) elicited significant commentary for its unabashed embrace of what the *Los Angeles Times* termed a "B-movie style," with bloody CGI graphics highly reminiscent of the campy film *300* (2006, directed by Zack Synder) and more full frontal nudity than even the most risqué of HBO series (including that network's own foray into the world of Roman antiquity, self-evidently titled *Rome* [2005–2007]) (Martin and Flint). Indeed, William Hamm, an executive of the network, explicitly stated in an interview with the *Los Angeles Times* that he and his colleagues did not want to follow in *Rome*'s footsteps, preferring the action-oriented nature of *Spartacus* to the more stately (one might even say highbrow) aspirations and storytelling conventions of HBO's historical drama (Martin and Flint). From its very inception, the series was seen as a linchpin in the network's efforts to make itself more competitive with HBO and Showtime, both of which have consistently overshadowed Starz in the premium-cable-channel landscape, not by offering the same sorts of dramas but rather a more visceral array of programming that appeals to a very different sort of cultural taste, what the *Los Angeles Times* referred to as "the baying crowd" (Martin and Flint)—a comment that reveals much about both the series' target audience and the types of pleasures it provides.

The efforts of Starz and the series' creators to deliver a product that would solidify the network's brand identity also generated a particular set of rules pertaining to what historian Robert Rosenstone has called "rules of engagement" with the world of the late Roman Republic. In the network's vision of antiquity, ancient Rome was a place where life, for both slaves and Romans, was often nasty, brutish, and short (if often quite sexy). Through three full seasons and a prequel—a miniseries set between the first and second seasons, commissioned to keep the series afloat while star Andy Whitfield underwent treatment for non–Hodgkin lymphoma—*Spartacus* followed both the titular character (played first by Whitfield and then by Liam McIntyre) and a band of gladiators as they struggle to survive in the *ludus* run by the villainous and cunning Batiatus (played by John Hannah) and his equally ruthless wife, Lucretia (played by Lucy Lawless). After leading a successful revolt at the end of the first season, Spartacus and his fellow gladiators entertain grander ambitions, and, after inflicting several severe defeats on the Romans sent to defeat them, including Spartacus' avowed nemesis Glaber (played by Craig Parker), they are eventually subdued and almost completely annihilated by the ruthless and cunning Roman general Crassus (played by Simon Merrells) and his able underling, Caesar (played by Todd Lasance).

Perhaps unsurprisingly, given its ancient-world setting (with its sexual mores that are, in many ways, significantly different from those of many of the series' contemporary viewers), *Spartacus* also featured several same-sex romances; each season featured at least one couple composed of two men united in sexual desire. These include Barca (played by Antonio Te Maioha) and Pietros (played by Eka Darville) in season one, Barca and Auctus (played by Josef Brown) in the prequel, and Agron (played by Dan Feuerriegel) and Nasir (played by Pana Hema Taylor) in seasons two and three. While the narrative trajectory of the early episodes ends in the all-too-familiar queer tragedy (what the popular website *TV Tropes* refers to as the "bury your gays" convention), with all of the queer male characters dead by the seventh episode of the first season, later episodes devote substantially more screen time to the ongoing development of the series' increasingly popular queer male couple, Agron and Nasir ("Bury"). Indeed, by the time the series ends, these two men are the only former slaves still alive, the rest having fallen victim to the Romans' attempts to utterly squash any further attempts at rebellion.

Accordingly, this essay argues that *Spartacus*—as a result of a complex series of social, industrial, and cultural forces—also generates a specific set of rules of engagement with a particularly *queer male* history. I use the term "queer" here deliberately, for it helps to avoid the act of historical flattening that often occurs in discussions of the world of antiquity and the sexual activities that occurred between men. In this series, engaging in same-sex sexual activity does not necessarily reflect on one's gender identity or on one's masculine performance. In fact, the series makes a concerted effort to ensure that the viewer does not understand these characters as the sad, young, effeminate men seen in so many dramas that are set in the past, nor as the deviant and pathological, often explicitly queerly coded characters encountered in many epic films that are set in antiquity. In doing so, however, it also heavily emphasizes the hypermasculine—which is to say, violent, muscled, sexually desirable and desiring—characteristics and credentials of its queer male characters, bringing them in line with the traditional conventions of the epic hero. Further, while the series does indulge in the queer tragedy narrative early on, it gradually eschews that narrative for one of male suffering and eventual triumph, at least for the two queer male characters Agron and Nasir. As a result, *Spartacus* suggests that only certain types of queer male sexuality can avoid the queer death narrative and thereby gain a place within the space of historical representation: If you want to survive in queer history, in other words, you have to be able to be as manly as the straight men. The series' glowing reception in many queer media outlets, including *The Advocate* and *Out*, suggests that it has indeed struck a chord with many gay male viewers, providing a significant corrective to both the absence of explicitly queer characters within action drama and the deviant queer that has so long been the cultural reminder of the consequences, and the perils, of queer male desire.

The Ecstasy and the Agony of the Historical Queer

Given the series' self-consciously camp style (a stylistic mark of several of the series' producers, who were also known for such high camp takes on antiquity as *Hercules: The Legendary Journeys* [1995–1999] and *Xena: Warrior Princess* [1995–2001]), as well as the rigorous emphasis on the male body on conspicuous (almost excessive) display, one can easily see how the series attempts to court a potential gay male audience. Just as importantly, the series fetishizes and idolizes a *particular type* of male body, one that exhibits the sort of defined muscularity and sculpted physique commonly deemed desirable within gay male culture. Anise Strong has compellingly pointed out that the series' "true innovation in the representation of female desire is its frequent depiction of women as sexually dominant figures who control not just the sexual encounters themselves but the *gaze and perspective of the audience*" (171, emphasis added). I would take Strong's point a step further to suggest that, in addition to privileging and seeking to cultivate a desiring female gaze, the series seeks to do the same for a desiring gay male one, in a way reminiscent of many films set it antiquity, which have consistently shown a desire to put the male body on conspicuous display even if, as Steve Neale has argued, such objectification and sexualization is often ameliorated by showing that body in action (18). However, as Susan Bordo has suggested, the rock-hard male body, so common in advertisements and in action cinema—both aesthetic traditions that *Spartacus* obviously taps into with its representational strategies—is specifically designed to appeal (presumably) to both straight female viewers and gay men. As Bordo so memorably puts it, "Images of masculinity that will do double (or triple or quadruple) duty with a variety of consumers, straight and gay, male and female, are not difficult to create in a culture like ours, in which the muscular male body has a long and glorious aesthetic history" (181–182).

Spartacus was not the first cable historical drama to solicit a desiring gay male gaze while also seeking to depict same-sex attraction between men in the past. Showtime's *The Tudors* (2007–2010), for example, depicts not only one but two separate same-sex romances between men, one between the composer Thomas Tallis (played by Joe Van Moyland) and the courtier William Compton (played by Kris Holden-Ried) and the other between the doomed George Boleyn (played by Padraic Delaney) and the court musician Mark Smeaton (played by David Alpay). The first romance between Tallis and Compton follows a trajectory similar to that delineated by Richard Dyer in his theorization of the figure of the "sad young man." Dyer argues that "the world before the sad young man offers four resolutions: death, normality, becoming a dreadful old queen, or, especially in the later texts, finding 'someone like oneself' with whom one can settle down" (132). The Early Modern world *The Tudors* depicts, of course, forecloses most of these possibilities by having William Compton perish from the sweating sickness, an affliction Basil Glynn argues has unfortunate similarities to that surrounding HIV/ AIDS in its coverage by the media (167). Although Tallis survives the death of his lover, he eventually ends up marrying a woman, clearly eschewing his brief foray into the realm of same-sex desire (though his smashing of a musical instrument on the grave of his deceased lover suggests that he has lost something of his muse with the death of Compton).

The relationship between George Boleyn and the musician Mark Smeaton is, in many ways, even more fraught and troubling than that of the largely asexual one between Tallis and Compton. As Glynn has compellingly argued, utilizing the term "sorry confusion" to describe the somewhat incoherent attitude *The Tudors* takes toward the expression of homosexual desire, these queer characters serve as the indication of what happens when male characters engage in behaviors deemed to be unacceptably masculine (167). In Boleyn's case, that confusion manifests itself as a sublimated and frustrated sexual desire that expresses itself through his brutal anal rape of his wife, Jane (played by Joanne King), who, in her turn, serves as one of the key witnesses against him when he is put on trial for committing incest with his sister (the implied connection between the two forms of "deviance" is subtle but nevertheless present). *The Tudors* thus creates a narrative chain of events that not only highlights the incompatibility of masculinity—equivalent here to the ability and desire to prove one's virility with women, as expressed again and again by the virile, muscular, irreverently heterosexual Henry and his best friend, Charles Brandon (played by Henry Cavill)—and male same-sex desire but also creates an impression that the queer male has no place in the processes of history. The queer tragedy narrative of the sad young man that this series evokes suggests that the queer male's life trajectory leads almost inevitably to death and to an erasure from history. The queer male, it seems, has no place in the historical imagination of the nation. While Henry and the other male members of his court brutally victimize and sexually exploit their women, their desires, at least at the level of narrative, gain the reward of maintaining their lives and their presence in history.

At first glance, *Spartacus* appears to fall into that same pattern. The two significant male-male relationships that emerge during the first season and a half both end in death. At the same time, it is important to note that in many regards the queer male relationships within the series' first two seasons do not resemble each other. Antony Augoustakis has argued that the relationship between Auctus and Barca seems to be much more strictly physical in nature, showing little of the nuance, tenderness, and complexity as that between Barca and Pietros (161). When Auctus dies at the hands of the new gladiator Crixus (played by Manu Bennett), for example, Barca does not show a great deal of grief and indeed even becomes quite good friends with the Gaul responsible for his lover's death. The sheer physicality of their relationship, as well as its relative emotional shallowness, suggests that, at least in this early stage of his development as a character, Barca is little more than a bundle of traditional male desires. Just as importantly, it suggests that it is precisely this masculine persona, this unwillingness or inability to engage emotionally and intimately with another person, that has allowed him to survive and thrive in the cutthroat and viscerally violent world of the arena, within which showing that type of vulnerability can only lead to an ignominious death.

However, it is important to note that, during his limited time in the series, Barca does gradually emerge as a complex character in his own right, at once a man who desires other men but, significantly, does not allow that desire to in any way jeopardize his position as a male figure. His backstory, related to Spartacus by his fellow gladiator Varro (played by Jai Courtney), significantly bolsters his male credentials. Known as the "Beast of Carthage" (itself a moniker laden with many layers of meaning, given that the character is played by a man of color), Barca was one of the last survivors of the fall of Carthage, ultimately forced to kill his former chieftain, who also happened to be his father. Unlike many of the other nameless gladiators, therefore, Barca is specifically given a fairly nuanced personality that is shaped by his tragic and violent past.

Perhaps unsurprisingly, therefore, Barca does not show many emotions, emerging throughout his narrative arc as a man who must guard his feelings and keep them under tight control, no doubt cognizant of the vulnerability inherent in the emotionality. The *ludus* emerges here as a space that not only encourages the men to constantly compete with one another but also to learn how to behave in ways that are masculine, if only to ensure their own survival, as it is made abundantly clear that the sands of the arena are not the only place where death can occur. The only gladiator (other than his lover Pietros) with whom Barca shares anything other than a terse, vaguely (and sometimes explicitly) antagonistic relationship is Crixus, the very man responsible for the death of his former lover. Time and again, the series shows Barca as a man of few words yet one capable of tremendous physical cruelty, as during the several instances when he serves as Batiatus' enforcer, inflicting pain (whether deserved or not) on those who have dared to cross the *lanista* in his various political and business dealings.

The only times Barca shows vulnerability and tenderness are when he plans on a future with Pietros, which in the series' diegetic chronology marks a significant development of his character from his earlier relationship with Auctus. In one of the most touching and evocative scenes of the first season, in the episode "Legends" the camera lingers almost lovingly on the two men as they tenderly care for a flock of birds, capturing them in medium close-up as they lean against a wall. The expression on Barca's face here is an especially significant one, as it is clear that, for this moment at least, he has managed to find a bit of a respite from the otherwise cold, harsh, and uncaring world of the *ludus* and of the Roman slave world of which it is an unfortunately accurate microcosm, a contrast made all the more acute by the editing, which juxtaposes this scene with the recounting of Barca's tragic backstory. Indeed, the tenderness with which he handles the bird in his arms—holding it to his face, stroking its feathers—suggests that the particular type of masculine behavior he has adopted is an unfortunate byproduct of the world around him, and that Pietros, as Augoustakis puts it, domesticates him in a way that Auctus, his lover from several years prior, does not (161). Pietros' youth and innocence, and his *genuineness*—made clear, for example, by his desire to show Spartacus at least a measure of respect and welcome rather than the outright antagonism he receives from most of the other gladiators— serve as a balancing and ameliorating influence on Barca, providing him with a reason to live beyond the certain (though perhaps glorious) death promised by a life in the arena.

This is not to suggest, however, that their relationship is a chaste or sexless one like that between Thomas Tallis and William Compton of *The Tudors*. One of the most intensely visceral and sexually explicit scenes of *Spartacus'* first season occurs in the episode "The Thing in the Pit," and it involves Pietros and Barca having sex in front of the other gladiators (albeit in their own cell). The shooting of this scene is consistent with the other displays of explicit sexuality found throughout the rest of the series; that is, there is no sense that the characters feel any sense of shame, nor do the other gladiators make any comment on the sexual practices of their brethren (though it is slightly implied that Spartacus feels a measure of discomfort at seeing such a public display of sexual behavior). Just as importantly, the attention the camera pays to the looks of pleasure evident on both men's faces (especially Pietros') suggests that this sexual relationship, unlike so many others in the world that *Spartacus* depicts, is mutually desired and indeed a source of pleasure for both parties.

This physicality, however, and the obvious affection it expresses are only a part of the relationship, as sex (like many other things in the world that *Spartacus* has created) ultimately becomes as much about power as it is about the unification of either physical or emotional desire. When threatened with the possibility that Spartacus may be attempting to steal away Pietros' affections, Barca remarks, somewhat offhandedly, that "my cock keeps him well filled." While his remark is in some measure a response to the world of the *ludus*—one in which admitting to anything so potentially unmanning or weakening an emotion as love would be dangerous at best and fatal at worst— it also reflects a very potent reality in terms of their relative positions within the school, positions determined in part by their age (it is implied that Pietros is significantly younger than Barca) but also by their martial ability and, by extension, their status as men. While Pietros has almost certainly engaged in this relationship willingly, and has likewise accepted his position as the receptive sexual partner, this does not of itself change the fact that, in the gender scheme of *Spartacus*, he occupies a less explicitly male position than his lover and protector. His youth, as well as his less physically defined physique—being notably smaller and slighter than the other gladiators, including and especially Barca—render him vulnerable. Indeed, the viewer never sees him fighting, instead watching him serve as the helper to the other gladiators, running errands rather than taking part in any of the physical training (a marked contrast, it should be noted, to his predecessor Auctus). Pietros, more than Barca, expresses his emotions and, perhaps because of his youth, has not yet had his sensitive nature entirely extinguished by the cruel world of the *ludus* and the emotional, mental, and physical violence it engenders in its prisoners.

Indeed, Pietros' tendencies toward sensitivity ultimately initiate the chain of events that will inexorably lead both queer male characters to their deaths. When Batiatus doubts that Barca was able to kill the young child of Ovidius (played by Matthew Chamberlain), one of his many political enemies, he questions Pietros, who unwittingly betrays the secret that his lover had told him: that he had not slain the boy. Of course, the steadfast Barca would never have let such a weak emotion as pity stir his heart for a complete stranger, or endanger the possibility of his eventually gaining his freedom and that of Pietros, but he lied to his lover in order to convince him that he was not, in fact, capable of the hardened cruelty that the viewer knows he can commit (and indeed, as events prove, actually *has* committed). This unfortunate moment of tenderness, this desire to prove that he has the sensitivity required to be a good partner to Pietros while also doing the bloody and ruthless deeds necessary to survive and thrive in the *ludus,* leads to his death as Batiatus, egged on by the cowardly slave Ashur (played by Nick E. Tarabay), cuts Barca's throat, making a mockery of his desire for freedom. Barca wounds or slays several of the men who have been ordered to take him down, but he has still sacrificed his life on the altar of narrative expediency.

The fact that Barca and Pietros had explicitly planned to start a life together outside of the *ludus* grants Barca's death a particular poignancy in keeping with the melodramatic mode that this series consistently evokes. As Linda Williams reminds us, one of the key ways by which melodrama renders its moral code visible is through the evocation of a space of innocence that the narrative seeks to replicate or reach by the end (28). The space of innocence in which Barca and Pietros sought to build a life outside of the confines of the *ludus* offers a tantalizing promise of a world outside the bonds of slavery and, as such, stands as a stark accompaniment to Spartacus' own desire to reunite with his wife, who was sold into slavery following the betrayal of the Romans. This space can never be attained, largely because the historical world the series creates does not have room for emotional sincerity nor for the type of life that would be untainted or uncomplicated by the sorts of political and sexual scheming that form such an essential part of the Roman worldview.

Given that Pietros stands as the more tender and vulnerable of the two queer men in the first season, it comes as no surprise that he finds it difficult, and eventually impossible, to survive in the harsh world of the Roman *ludus,* at least without the protection that Barca consistently offered him. Deceived by the villainous Ashur into believing that Barca cared nothing for him and left without a thought for their shared freedom, Pietros is also subjected to the physical—and, it is implied, sexual—abuse of one of his fellow gladiators, Gnaeus (played by Raicho Vasilev). Spartacus quickly notes the bruises on his face, and the scene encourages the viewer to contrast this new form of abjection with the powerful and affective bond shared between Barca and Pietros. This new relationship is precisely the kind of fraught one that Barca and Pietros largely avoided. Unsurprisingly, Pietros slips into that most long-standing and pernicious of media stereotypes, the suicidal queer, what *TV Tropes* refers to as the "too good for this sinful earth trope," to which I would add "not masculine enough" to survive the cold hard world of the *ludus* ("Too Good"). In taking his own life, Pietros makes the series' general point overtly clear: this is not a world that can accommodate a sensitive male figure, nor will it allow any sort of genuinely emotional relationship to survive and thrive, including (and especially) queer male love.

To drive home its point that only certain types of masculine behavior enable survival within this harsh and brutal world, the early seasons of *Spartacus* suggest that even a paragon of (almost excessively) violent, powerful, muscular masculinity like Barca can be brought down by the overwhelming and weakening desire to find a measure of happiness, peace, and tranquility in this particular world. While none of the main characters find romantic fulfillment in the first season (e.g., Spartacus' wife dies at the cusp of their reunion, Crixus and Naevia [played by Cynthia Addai-Robinson] have their romance torn apart by the scheming of Ashur and the vicious jealousy of Lucretia, etc.), only Barca and Pietros ultimately *die* as a result of their romance. While *Spartacus* may have broken some new gay-television ground by so self-consciously courting a queer male spectatorship and by so unflinchingly portraying same-sex physical desire, in its first season and a half it unfortunately fell all too easily into the same representational strategies utilized by so many other television series, sacrificing the queer characters in order to provide their avowedly opposite-sex-attracted characters with another motivation for ultimately rebelling against their Roman masters.

Agron and the Rehabilitation of the Historical Queer

Although the first season and a half of *Spartacus* saw the only queer male figures die, the second and third full seasons devoted substantially more attention to *their* queer male characters, even going so far as to allow both of them to survive the final battles that kill the rest of their fellow former gladiators. This second couple, Agron and Nasir, is given more screen time to grow and develop, and, while the series still adheres to some of the representational patterns it established earlier (i.e., the men are of different ages, occupy different statuses within the group of escaped slaves, and exhibit very different styles of masculinity), the fact that they do not fall as easily into the queer tragedy narrative as their predecessors suggests, at some level, the series' attempt to rehabilitate the figure of the queer male of antiquity, to rescue him from the abjection of such figures as Pietros and the tragic yet über-masculine Barca.

Throughout these later seasons, Agron in particular attains substantial character and psychological development, serving as a complementary epic hero to Spartacus, his own journey mirroring that of his leader. Although Agron was initially introduced in the first season, when he entered the *ludus* with his brother (who was slain during the revolt that brought down the

House of Batiatus), it is not until the start of the full second season, subtitled *Vengeance*, that he begins to emerge as a character in his own right, exhibiting many of the attributes of the traditional epic hero that has maintained a consistent presence in representations of antiquity, serving an important cultural and social function as a representational figure. Derek Elley refers to this hero as the "muscle-man, the perfect mythic physical/sexual stereotype" (21), and Robert Burgoyne further points out the ways by which the epic hero functions to resolve various contradictions "between slavery and masculinity, between individual subordination and collective agency" (86). This gay action hero, as he would later be called, must also mediate between his own desires and those of the people he supposedly fights for, as well as between his desire for vengeance and the possibility of a better future.

At the beginning of his later story arc, however, Agron exhibits many of the characteristics that are the darker side of the epic heroic figure; unlike Spartacus, who sees value in all of the people who have come under his care, Agron argues that they should focus on caring for those who are most able to fight. This tension between Spartacus and his general continues throughout much of the season, exacerbated by the reality that Agron also frequently clashes with Crixus, who, along with Spartacus, stands as one of the most powerful and most respected gladiators among the army. Agron frequently represents the darker vision of the movement that Spartacus has started, eager for little more than revenge and with little thought for the development of an organized and peaceful society, hence his belief that only those able to fight should be the focus of attention. He is more ruthlessly pragmatic than either of his fellow generals, willing to do whatever is necessary to exact vengeance for his brother. In many ways, then, Agron spends the majority of the second season behaving in a fashion similar to Barca; though freed from the bonds of Roman slavery, he still finds it difficult to think of anything beyond the immediate goal of engaging in a measure of violence that grants some measure of meaning to his suffering at the hands of the Romans. He stands as the exemplar of masculinity gone wild, untamed and uncontrolled. The arrival of Nasir, a Syrian slave boy in the house of a noble Roman, begins to change this, as Agron finds himself inexorably drawn into desire for the younger man. Like Barca, same-sex love acts as a means of containing and channeling his masculinity. However, he still very much occupies the dominant position in the relationship, both socially and sexually.

In true epic-hero fashion, Agron undergoes significant pain in his effort to overthrow the Romans. In the third-season episode "The Dead and the Dying" (the penultimate episode of the series), after his capture by the general Crassus he, along with several other prisoners of war, suffers that most distinctly Roman method of execution: crucifixion. Indeed, the series goes to great lengths in order to enable the viewer to experience the visceral, bodily terror of his presumptive execution, utilizing quick cuts and rigorous close-ups to reveal every grisly detail of the process, thereby evoking the contra-dictory pleasures often associated with the representation of the afflicted male body so common in historical dramas. As Paul Willemen famously put it: "The viewer's experience is predicated on the pleasure of seeing the male 'exist' (that is, walk, move, ride, fight) in or through cityscapes, landscapes, or, more abstractly, history, and on the unquiet pleasure of seeing the male mutilated ... and restored through violent brutality" (16). Like the earlier Spartacus from the 1960 film directed by Stanley Kubrick, Agron must suffer the utmost in order for his fighting, and his sacrifice, to have the greatest possible emotional and symbolic weight. Unlike that earlier sacrificial victim, however, and indeed like all of the other male gladiators with whom he has shared the bonds of brotherhood, he manages to escape death, though his body will forever bear the marks of his emasculation. He may survive, but his days as a warrior have effectively come to an end.

While Agron occupies a substantial position as one of Spartacus' chief generals, his lover, Nasir, also gains complexity and nuance as a character as he struggles to overcome the legacy of his slavery to the Romans and prove his masculinity. Even here, though, the series seems unable to break away from its reliance upon masculinity as a means of articulating its particular vision of queer male sexuality. Like Pietros in the earlier season, Nasir finds his masculinity constantly threatened by the other members of Spartacus' army, who consistently refer to him as Agron's "boy" (typically in an attempt to goad his older lover); as a result, he attempts to recover his masculinity by learning the same martial skills as his fellows. His journey as a character, therefore, is as much about the transition from a boy to a martial male figure as it is about the transition from a slave to a freedom fighter, a transformation made difficult by the sexual politics the series has created through the rela-tionship of Barca and Pietros (with its consistently evoked power relations), and also through the gendered power that constitutes a part of the slave soci-ety Spartacus and his fellows establish throughout the last two seasons. His sexual and social positioning always remain in some measure liminal, cir-cumscribed by a system that only permits certain types of men to move from "boy" to "man."

"The Gay Action Hero": Queer Masculinity Finds Its Adoring Audience

The gay press has particularly praised the character of Agron for serving as, in the assessment of *Out* magazine, the new gay action hero that many gay men have eagerly looked for but found so uncommon in both television and film (indeed, the title of the article profiling the actor who plays Agron, Dan Feuerriegel, is "The Gay Action Hero") (James). A related interview between Feuerriegel and the influential magazine *The Advocate* reveals a great deal about the relation between masculinity and gay men, both within the series' diegesis and the larger cultural conversation occurring around the series. For example, when asked how he reacted when he learned that he would be playing a gay gladiator, the actor responded,

> It didn't make any difference to me. I would have played him the exact same way whether he was interested in women or men. His personality wouldn't change. They just wanted me to make him really fierce and a hard-ass, but then open up and have a soft, sensual side when he's alone with the people he loves. His sexuality doesn't change that as far as I'm aware [qtd. in Peeples].

One hears in these words an echo of the desire of so many high-profile gay men to be "just like everyone else," to not have one's sexuality define either one's entire personality or one's public persona but rather for it to be just one aspect of that persona. As Feuerriegel states later in that interview, the relationship between Agron and Nasir "shows that love is everywhere. Regardless of who you are or who you like, love is love" (qtd. in Peeples). While Feurriegel acknowledges his own sense of gratification that so many gay fans have felt drawn to his character as a screen hero, he continually attempts to deflect attention away from the queer specificity of Agron and his relationship with Nasir.

There seems to be an unspoken tension within this interview between celebrating the type of queer representation that the actor has produced—rendering Agron a "hard-ass" who nevertheless has the ability to love and be gentle and caring with those he loves—and identifying that representation as being specifically *queer*, as a mode of desire and gender presentation that exists outside of the heteronormative. Such a desire to appear "normal" clearly partakes in a longer tradition of masculine figures in popular television, for as Joe Wlodarz has shown, figures such as the gay jock and other traditionally masculine television types engage in a "universalizing approach that inadvertently functions to queer patriarchal norms and institutions, particularly sports" (94), even as it seeks to avoid that queer affect. In many ways, then, the discourses surrounding *Spartacus* use masculinity, and the expression of it through both physical hardness and emotional fortitude, as the means by which queer sexual desire becomes normalized.

The rhetoric used by Alexander Stevenson in his list of the best gay TV characters further reveals the ways that traditional masculinity still stands as an ideal among many gay men, at once something to be sexually desired and (implicitly) a set of characteristics to desire to achieve. Agron appears at number five on this list of gay characters. The way he is described illuminates the relationship that gay male audiences form with their televisual representations:

And yet, Agron was something wholly new to modern audiences: he's here, he's queer, and yes, he will kick your butt if you don't like it. We've seen "tough-guy" gays before, but with Agron, we get that gay tough guy without all the usual accompanying baggage. What a breath of fresh air. Agron is the jock boyfriend we all hope to have: fiercely protective, unafraid to love, and yes, rippling with muscles [Stevenson].

Note the evocation of "we're here, we're queer" repurposed for association with the particular kind of almost brutish, excessively violent masculinity that Agron represents. Stevenson's list remains frustratingly vague about the specific sorts of baggage that are typically associated with the tough-guy gay character type, but even more revealing is the consistent use of the pronoun "we" in order to position the presumably queer reader with a particular kind of queerness and with a particular type of queer male desire. Indeed, David Simmons has suggested that the images of hypermasculine male bodies in *Spartacus* "function as a means of imaginative empowerment, a vehicle of identification for those experiencing feelings of powerlessness" (151). While he goes on to argue that the series perhaps does not take its hypermasculine figures too seriously, the rhetoric discussed above suggests that the stakes for at least some gay viewers are significantly higher than simply taking an ironic stance regarding the masculinity on display. Agron is thus not simply an action hero, he is also the "jock boyfriend we all hope to have," the "we" presumably being the less masculine gay men in the audience, the ones who position Agron as both the object of sexual desire (hence the wanting him as a boyfriend) and, somewhat paradoxically, the model of masculinity that one, it seems, would also like to attain (hence his status as the gay action hero, the figure with which gay male viewers can identify and to which they can aspire).

Conspicuously absent from much of this discussion is, of course, Nasir, the significantly less martial partner and, it must be pointed out, sexual bottom in this pairing. Of course, the elevation of the top as an object of sexual desire is nothing new within gay male culture, for a host of sociocultural reasons, among them the fact that to embrace the bottom position in gay sex is, as scholars have consistently noted, to embrace the abjection that comes from accepting the penetrated position during sex. As Leo Bersani so famously put it, the rectum is the grave of the traditional masculine ideal (222). It is perhaps no accident that similar attitudes prevailed in antiquity, nor indeed should it surprise that they continue to exist within many segments of the contemporary gay male cultural and sexual landscape. As David Halperin has ably demonstrated, "The notion that anal intercourse, or any kind of bodily 'penetration,' is incompatible with masculinity and therefore out of keeping with any dignified form of male intimacy among men seems to have provided the basis for a number of online gay male communities" (508). Nasir, even more than Agron, represents the complex relation between gay male subjectivity and masculinity as well as the difficulty entailed in imagining same-sex relationships, even those set in the distant past, in terms that do not rely on patterns and relations of power predicated on the ability to perform a particular type of masculinity.

Such a valorization of the gay action hero and the concomitant desire to position him as an object of desire and adulation, with the simultaneous sidelining of the more effeminate (or at least sexually receptive) partner, is not surprising, especially given the ways by which gay men in particular have been presented within representations of antiquity in the cinema. Although, as Harry Benshoff and Sean Griffin have noted, the epics of the 1950s and 1960s (and, one might add, those of the turn of the millennium) offer plenty of visual spectacle to the gay male spectator, it is equally true that the epic has consistently also positioned the queer/failed male as a source of political, social, and sexual disorder and deviance (101–102). And as Jerry Pierce convincingly argues of the millennial cycle, "By presenting the masculinity and heterosexuality of the heroes as normative, the narrative arc of these movies also implies that it is this very type of masculinity that will save their families and their societies from the threat posed by unmanly men" (41).

While Pierce focuses on the millennial resurgence of the epic, the deviant queer male figure has deep roots in the genre, especially in the story of Spartacus. *Spartacus,* the 1960 film starring Kirk Douglas in the titular role, contains one of the most infamous scenes of same-sex eroticism in which the Roman general Crassus (played by Laurence Olivier), in a moment dubbed the "oysters and snails scene," attempts to seduce his young slave Antoninus (played by Tony Curtis). Although originally cut from the theatrical release due to censorship concerns, this scene is a crucial component of Crassus' sexual deviance, which the film aligns with the general decadence, corruption, and political despotism of ancient Rome and which, as scholars including Alison Futrell and Ina Rae Hark have noted, stands diametrically opposed to the more genuine, rigorously heterosexual Spartacus and his fellow freedom fighters. The queer male, this film asserts, stands as a force of chaos and disorder that must constantly be disavowed, and if possible defeated, by the epic hero. Monica Cyrino makes the astute observation that "in *Spartacus* the scope of 'normal' sexuality is defined by the titular hero, the life-affirming and heteronormative father figure, the rebel slave, Spartacus, against the death-obsessed, family-less, and sexually 'deviant' elite Roman Crassus" (619). Not surprisingly, given the context in which the film was released, same-sex desire leads inevitably to death, not necessarily for Crassus, but for those who oppose him. The film encourages the viewer to understand him as the distilled impression of Roman tyranny, his flawed masculinity radiating outward to create a despotic state that has no care for human life.

Conclusion

Given both this troubling representational history and the continued (if somewhat contradictory) relation between gay men and masculinity, it comes as no surprise that, throughout its run, the television series *Spartacus* sought to rehabilitate the historical queer by aligning him so thoroughly with the epic hero. Through this rehabilitation, *Spartacus* has done a great deal to disentangle the deeply entrenched link between same-sex desire and deviance in historical representation. Doing so, however, has also brought with it a significant number of other issues that are not so easily done away with. Although the series eventually overcame its reliance on the queer tragedy narrative, it nevertheless continued to rely on demarcating queer male sexuality according to particular performances of masculinity. In the vision of antiquity presented here, the world of the late Roman Republic was a dark, dangerous place, with sex and violence continually intertwined. As Cyrino suggests, *Spartacus* in particular makes these connections abundantly clear in most of its seasons, frequently intercutting scenes of graphic sex with explicit violence (626). In such a harsh world, one must adopt the conventions of the epic hero and his martial abilities in order to survive. Thus, while Pietros is ultimately sacrificed in order to reveal the harshness of life in the *ludus,* Nasir, due to both his slowly acquired martial abilities and his freedom, can survive.

Just as importantly, however, the series also marks a significant reworking of the negative consequences so often equated with queer desire. Whereas before, male same-sex desire was associated with death and the downfall of a diseased state, here that situation has been reversed, and this is especially significant given the ways in which the cinematic version of *Spartacus* continues to exert such a substantial influence on contemporary understandings of the Spartacus myth in general. The end of that film sees Varinia (played by Jean Simmons), the wife of Spartacus, holding up the son of the crucified gladiator to his father before riding off with the reformed Batiatus (played by Peter Ustinov), the viewer left feeling certain that she will raise her son with the proud knowledge of his father's sacrifice so that others might live freely. The ending of the Starz series, however, differs substantially, for it is Nasir and Agron who oversee the burial of their fallen leader, far from the prying eyes of the Romans (thus depriving them of the opportunity to showcase his death to the rest of the slave population). Spartacus' remaining love interest is given only passing attention by the camera, which focuses instead on the two male lovers, mourning their fallen comrade, as well as all of the others who have lost their lives, all victims of Roman cruelty. Given the lengths to which the series has gone to valorize genuine emotion over the brutalizing and dehumanizing sexual desires of the Romans, this final moment gains greater symbolic weight for the queer viewer. The queer male has now been thoroughly rehabilitated, allowed to represent the birth of a new world and a new society, one based on mutual love and affection rather than tyranny, deviance, and slavery.

WORKS CITED

Augoustakis, Antony. "Partnership and Love in *Spartacus: Blood and Sand (2010)*." *Screening Love and Sex in the Ancient World*. Ed. Monica S. Cyrino. New York: Palgrave Macmillan, 2013. 157–165. Print.

Benshoff, Harry M., and Sean Griffin. *Queer Images: A History of Gay and Lesbian Film in America*. Lanham, MD: Rowman & Littlefield, 2006. Print.

Bersani, Leo. "Is the Rectum a Grave?" *October* 43 (1987): 197–222. Print.

Bordo, Susan. *The Male Body: A New Look at Men in Public and in Private*. New York: Farrar, Straus and Giroux, 1999. Print.

Burgoyne, Robert. *The Hollywood Historical Film*. Malden, MA: Blackwell, 2008. Print.

"Bury Your Gays." *TV Tropes*, n.d. Web. 15 October 2014. http://tvtropes.org/pmwiki/pmwiki.php/Main/BuryYourGays.

Cyrino, Monica S. "Ancient Sexuality on Screen." *A Companion to Greek and Roman Sexualities*. Ed. Thomas K. Hubbard. Malden, MA: Blackwell, 2014. 613–628. Print.

Dyer, Richard. *The Culture of Queers*. London: Routledge, 2002. Print.

Elley, Derek. *The Epic Film: Myth and History*. New York: Routledge, 1984. Print.

Futrell, Alison. "Seeing Red: Spartacus as Domestic Economist." *Imperial Projections: Ancient Rome in Modern Popular Culture*. Ed. Sandra R. Joshel, Margaret Malamud, and Donald T. McGuire, Jr. Baltimore: Johns Hopkins University Press, 2001. 77–118. Print.

Glynn, Basil. "The Conquests of Henry VIII: Masculinity, Sex, and the National Past in *The Tudors*." *Television, Sex, and Society: Analyzing Contemporary Representations*. Ed. Basil Glynn, James Aston, and Beth Johnson. New York: Continuum, 2012. 157–173. Print.

Halperin, David M. *How to Be Gay*. Cambridge: Belknap Press, 2012. Print.

Hark, Ina Rae. "Animals or Romans: Looking at Masculinity in *Spartacus*." *Screening the Male: Exploring Masculinities in Hollywood Cinema*. Ed. Steven Cohan and Ina Rae Hark. New York: Routledge, 1993. 151–172. Print.

James, Diego. "The Gay Action Hero." *Out*, 5 January 2013. Web. 1 November 2014.

Martin, Denise, and Joe Flint. "Spicy 'Spartacus' Slays 'Em for Starz." *Los Angeles Times*. Los Angeles Times, 23 March 2010. Web. 29 September 2014.

Neale, Steve. "Masculinity as Spectacle: Reflections on Men and Mainstream Cinema." *Screening the Male: Exploring Masculinities in Hollywood Cinema*. Ed. Steven Cohan and Ina Rae Hark. New York: Routledge, 1993. 9–20. Print.

Peeples, Jase. "The Gay Action Hero on *Spartacus* Is Back." *Advocate*, 24 January 2013. Web. 12 December 2015.

Pierce, Jerry B. "'To Do or Die Manfully': Performing Heternormativity in Recent Epic Films." *Of Muscles and Men: Essays on the Sword and Sandal Film*. Ed. Michael G. Cornelius. Jefferson, NC: McFarland, 2011. 40–57. Print.

Rosenstone, Robert A. *History on Film/Film on History*, 2d ed. New York: Routledge, 2013. Print.

Simmons, David. "'By Jupiter's Cock!' *Spartacus: Blood and Sand*, Video Games, and

Camp Excess." *Of Muscles and Men: Essays on the Sword and Sandal Film.* Ed. Michael G. Cornelius. Jefferson, NC: McFarland, 2011. 144–153. Print.

Stevenson, Alexander. "The 50 Greatest Gay TV Characters." *NewNowNext.* 7 October 2013. Web. 12 December 2015. http://www.newnownext.com/greatest-gay-tv-characters/10/2013/.

Strong, Anise K. "Objects of Desire: Female Gazes and Male Bodies in *Spartacus: Blood and Sand (2010)." Screening Love and Sex in the Ancient World.* Ed. Monica S. Cyrino. New York: Palgrave Macmillan, 2013. 157–165. Print.

"Too Good for This Sinful Earth." *TV Tropes,* n.d. Web. 15 October 2014. http://tvtropes.org/mwiki/pmwiki.php/Main/TooGoodForThisSinfulEarth.

Willemen, Paul. "Anthony Mann Looking at the Male." *Framework: The Journal of Cinema and Media* 15–17 (1981): 16. Print.

Williams, Linda. *Playing the Race Card: Melodramas of Black and White from Uncle Tom to O.J. Simpson.* Princeton: Princeton University Press, 2001. Print.

Wlodarz, Joe. "'We're Not All So Obvious': Masculinity and Queer (In)Visibility in American Network Television of the 1970s." *Queer TV: Theories, Histories, Politics.* Ed. Glyn Davis and Gary Needham. New York: Routledge, 2009. 88–107. Print.

Leonardo's Paradoxical Queerness

Da Vinci's Demons *and the Politics of Straightwashing*

DRAGOS MANEA

Despite being the first television series to depict Leonardo da Vinci romantically kissing another man, the Starz series *Da Vinci's Demons* (2013–2015), an ongoing historical fantasy, has widely been denounced for straightwashing its main character. While I agree that the accusations are entirely warranted and discuss them in detail, I go beyond a rigid focus on the series' reception in the gay community, attempting to understand the larger approach to the adaptation of historical narratives that informs the series' production as well as its relation to queer cultural memory. I thus attempt to elucidate Leonardo's paradoxical queerness by exploring three fundamental questions: How do traditional historical adaptations serve to reconcile viewers to normative, contemporary ways of being while at the same time suppressing both authentically historical and alternative, contemporary values and social practices? How does queer cultural memory resist acts of mnemonic erasure? And what exactly is the underlying cultural logic that governs the practice of straightwashing?

Having entered its third (and final) season in October 2005, *Da Vinci's Demons* is, in a number of ways, a follow-up to the earlier Starz series *Spartacus* (2010–2013). Both are historical dramas filled with moments of action-adventure and centered on famous, strong figures from Western history, but while *Spartacus* offered viewers a tragedy that carefully pondered the burden of revenge, *Da Vinci's Demons* is content with giving audiences less grandiose thrills. The series presents the exploits of the young Leonardo da Vinci (played by Tom Riley) as he navigates the treacherous politics of Renaissance

Italy, coming into the employ of Florence's rulers, the Medici family, as a war engineer during their conflict with Rome's tyrannical Papacy. Leonardo is assisted in his adventures by his apprentice, Nico (played by Eros Vlahos), who is later revealed to be a young Niccolo Machiavelli; his best friend, Zoroaster (played by Gregg Chillin); an ethnically ambiguous rogue, Vanessa (played by Hera Hilmar), a former nun who left the monastery after being deflowered by Leonardo; and his old master, Verrocchio (played by Allan Corduner), who runs an important Florentine workshop (in which fellow painter Botticelli [played by Jack Farthing] is also employed, although he appears only briefly). Because of his skills as both a war engineer and a brilliant painter, Leonardo gradually becomes a trusted advisor to Lorenzo de Medici (played by Elliot Cowan), a relationship later complicated by the fact that they both find themselves involved with the same woman, Lucrezia (played by Laura Haddock), a papal spy. The republic of Florence, which the series presents as a very progressive city-state, is in conflict with Rome, a theocratic regime governed by the brutal and lecherous Pope Sixtus IV (played by James Faulkner), who is later revealed to be the real Pope's twin brother and Lucrezia's uncle. Both Leonardo and the Pope, most often represented by his agent, Count Riario (played by Blake Ritson), are after the *Book of Leaves*, a lost depository of ancient knowledge. While Leonardo's motives are more pure (i.e., he hopes to be reconciled with his mother, who has hidden the book with the Incas), the Pope wants only to use the book to strengthen his hold on power.

This pulpy plot is matched by a hero who is by turns a technological genius whose experiments sometimes save the day (and almost always put his friends in harm's way), a swashbuckling rogue well versed in fisticuffs and brawling, and a sensitive painter and natural philosopher, always attentive to the complex beauty of the world around him. Equal parts pragmatist and romantic, Leonardo is seldom bested in physical or intellectual combat. He possesses an eidetic memory that allows him to remember the minutiae of daily existence, and he is presented as a seductive and competent lover whose charms cannot be resisted. In a sense, Leonardo comes to embody his own Vitruvian man.

However, unlike the historical Leonardo, the hero of *Da Vinci's Demons* is first and foremost a lover of women: from his playful trysts with Vanessa to his intense love affair with Lucrezia to his brief and advantageous marriage to Inca High Priestess Ima (played by Carolina Guerra), the women Leonardo beds play a central part in the unfolding of the plot, while his homosexual relationship with the model and prostitute Jacopo Saltarelli (played by Christopher Elson) occurs, save for one brief kiss, entirely off-screen. This state of affairs has understandably drawn the ire of the online gay community, which has (rightfully) understood it to be an instance of straightwashing, as

I discuss in greater detail later. But the purpose of this essay requires that I make one preliminary statement: Leonardo di ser Piero da Vinci (1452–1519) was a man whose life was undoubtedly shaped by same-sex desire, a fact that has by now become widely accepted among biographers and historians. He was publicly accused of sodomy twice, had lifelong male companions whom he showered with affection, showed no erotic interest in women, and was depicted by at least one contemporary writer as a proponent of *l'amore masculino*: male love (for further reading I recommend the works of Crompton, Feinberg, Kemp, Rocke, and Wittkower and Wittkower, on whom I largely draw for historical information). Nevertheless, Leonardo's fictional afterlife has largely been heterosexual or, at least, heteronormative, as the three most recent television adaptations of the life of the Renaissance polymath serve to attest.

In addition to *Da Vinci's Demons*, both the British television series *Leonardo* (2011–2012) and the French–German–Czech series *Borgia* (2011–2014) further what has by now become the classic approach to straightwashing Leonardo. The former, a children's series depicting the young artist (played by Jonathan Bailey), has him falling in love with the beautiful Valentina (played by Emily Child) while hinting that he and Lisa (played by Flora Spencer-Longhurst)—of future Mona Lisa fame—are destined to be together, a decision that led to the BBC being criticized for furthering LGBT discrimination (Mason). The latter series, a chronicle of the exploits of the notorious Borgia family, introduces Leonardo (played by Paul Rhys) in its second season as an artist and war engineer under the employ of Cesare (played by Mark Ryder), of whom he speaks with fondness, describing him in the third-season premiere episode, titled "1495," as a man who is "free from all prejudice against one's sexual appetite"; as such, Leonardo's sexuality is thus reduced to a knowing hint while the series engages in numerous depictions of orgiastic heteronormative intercourse. Either by turning a historically queer character straight or choosing not to depict his sexual life, these series do violence to LGBTQ visibility and cultural memory. In this essay, therefore, I address the ways by which historical writing and fiction have tackled the conceptualization and representation of queerness, discuss the reception of *Da Vinci's Demons* in the online LGBTQ community, and offer a critique of the series' regressive approach to sexual politics.

The Whig Interpretation of Sexual History

Da Vinci's Demons is but one recent television series that furthers a negative image of the Middle Ages as a period of obscurantism, tyranny, and thoroughgoing repression, mercifully ended by the flowering of the Renaissance. The series stands as further proof of the pervasive endurance of the Whig interpretation of history and of the Great Man theory in Anglo-American popular culture, the two intertwining modes by which historical narratives are still predominantly framed outside of academia.

In a seminal 1931 study, the British historian Herbert Butterfield defined the Whig interpretation of history as the common tendency of many historians "to write on the side of Protestants and Whigs, to praise revolutions provided they have been successful, to emphasize certain principles of progress in the past and to produce a story which is the ratification if not the glorification of the present" (Butterfield). I take that last part to be of crucial importance: such an interpretation is driven by a desire to imagine past events as foundational or transformative for a given community, followed by a profound identification by members of that community with the main characters involved in the events thereby interpreted. This immediately creates two further complications: (1) the characters themselves must be of great importance, otherwise they could not have effected the change necessary for the event to be foundational or transformative; and (2) it is here that we can locate an affinity between such an interpretation and the Great Man theory. Historical fiction of this kind does not spare even the most minor of historical characters from becoming great (see, for example, the HBO series *Rome* [2005–2007], within which the main characters Lucius Vorenus [played by Kevin McKidd] and Titus Pullo [played by Ray Stevenson], whose historical significance amounts to brief mentions by Caesar in his Commentaries, come to be responsible, in one way or another, for the fate of the Roman Republic).

There is yet another complication of note: such an interpretation of history is grounded upon the act of identification. Past characters must be interpreted in such a way as to be recognizably similar to ourselves—their norms, values, even outward appearances to some degree need to be compatible with our own. This enables members of the audience to project themselves back into the past, to imagine themselves as both the architects of the past and its successors. The vast distance between past and present is collapsed, and a strange continuity is achieved whereby past events serve to foretell the present while being brought about by an altogether contemporary consciousness. But to achieve this paradoxical continuity, an interpretation must strive not to lose the allure of historical verisimilitude (i.e., the ability to make itself understood as historical). It must be careful to delineate between characters that are like us (and are therefore familiar) and characters that are not (and are therefore foreign or strange): a self-image and a hetero-image are always produced within the act of historical identification.

To my mind, there are two approaches to the adaptation of historical narratives that are, to a certain extent, compatible with a gay agenda (and which *Da Vinci's Demons* thoroughly avoids). The first is essentialist and pre-sentist, and it does not differ substantively from the traditional approach to historical fiction that I outlined above but rather merely places the homo-sexual subject at the center of its narrative, while proposing a moral universe wherein homosexuality is either neutral or good in terms of ethical value. It imagines homosexual desire as universal and transhistorical, and it super-imposes a contemporary consciousness onto historical characters that drives them to achieve their goals. Such an approach is inherently familiarizing and founded on a logic of reconciliation, to the extent that it accepts the existence of a coherent homosexual history and a coherent homosexual subject both within and outside of history—a homosexual subject it then proposes as a locus of identification for contemporary gay and lesbian viewers. From *Wilde* (1997, directed by Brian Gilbert) to *De-Lovely* (2004, directed by Irwin Win-kler) to *Milk* (2008, directed by Gus Van Sant), biographies of modern homo-sexuals are far from rare or unprofitable, in part because the mores they depict are easily recognizable to contemporary audiences. By contrast, Derek Jarman's *Caravaggio* (1986) is a rare example of a film centered on a pre-modern or early modern homosexual subject, while television examples include the (non-central) relationships between Agron (played by Daniel Feuerriegel) and Nasir (played by Pana Hema Taylor) on *Spartacus* as well as Renly Baratheon (played by Gethin Anthony) and Loras Tyrell (played by Finn Jones) on *Game of Thrones* (2011–), although the latter's medieval society is entirely fictitious. Nevertheless, the three all share a belief in the transhis-torical nature of the homosexual subject, and the romantic actions of their characters are shaped by modern structures of desire.

Such an approach to history is endemic in the American mainstream. Ranker.com offers a list of more than 1,800 famous gay men from antiquity to the present day ("Famous"), Wikipedia labels individuals from different historical periods as LGBT, and popular encyclopedias such as Keith Stern's *Queers in History* promise (as stated on its front cover) "innuendo, … sar-casm, and schmooze" while delivering biographies of various individuals from Socrates to Neil Patrick Harris. This discourse is also to a certain extent informed by academic history. From K.J. Dover's groundbreaking 1978 study *Greek Homosexuality* and John Boswell's influential work in the 1980s and 1990s; to 2003's towering world history of same-sex desire, *Homosexuality and Civilization*, by Louis Crompton; to, more recently, 2011's less grand though not less argued *A Queer History of the United States* by Michael Bron-ski, an important strand of researchers working in the field have accepted the existence of the homosexual subject as a universal category, one that might find its particular historical expression in various ways in different cultures but is nevertheless not the product or construct of history. As Boswell once put it, "If the categories 'homosexual/heterosexual' and 'gay/straight' are the inventions of particular societies rather than real aspects of the human psyche, there is no gay history" (20).

In contrast, some queer historians and especially queer theoreticians have argued, following Michel Foucault, that sexuality is an inherently modern phenomenon, the result of the development of Western bourgeois culture in the long 18th century (Halperin, "Sex" 42). Such a constructionist and historicist approach stresses the contingency of structures of desire and the crucial role played by language and discourse in the formation of the self, and it denies the applicability of presentist categories such as "homosexual" to pre-modern or early modern individuals. Unlike the essentialist paradigm, still dominant in the American mainstream, social constructionism remains foundational and hegemonic in queer theory but has had little impact on popular historical writing (Hall 43). To encounter the pre-modern or even the early modern is to have a profoundly defamiliarizing experience as we are confronted with a radically different way of being—one that may further enable us to "bring more clearly into focus the ideological dimension—the purely conventional and arbitrary character—of our own social and sexual experiences," as David Halperin argues ("Is There" 417). Yet at the same time, in resisting totalizing metanarratives, it does violence to the possibility of having a coherent universal queer history or cultural memory, which significantly reduces its political efficacy in modern liberal societies.

For the purposes of historical writing, it might be better to understand essentialism and constructionism not as absolute polar opposites but rather as part of an interconnected spectrum. Most historical writing is neither radically essentialist nor radically constructionist; instead, it occupies a space in-between. Bronski's approach in writing *A Queer History of the United States* is a good example of this eminently pragmatic middle position. About his use of the term "sexuality," the historian writes:

> Here "sexuality" connotes the never-ending constellation of factors that inform how people understand their sexual desires and actions. My use of the term is meant to connect the present with the past so that we can better understand both. Whatever sexuality means today and did not mean before, the word, like others before it, has always attempted to describe something we know is not reducible to a word, an identity, or even a set of behaviors [xviii].

While I am yet to be convinced that this "something" exists as a real ontological given, its pragmatic importance is fairly unobjectionable: it allows for a coherent, yet non-totalizing, history of homosexuality, one that is not entirely beholden to simple metanarratives but rather retains the power to challenge and discover historical fact while simultaneously accepting the real and palpable strangeness of the past. In other words, it preserves the unfamiliarity of historical experiences and events without denying our ability to understand their non-discursive reality, or the fact that they possess a non-discursive reality in the first place. Such an approach might, for instance, lead us to understand that Leonardo di ser Piero da Vinci was perhaps not a modern homosexual, but that his life was driven and structured by same-sex desire in a way that we might find profoundly unconventional by our current standards. It might lead us to further understand that his way of being was part of the habitus of his age and governed as such by the various norms of Early Modern Italian society (which could lead to terrible discrimination against contemporary "sodomites," including capital punishment and imprisonment). And it might finally make us reflect on the continued conventionality of our own existence and the roles played by structures of desire without denying the fact that these structures do impact something that is not entirely their construction.

Yet historical fiction, by virtue of poetic license, is not as beholden to the reality of the past (if such a reality could ever fully be grasped). While I may argue for the political and aesthetic merits of a poetics of estrangement, the fact remains that for most producers and consumers of historical fiction, the genre is eminently presentist. The past is there to give meaning to present concerns and to voice future possibilities; to weave subtle allegories or to present foundational events; to hold an irrevocably bent mirror up to contemporary society. Historical fiction, as such, is seldom about history for its own sake—it is always complicated by issues of politics and cultural memory, as the reception of *Da Vinci's Demons* in the online gay community clearly testifies.

Straightwashing and the Struggle for a Queer Cultural Memory

Da Vinci's Demons had yet to air and its trailer had already angered gay commentators. To the beat of heavy metal drums, the preview offered viewers brief glimpses of Leonardo bedding a traditionally attractive woman inserted amid images and events that are clearly meant to excite: sword fights, a huge cannon, and a young man gliding in Leonardo's famed (and non-functional) flying machine. The trailer ends with a scene of the same young woman, her hand drawing closer to Leonardo's shadowed pelvic region, as she mouths, "I thought danger was the appeal for you." Heterosexual desire is thus directly connected with peril and bravado, the two main elements of the action-adventure plot. From the very beginning, it is posited as one of the series' core elements ("Da Vinci's").

To counter growing accusations of straightwashing (including Daniel Mikelonis' bitingly satirical article "Leonardo's Sexuality in 'Da Vinci's Demons' and Famous Gay Folks That Could Be Straight-Washed," published before the trailer's premiere as rumors of the series' sexual politics began to emerge), leading man and future co-producer Tom Riley was quick to comment that his character is not "constrained by sexuality," and series creator and showrunner David S. Goyer insisted that Leonardo "was not a man that could be confined" and, as such, the series would "embrace his many complexities" (qtd. in Mikelonis, "Why Leonardo's"). In an interview with the gay entertainment website AfterElton (weeks before it was rebranded as The Backlot, and then again later as NewNowNext), Goyer continued to deny the trailer's apparent commitment to a heteronormative image of Leonardo, promising a more gay-friendly version of the Renaissance polymath (Halterman, "Creator"). Although he was taken to task in the comments for stating that Leonardo's sexuality should be irrelevant and that it seemed to have been so during his time (a statement hard to reconcile with the fact that a record one hundred sixty-one individuals were convicted of sodomy in Florence just four years before Leonardo's own denunciation in 1472 [Crompton 265]), the series' weekly coverage on The Backlot was originally optimistic. Reviewing the first episode, Daniel Mikelonis, who had expressed his hopes that Leonardo would be one of the first bisexual protagonists after viewing the trailer ("Why Leonardo's"), declared his enjoyment of the series, even though it had yet to fulfill its queer promise (which the reviewer had been informed it would do later in the season), and he largely glossed over the problematic nature of the first two overtly homosexual scenes ("Well, Apparently").

The promise of Leonardo's queerness was supposed to be fulfilled in the series' fifth episode, "The Tower." Shortly before it aired, Riley gave another interview to The Backlot, in which he stated that "the online vitriol regarding 'straightwashing' has been very tough to read" and that he was committed in his portrayal of Leonardo to preserving the man's historically documented refusal to obey the sexual norms of his day (Halterman, "Defining"). "The Tower," which chronicles Leonardo's trial for sodomy, proved a great disappointment even to the queer commenters on The Backlot who had yet to lose faith in the series, and Riley and Goyer's post-mortem follow-up elicited little sympathy (Halterman, "Sodomy Trial"). *Da Vinci's Demons* appeared to have reduced Leonardo's homosexuality to one brief bi-curious entanglement, now safely in the past. As a result, the website's reviews grew increasingly sardonic—culminating in a wonderful parody of straightwashing, *Einstein's Evils*, featuring gay couple Albert Einstein and Franklin Delano Roosevelt doing battle against the Third Reich (Mikelonis, "Sleeping Geniuses")—before The Backlot decided to cease its coverage of *Da Vinci's Demons* in January 2014, dramatically "banishing" the series (Ayers). Goyer's promise that the series would not back away from Leonardo's bisexuality but that there was no room for it in season two for plot-related reasons (homosexuality, unlike heterosexuality, is apparently gratuitous, according to Goyer) largely fell on deaf ears (Nededog).

I offer a detailed reading of the series' sexual politics further on, but for the moment I would like to discuss its reception in greater detail. "Straight-washing" is a term that has gained a great deal of discursive traction in recent years, offering a visually powerful metaphor for the practice of erasing LGBTQ characters, characteristics, and/or events. As a play on the term "whitewash," the concept implies both censorship (the term's older meaning) and an intersectional link with the similar discrimination faced by people of color (as the term is more often used today). Instances of straightwashing include, but are certainly not limited to (1) turning an LGBTQ character straight (this can affect historical characters such as Leonardo, as well as fictional ones, as attested by Goyer's more recent controversy over the apparent heterosexuality of bisexual magician John Constantine [played by Matt Ryan] in *Constantine* [2014–2015], NBC's adaptation of the *Hellblazer* comic series [Cruz]); (2) downplaying a character's queerness so as to appease conservative audiences (see the recent example of *The Imitation Game* [2014, directed by Morten Tyldum], in which Alan Turing [played by Benedict Cumberbatch] is shown to be romantically involved only with Keira Knightley's Joan Clarke [Richards]); (3) erasing a film's queer content in marketing for the same reason (as happened to the trailer for Tom Ford's *A Single Man* [2009], which was re-edited to remove all but a few hints of homosexuality, and to the U.S. DVD cover for Matthew Warchus' more recent *Pride* [2014], which airbrushes a banner proclaiming "lesbians and gays support the miners" and refers to the film's queer activists as merely "a group of London-based activists" [Shari-atmadari]); and (4) rewriting entire historically non-heteronormative societies to fit contemporary straight standards (and here Zack Snyder's *300* [2006] is perhaps the worst offender, but such an approach is almost endemic in popular historical fiction). Quite clearly, straightwashing is a problem for LGBTQ visibility in the present, but it is also a serious blow to queer cultural memory. Leonardo, Turing, Sparta—all are constitutive elements of an alternative, non-heteronormative collective memory and identity that is either erased or ignored by mainstream U.S. media. Straightwashing is thus a form of what Charles Morris III has called "queer mnemonicide": the erasure of LGBTQ memory sites in order to assuage heteronormative anxieties (103). The reception of *Da Vinci's Demons* in the online gay community should be understood as a response to this type of erasure, which has led to calls for alternative queer historical series. Or as Jerry, a commenter on The Backlot, put it, "Why doesn't LOGO get rid of just one of it's [sic] more awful shows and create a piece of historical fiction about just one of our gay forefathers?" (Ayers).

The need for "gay forefathers" lies at the heart of the series' reception in the online gay community, and the rhetoric employed is manifestly presentist and essentialist. It largely follows the logic of the first approach to the adaptation of historical narratives that I outlined earlier in presuming the existence of a coherent, transhistorical homosexual subject that can be represented and performed. In addition to The Backlot's commentary, critiques of the series on other sites reflect the same underlying logic. In arguing that "sexuality is an important part of every persons [sic] life" (Bowen) or that "much of history denied the existence of the identity itself and denied us a coherent language with which to define that identity and personhood" (Sparky), the commentators run the risk of imposing contemporary normative boundaries on historical characters and events—boundaries that are then universalized in the act of imagining them as transhistorically applicable. When Bowen posits the question "Would not da Vinci himself be insulted to know that his homosexuality was to be straightwashed this way, especially considering he himself even broke laws and was tried in his time in order to participate in a gay relationship?" he is already engaging in a crucial presentist assumption: that anything resembling a modern "gay" relationship could have been possible in Renaissance Italy, at a time when homosexuality was considered "an activity, rather than an identity" (Feinberg 60). As Michael Rocke notes, homosexual relations, while not governed by a fixed conceptual category with regard to sexual object-choice—a clear homosexual identity—were nevertheless extremely frequent in Renaissance Florence and largely followed the ancient Mediterranean pattern of same-sex intercourse between a mature "active" partner and an adolescent "passive" partner (12–13). This was a hierarchical, role-bound structure of male erotic desire, within which role reversal was only permitted among adolescents and "sex between mature men was, with very few exceptions, unknown" (Rocke 13).

As such, if *Da Vinci's Demons* were to be historically accurate, a relationship between Leonardo and his assistant, the adolescent Niccolo Machiavelli, would be far more appropriate—and would clearly contravene contemporary sexual norms. The homosexual Leonardo desired by most gay viewers is not the Leonardo of later Renaissance art critic and theorist Gian Paolo Lomazzo's (1538–1592) treatise on *l'amore masculino*, in which interlocutor Phidias asks a fictive Leonardo whether he has played "the game in the behind that the Florentines love so much" with his apprentice Salai (a real historical character who had entered his employ at the age of ten); his answer is "And how many times! Have in mind that he was a most beautiful young man, especially at about fifteen" (Crompton 267). Such a depiction of Leonardo would prove shocking and estranging to contemporary audiences, and it would hardly allow LGBTQ viewers to identify with him—and with the mechanism of identification broken, Leonardo's importance to queer cultural memory would be greatly reduced. To escape this conundrum, we must move beyond a presentist understanding of history and accept that regardless of the universality of same-sex desire, its expression is always historical and cultural, and we must likewise recognize that historical fiction should not be—and perhaps cannot be—as rigid and accurate as historical writing. What it should do, and what *Da Vinci's Demons* has failed to do for the queer community, is give productive meaning to present and future concerns.

Da Vinci's Demons *and the Aesthetics of Heterosexual Anxiety*

As I have already suggested, traditional historical fiction depends on the act of identification: it proposes characters and communities whose values are compatible enough with our own so as to ensure viewer familiarity, and it generally presents their actions as ethically correct, in contrast to those of their more historically accurate adversaries. What animated the online gay community's incensed reception of *Da Vinci's Demons* is precisely that it proposes a collective identity that is profoundly heteronormative. This identity emerges in relation to Leonardo and is established around the Republic of Florence. The very first episode, titled "The Hanged Man," gives viewers this description of the Italian city state (voiced by Leonardo):

> Where else could we practice our flights but in Florence? Anywhere else, we'd just be burnt at the stake for our efforts. But here? I'm just another free-thinking heretic. Chaos. Culture. It's all celebrated within these walls. Florence only demands one thing of its people: To be truly awake.

And later, in the third episode of season two (titled "The Voyage of the Damned"), Lorenzo de' Medici (who by this time has become one of the most focalized characters, and who has been inscribed in the narrative logic of the series as being someone trustworthy) utters these words: "Florence creates the future." Florence is situated within the narrative as both a place of enlightened attitudes—with regard to social advancement, sexual mores (as long as only straight sexuality is depicted for viewer enjoyment), and the worth of science and art—and a space of futurity: a location where modernity has already taken shape and is going to evolve—at least unless Leonardo and his allies are thwarted—into our future. This, as I suggested earlier, is a rhetorical strategy by which audience members are made to identify with the Florentine collective identity: in the act of identification they are both laying the foundations of Western modernity and enjoying the fruits of their vicarious endeavors. Florence functions as the locus of a transcultural collective identity available to all who buy into the logic of heteronormative modernity.

This proves all the more disappointing as *Da Vinci's Demons* premiered on the same network that had aired *Spartacus*, perhaps the most gay-friendly of all action series, and it benefitted from an early ratings boost by following the latter's finale and later taking over its time slot. In addition to copious scenes of barely dressed buff men, *Spartacus* offered an altogether rarer commodity: a mature homosexual romance. Agron and Nasir's relationship has yet to be matched in genre television in terms of intimacy and authenticity, and, in a series in which most heroes met a tragic end, the two were allowed to walk happily into the sunset. As they cross the Alps and leave Roman territory for good, leading a band of women, children, and wounded veterans, the two are the only couple to survive. In their newfound adamic dimension, the two herald the potential for what José Esteban Muñoz referred to as a "queer futurity." Writing against the future as a "fantasy of heterosexual reproduction," the late theoretician argued that "heterosexual culture depends on a notion of the future" that it normatively enforces (49). Yet he also found hope in the potential of "anticipatory illuminations," a term he took over from Ernst Bloch, to reveal a utopian horizon and to imagine a future beyond heteronormative conventions (Muñoz 7). *Da Vinci's Demons*, like most historical fiction, only evinces counterfeit anticipatory illuminations that serve to reproduce the normative structures of contemporary society.

When these structures are threatened—when characters crucial to cultural memory are depicted as queer, for example—the mainstream response is often driven by panic and anxiety. Documenting the conservative reception (both by professional historians and members of the public) to Larry Kramer's allegation of Abraham Lincoln's homosexuality, Morris writes:

> I turn to the notion of homosexual panic, the homophobic terror of guilt by homosexual association that subtly governs our social bonds and warrants visceral and vicious responses to any potential encroachment by the queer contagion. In view of the magnitude of Lincoln's memory in forging our collective, national identity, with obvious implications for individual identity, conviction of his homosexuality would necessarily implicate us all, by means of this inescapable heritage, as practitioners and progenitors of same-sex love [103].

Morris' dual model of "practitioners and progenitors" largely corresponds with my own understanding of the role played by identification in historical adaptations, and I think his emphasis on homosexual panic as the impetus behind straightwashing is very much warranted. To counter Leonardo's "inescapable heritage," *Da Vinci's Demons* constructs its heteronormative futurity, employing an aesthetics that is largely governed by homosexual panic. As I will show, the series routinely frames queer encounters negatively and repetitively assures viewers of Leonardo's heteronormativity, even as it allows him to engage in homosexual activity. Why it even portrays such activity in the first place can, I believe, be attributed to the fact that its ideal audience is liberal and secular (the series presents religion as a corruptive force and patriarchy as damaging to women's natural abilities, places particular emphasis on an individual's ability to effect progressive political change, and features frank sex scenes and violent content) and that it presumably has access to a source even as rudimentary as Wikipedia. I would also argue that the producers' interviews with The Backlot should not simply be read as cynical attempts to dupe gay viewers; instead, I would like to entertain the possibility that they genuinely believed that their depiction of Leonardo's sexuality was respectful and inclusive of gay viewers, and that their failure in turn betrays contemporary American society's deep-seated heteronormative assumptions. But while the producers may have paid lip service to the idea of a gay Leonardo, such an understanding remains altogether absent from the series itself.

The very first episode of the series includes two homosexual encounters, and both are framed as negative, transgressive interactions. The first of these scenes begins provocatively with the Duke of Milan (played by Hugh Bonneville) curtly dismissing a much younger male sexual partner in the morning, only to be surprisingly stabbed in the neck soon after, at a Palm Sunday church service by an agent of the Vatican Secret Archives (the Pope's intelligence agency, as it were). The casting of Bonneville as the Duke exploits the fame he had achieved by playing another aristocrat, the Earl of Grantham, on the hit series *Downton Abbey* (2010–) in order to thwart viewers' expectations: unlike the stiff, mild-mannered English patriarch, the Duke is boorish, vulgar, and sexually promiscuous—a suggestion to audiences that they should not be expecting a conventional historical drama. The Duke is introduced in one of the towers of his fortress (the room itself is beautifully furnished, if ravished by what appears to have been a night of debauchery). He is naked and urinating in a kind of Renaissance chamber pot. He has a strong, traditionally masculine body, the heteronormative luster of which is marred slightly by middle age and the presence of a gut. He appears to be thoroughly unashamed of the situation as he kicks his catamite out of bed, dismissively referring to him as "boy." The young man is not even given a chance to put his clothes on before the Duke again orders him to go, slapping him on the buttocks in front of a small Christian shrine. The tone is jovial and satirical. A short conversation with his butler informs us that the Duke is married with children and that they are waiting for him at church—where the duke will soon meet his abrupt end. This brief scene already connects homosexuality and Christianity, and the Duke's death at the hands of an agent of the Vatican might have suggested that his death serves as punishment for immoral behavior, had the series not thoroughly discredited the Papacy as a moral center by the end of the same episode in a scene that also employs homosexuality for shock value.

Pope Sixtus IV is introduced alongside a male lover, only this time the boy appears to be strikingly younger, and the Pope holds a dagger to his neck as they are both submerged into one of the Vatican's sinister underground swimming pools. The tone is appropriately creepy, as the scene opens to a close-up of an older, bald man holding a boy in his arms (Matthew Tennyson, who plays the character referred to simply as "altar boy" in the credits, would have been in his early twenties, but his small stature, hairless body, and adolescent facial features make him look about fourteen [Curtis]). The boy's back rests on the man's chest, and the man caresses the boy's jaw with his left hand while holding a knife to his neck with his right. Both are naked, but the water shadows the boy's genitalia. The man asks if the boy is frightened and the boy answers that he is not, calling the man "Most Holy Father." The boy is clearly uncomfortable, as he fixes his gaze upward and twitches when the man caresses his face. The man entertains a theological argument, as he moves his left hand toward the boy's genital area and out of the shot. He tells the boy that "lying is a sin … it separates us from God's grace," and the entire scene builds up to a forced half-kiss, after the man commands the boy to answer truthfully whether he wants to enter the kingdom of God. They are interrupted by the Pope's lieutenants, who report that they have been successful in assassinating the Duke (an ally of the Medici) and that Florence "is ripe for the picking." As the Pope exits the swimming pool, viewers are given a better view of his body (old, with rather scrawny arms and an air of general flabbiness) and a brief glance of his flaccid penis. He leaves the room after discussing plans for toppling Florence and one of the men, whom the Pope has identified as his nephew (Count Girolamo Riario, later revealed to be his son), cuts the boy's throat for having heard their plans (and not because he was the Pope's victim, which suggests that his sexual proclivities do not need to be protected). The scene embraces a number of anti–Catholic prejudices—pedophilia, abuse of power, the corrupting and absolute influence of the Pope—all of which are still present in American cultural memory.

While the two homosexual relations are presented as shocking and ethically dubious, the series clearly makes a distinction between them, portraying the latter as substantially worse. The boy is younger, he appears to be taken against his will, the threat of violence is far more readily apparent, and, of course, the former is only suggested while the latter is shown. The contrast between the two older men is also worth noting: while the Duke is generally fit and leonine, the Pope appears almost impotent (both literally, as attested by his flaccid penis, and figuratively, as he leaves the boy's murder to Riario). It seems that the farther one is from Florence's best interests, the worse one's actions are: the ally is dubious but amusing, the adversary is a complete monster. In order to strengthen viewer identification, the series constructs a moral universe with Florence and ultimately Leonardo at its center.

The two homosexual relations are fairly historically accurate with regard to Renaissance sexual norms: the active partner is a mature man and the passive partner an adolescent boy, and this serves to mark them as strange and unfamiliar. In contrast, almost all of the main heterosexual relationships are familiarizing and written from a presentist perspective, with both partners presented as equals enjoying a rewarding experience. Heterosexual love even often appears as a form of salvation: Lucrezia is literally saved by Leonardo (and made better by his love), Vanessa's relationship with Giuliano de' Medici (played by Tom Bateman) helps her to transcend her low social status, and the adultery of Clarice Orsini (played by Lara Pulver) with Carlo de' Medici (played by Ray Fearon), her husband Lorenzo's illegitimate uncle, helps her to amass and consolidate power unthinkable for a woman of her time. Ultimately, all of these relationships are shaped by contemporary structures of desire and exist in the service of the series' counterfeit anticipatory illumination: they posit modern heteronormative love as one of the loci of our present futurity.

At the same time, this first episode erases or obscures much of Leonardo's own homosexuality. An early scene meant to give viewers a better understanding of his character has him painting a topless Vanessa, as he recounts a memory from when he was six months old: after his mother had left his cradle in the field, a falcon flew down, perched on the cradle's handle, and stared at the babe, "almost as if it were trying to reveal some kind of mystery," as Leonardo puts it. Aside from a later passionate kiss between the two, which appears to be there solely to establish Leonardo's interest in women, the scene seems relatively unproblematic—yet it conceals one of the most powerful rewritings of historical fact. In the passage from the *Codex Atlanticus* on which the event is based, Leonardo describes being attacked by a kite as an infant, which opened his mouth with its tail, and which proceeded to strike him a number of times with its tail against his lips, a passage that was famously read by Sigmund Freud as a passive homosexual fantasy and opened up the subject of Leonardo's sexual nature to discussion (Crompton 266). As such, the scene erases a foundational moment for Leonardo's link to queer cultural memory—and then further suppresses it by following it up with a heterosexual kiss. If straight anxiety has not been sufficiently assuaged, by the end of the episode, Leonardo has already bedded his love-at-first-sight Lucrezia in a fairly graphic sex scene (which is also quite glamorous and clearly meant for viewer titillation, unlike the two homosexual scenes).

There is one brief hint in the first episode that Leonardo might have at least a little sexual interest in men: at a bar with Nico and Zoroaster, he is propositioned by an effeminate, young model/hustler, whom he curtly dismisses, although not without later admitting that the youthful male is "pleasing to the eye," a line Riley delivers with a wry, knowing smile. The same young man, Jacopo Saltarelli, returns in the fifth episode of the series, titled "The Tower," and testifies before court that Leonardo had sodomized him, as part of a papal plot to discredit the artist. The episode largely follows the same narrative logic of undermining Leonardo's homosexuality while assuaging viewers of his fundamental straightness. In an early court scene (the Renaissance judicial system is updated so as to be perfectly intelligible to contemporary viewers), Leonardo offers an impassioned defense of the right to intimacy and describes accusations of sodomy as stemming "from a wellspring of ignorance." This is hardly a radical defense of queerness, but the series nevertheless feels it necessary to follow it with a quick banter between Vanessa and Zoroaster which reminds viewers that Leonardo had deflowered her when she was a nun. Later, after Leonardo is cleared of his crime (in a plot development that involves a naked judge tied to a pig and projected over the Florentine night sky via an early camera obscura), Jacopo confronts him once more and reveals that he had clear proof of Leonardo's deed (a drawing of Jacopo with an erect penis), but that he wanted him exposed and not killed. He accuses Leonardo of only being with women out of fear, but the latter claims that desire "is not as simple as one sex or the other," apologizes to Jacopo (having realized that his "experiments and curiosities ... are not always without cost"), and kisses him goodbye. The episode cuts to a scene of Leonardo and Lucrezia naked in a bathtub, as she shaves and cleans him following weeks of detention. A grateful Leonardo mouths a double entendre, reaches for her genital area, and the scene later ends, characteristically, in straight sex. *Da Vinci's Demons*, therefore, manages the paradoxical feat of being the first television series to depict Leonardo kissing another man while simultaneously making it feel completely inconsequential, if not downright insulting. Besides reducing his homosexuality to an experiment or curiosity, the series, ever faithful to a narrative logic governed by gay panic, follows it up with a scene in which heterosexuality can easily be read as cleansing and restorative—as a final excision of the "queer contagion." In the thirteen episodes that followed during the remainder of season one and all of season two, the series apparently did not feel the need to revisit the question of Leonardo's queerness—or to give space to LGBTQ visibility, for that matter.

   Da Vinci's Demons remains a series deeply animated by the politics of straightwashing. In reducing Leonardo's queerness to one brief experiment, the series proposes a heteronormative version of the Renaissance polymath, governed by a narrative logic of appeasing heterosexual anxiety and avoiding gay panic. Ultimately, *Da Vinci's Demons* creates a space within which its audience can project itself and vicariously relive the birth of the modern world. However, the world it contains as well as the one it foreshadows leave little room for either the queer subject or the queer viewer.

ACKNOWLEDGEMENT

My research for this essay was enabled by UEFISCDI grant PN-II-RU-TE 2014–4-0609, *Representations of Violence in Contemporary American Popular Culture* (Project Coordinator: Associate Professor Mihaela Precup).

WORKS CITED

Ayers, Dennis. "Banishing 'DaVinci's Demons.'" *The Backlot*, 12 January 2014. Web. 28 February 2015. http://www.thebacklot.com/banishing-davincis-demons/01/2014/.

Boswell, John. "Revolutions, Universals, and Sexual Categories." *Hidden from History: Reclaiming the Gay and Lesbian Past*. Ed. Martin Duberman, Martha Vicinus, and George Chauncey, Jr. New York: Meridian, 1989. 17–36. Print.

Bowen, Daniel. "Da Vinci, Lincoln, and Liberace: Why 'Straight-Washing' Homosexuality in the Media Needs to Stop." *What Culture*, 14 January 2013. Web. 28 February 2015. http://whatculture.com/tv/da-vinci-lincoln-and-liberace-why-straight-washing-homosexuality-in-the-media-needs-to-stop.php.

Bronski, Michael. *A Queer History of the United States*. Boston: Beacon Press, 2011. Print.

Butterfield, Herbert. *The Whig Interpretation of History (1931)*. Electronic Library of Historiography. N.pag. February 2002. Web. 25 October 2014. http://www.eliohs.unifi.it/testi/900/butterfield.

Crompton, Louis. *Homosexuality and Civilization*. Cambridge: Belknap Press, 2003. Print.

Cruz, Eliel. "Op-Ed: NBC's Straight-Washing of John Constantine Is Bi Erasure." *Advocate*, 28 July 2014. Web. 28 February 2015.

Curtis, Nick. "Bright Young Things." *Evening Standard*, 20 November 2012. Web. 28 February 2015.

"Da Vinci's Demons—Trailer." *YouTube*, 18 January 2013. Web. 28 February 2015. https://www.youtube.com/watch?v=vgg9nnALFGA.

Dover, K.J. *Greek Homosexuality*. Cambridge: Harvard University Press, 1978. Print.

"Famous Gay Men: List of Gay Men Throughout History." *Ranker*, n.d. Web. 12 December 2015. http://www.ranker.com/list/famous-gay-men-list-of-gay-men-throughout-history/famous-gay-and-lesbian?page=24.

Feinberg, Larry J. *The Young Leonardo: Art and Life in Fifteenth-Century Florence*. New York: Cambridge University Press, 2011. Print.

Freud, Sigmund. *Leonardo da Vinci: A Psychosexual Study of an Infantile Reminiscence*. Trans. A.A. Brill. New York: Moffat, Yard, and Company, 1916. *Project Gutenberg*, 12 November 2010. Web. 1 March 2015. http://www.gutenberg.org/files/34300/34300-h/34300-h.htm.

Hall, Donald E. *Queer Theories*. New York: Palgrave Macmillan, 2003. Print.

Halperin, David M. "Is There a History of Sexuality?" *The Lesbian and Gay Studies Reader*. Ed. Henry Abelove, Michèle Aina Barale, and David M. Halperin. New York: Routledge, 1993. 416–431. Print.

_____. "Sex Before Sexuality: Pederasty, Politics, and Power in Classical Athens." *Hidden from History: Reclaiming the Gay and Lesbian Past*. Ed. Martin Duberman, Martha Vicinus, and George Chauncey. New York: Meridian, 1989. 37–53. Print.

Halterman, Jim. "'Da Vinci's Demons' Creator David S. Goyer Talks Not 'Shying Away' from Anything." *The Backlot*, 8 January 2013. Web. 28 February 2015. http://www. thebacklot.com/davincis-demons-creator-david-s-goyer-talks-not-shying-away-from-anything/01/2013/.

_____. "'Da Vinci's Demons' Sodomy Trial Post-Mortem: Tom Riley and David S. Goyer." *The Backlot*, 13 May 2013. Web. 28 February 2015. http://www.thebacklot. com/da-vincis-demons-interview-tom-riley-david-s-goyer/05/2013/.

_____. "Defining Da Vinci: Tom Riley Previews This Week's Revealing Episode." *The Backlot*, 9 May 2013. Web. 28 February 2015. http://www.thebacklot.com/defin ing-da-vinci-tom-riley-previews-this-weeks-revealing-episode/05/2013/.

Kemp, Martin. *Leonardo da Vinci: The Marvellous Works of Nature and Man*. New York: Oxford University Press, 2006. Print.

Mason, David. "Comment: Continued LGBT Discrimination at the BBC Would Let Down a New Generation." *PinkNews*, 2 April 2012. Web. 28 February 2015. http:// www. pinknews.co.uk/2012/04/02/comment-continued-gay-discrimination-at-the-bbc-would-let-down-a-new-generation/.

Mikelonis, Daniel. "'Da Vinci's Demons': Let Sleeping Geniuses Lie." *The Backlot*, 1 June 2013. Web. 28 February 2015. http://www.thebacklot.com/davincis-demons-let-sleeping-geniuses-lie/06/2013/.

_____. "'Da Vinci's Demons': Well, Apparently History Is a Lie." *The Backlot*, 13 April 2013. Web. 28 February 2015. http://www.thebacklot.com/davincis-demons-recap-well-apparently-history-is-a-lie/04/2013/.

_____. "Leonardo's Sexuality in 'Da Vinci's Demons' and Famous Gay Folks That Could Be Straight-Washed." *The Backlot*, 1 November 2012. Web. 28 February 2015. http://www.thebacklot.com/leonardos-sexuality-in-da-vincis-demons-and-famous-gay-folks-that-could-be-straight-washed/11/2012/.

_____. "Why Leonardo's as Yet Undefined Sexuality in 'Da Vinci's Demons' May Be a Step Forward." *The Backlot*, 7 November 2012. Web. 28 February 2015. http:// www.newnownext.com/why-leonardos-as-yet-undefined-sexuality-in-da-vincis-demons-may-be-a-step-forward/11/2012/.

Morris, Charles E., III. "My Old Kentucky Homo: Abraham Lincoln, Larry Kramer, and the Politics of Queer Memory." *Queering Public Address: Sexualities in American Historical Discourse*. Ed. Charles E. Morris III. Columbia: University of South Carolina Press, 2007. 93–120. Print.

Muñoz, José Esteban. *Cruising Utopia: The Then and There of Queer Futurity*. New York: New York University Press, 2009. Print.

Nededog, Jethro. "'Da Vinci's Demons' Creator Says 'We're Not Backing Away' from Leonardo's Bisexuality." *The Wrap*, 11 January 2014. Web. 28 February 2015. http:// www.thewrap.com/starz-davincis-demons-gay-bisexual-leonardo-season–2/.

Richards, Stuart. "*The Imitation Game* and the 'Straightwashing' of Film." *The Drum*, 6 January 2015. Web. 28 February 2015. http://www.abc.net.au/news/2015–01–06/richards-the-imitation-game-and-the-straightwashing-of-film/6001864.

Rocke, Michael. *Forbidden Friendships: Homosexuality and Male Culture in Renaissance Florence*. New York: Oxford University Press, 1996. Print.

Shariatmadari, David. "Straightwashing at the Movies: The Pride DVD Shows Gay People Still Make the Film Industry Nervous." *Guardian*, 6 January 2015. Web. 1 March 2015.

Sparky. "Straightwashing GBLT Characters." *Fangs for the Fantasy*, 17 May 2013. Web. 28 February 2015. http://www.fangsforthefantasy.com/2013/05/straightwashing-gblt-characters.html.

Stern, Keith. *Queers in History: The Comprehensive Encyclopedia of Historical Gays, Lesbians, Bisexuals, and Transgenders*. Dallas: Benbella, 2009. Print.
Wittkower, Margot, and Rudolf Wittkower. *Born Under Saturn: The Character and Conduct of Artists (A Documented History from Antiquity to the French Revolution)*. New York: New York Review Books, 2007. Print.

Racial Homophily and Homogeneity as Post-Racial Commodification in *BrokeStraightBoys.tv*

Michael Johnson, Jr.

The emergence of reality TV presaged a new era in U.S. television. Today, viewers' familiarity with the genre has resulted in a decline in its popularity. However, this essay examines a new incarnation of the genre with the emergence of *BrokeStraightBoys.tv* (2014–), also known simply as *Broke Straight Boys* as well as *Broke Straight Boys TV*, on the Here TV channel. But its appearance there is not quite what it may seem, given that viewers do not access this new reality series through a typical cable network provider. Instead, in lieu of that sort of traditional distribution system, viewers pay a monthly subscription fee to access the Here TV Premium channel on YouTube, where the series airs. During the series' first season, subscribers were granted access to a total of eight episodes of drama-filled reality programming, ranging in length from twenty to forty minutes each, totaling approximately three hours of content (Here).

Until very recently, pornography was something regarded as socially unacceptable by most members of "polite society"—porn stars remained social outcasts and were usually associated with prostitution, and, as a consequence, pornography was something one watched in private but did not talk about in public. Because *BrokeStraightBoys.tv*'s target demographic is primarily gay men, the significance posed by this challenge cannot be overstated, especially given the relative importance that adult film has for the gay male demographic in the United States during an era punctuated by easy and ready technological accessibility like that available through the Internet (Dixon; Jensen; Thomas). Indeed, according to Joe Thomas, by 2010

> the important studios had expanded their web presence—offering pictures, streaming video, and downloads—to the point that Falcon [a major gay pornography studio] expected Internet revenues to exceed wholesale [revenues].... Entirely new studios also emerged with products that were exclusively available as subscription services on the web.... In fact, the Internet soon became major competition to the established studios [75].

Thomas ultimately argues that with the "explosion of Internet porn and the growth of overseas studios, gay porn is clearly a full participant in the new globalized economy" (81). The popularity of pornography in gay culture is related to an identity-making practice, and at least one study has found that gay men view pornographic videos and Internet pornography at more than twice the rate of heterosexual men (Duggan and McCreary 51–52).

According to Thomas, among members of the gay male demographic, pornography has historically enjoyed an elevated position of worth relative to other types of media depictions of same-sex desire. He states, "Porn has always held a more accepted, even exalted position in gay culture than in straight; as sexual outlaws, gays were less concerned about being called perverts.... What better way to assert a gay identity than by the open, casual acceptance and celebration of homophobically dreaded sex acts?" (Thomas 82). Thomas' assertion is supported by other scholars including Michael Bronski, who argues that the "omnipresence of sexual imagery in gay media— even beyond pornography—has been explained as a way for gays to create a 'positive definition' for themselves" (166). Given the foregoing importance that gay pornography has in the popular consciousness of many (though admittedly not all) gay men, it makes sense that a reality TV series like *BrokeStraightBoys.tv* would generate a significant degree of interest among, if not also have a profound impact on the viewing habits of, its target viewers.

As I have argued elsewhere, "Within the wider cultural framework, mainstream gay pornography has a special relationship with the subculture to which it caters.... For gay men, [this relationship becomes] constituted and cemented in the popular consciousness explicitly through the influential discourses of same-sex desire and sexuality depicted in gay pornography" (182–183). *BrokeStraightBoys.tv* accomplishes this same goal, albeit through a different mechanism that leverages audience members' interest in gay porn actors—except without the explicit depiction of sexual acts. It is precisely because the series is "explicitly asexual" that gay men may be even more attracted and incentivized to watch these actors' non-performative behaviors as a potential insight into their "authentic" selves (presumably an identity only perceivable outside of the sexual settings of their employment). Increasingly, gay porn has moved beyond simple scenes of sexual activity to focus more on plot devices, story arcs, character development, and even serialization in order to remain relevant in the highly competitive digital era, giving rise to viewer interest in actors' off-screen lives.

This phenomenon, whereby the subject of the *straight* male porn actors' lives are examined in much closer detail, in circumstances explicitly outside of the pornographic scenes that viewers are typically accustomed to, makes the series especially titillating and provocative because of its illusion of behind-the-scenes intimacy. What follows is my assessment of both the influence of the series in terms of the messages it communicates to its target audience and the political economic meanings associated with those messages. This essay will also investigate the series' messages about the humanity of its employee/actor/cast members' sexual labor within a highly competitive milieu of mass-mediated commodities and the influence such competition has on televisual racial diversity in an allegedly "post-racial" society.

First, I describe the theoretical background and methodologies employed in this research. Second, I briefly summarize the literature on reality TV and its application to this series. Third, I diagram and explain the complex negotiations that straight men face in their capacity as "gay-for-pay" pornographic actors and in regard to the corresponding economics of their performance. Finally, I conclude with an assessment of the series in terms of its racial politics as applied to its production, distribution, and conspicuous consumption. Although *BrokeStraightBoys.tv* offers only the briefest glimpses of pornographic scenes and alludes to the choreographed preparation required for them, the series itself is intrinsically wedded to the employment of its actors and the ensuing personal and socioeconomic struggles that arise from their unique choice of employment.

Sharif Mowlabocus contends that "gay porn is securing the parameters of gay identity, forming ever more impenetrable boundaries and validating a set of identifications and practices at the expense of all others. If the potential of homosexual pornography is to *queer* reality, then the reality of gay porn serves to condense homosexuality into a single overarching identity; one that does little to challenge hegemonic norms or liberate sexuality" (71, original emphasis). However, I would argue that *BrokeStraightBoys.tv* attempts to illustrate the normalcy of a type of *heterosexualized* liberation from the traditional homonormative foundations of gay pornography by bringing to the screen depictions of gay-for-pay performers as human beings irreducible to their bodily, sexual functions, complete with life goals, aspirations, and problems that most people face outside of the bedroom and other sexual settings. Of course, this is not to say that the series does not suffer from a number of equally problematic issues which, to some extent, undermine its liberatory potential. Ron Becker suggests that there is plenty of evidence to explain how this liberation has come to pass:

Television's queer straight guys certainly suggest that the relationship between hegemonic masculinity and (homo)sexuality is shifting. It would be surprising if it weren't, since LGBTQ political activism and cultural visibility [have] destabilized elements important to certain heteronormative configurations of gender, desire, and identity.... LGBTQ politics ... have advanced alternative ways to think about the purposes of erotic pleasure and have helped normalize a wide range of sexual practices [124].

Becker ultimately wonders "how different straight male sexuality might look in an actually realized post-closet culture where being gay is defined by one's cultural identity rather than one's sexual practice, where the line between gay and straight is assumed secure, and where one's masculinity is not defined by one's repudiation of homosexuality or haunted by the closet" (133). As such, he raises an intriguing and difficult question. One answer might lie in the proliferation of gay-for-pay male actors in the gay porn industry, given the increasing frequency with which these straight men willingly perform gay sex acts (to varying degrees of consumer persuasiveness), especially when they conceive of their gay sex acts perpetually through "heterosexual lenses" of performativity.

BrokeStraightBoys.tv is rife with examples that attempt to answer Becker's question. In the first episode of the series, Denver Grand enthusiastically defines his job as follows: "I have sex with guys, *like they're girls*. That's what I do." For Denver at least, his gay sex acts represent a type of heterosexualized sex, albeit with a male substitution. Another example includes the developing romance between Paul Canon and Damien Kyle, which is featured in the eighth episode. Although Damien has consistently maintained his bisexuality, Paul's original heterosexual identity is depicted as changing to a more fluid one only *after* he has become employed with BluMedia's *BrokeStraightBoys.tv*. But before going into further detail about the depictions offered to viewers through *BrokeStraightBoys.tv* and the concomitant inferences one might draw from the scenes between its performers, I must first explain both the theoretical and methodological approaches utilized in this research. For the purposes of this analysis, given the ways by which this reality television series is both branded by its creators and marketed to consumers, I adopt Jonathan Gray's argument of interpreting popular telenarratives as "entertainment" commodities (811). To that end, I employ a mixed methodology that combines both textual and political economic analysis.

Methodology

Textual analysis, which focuses on discursive forces present in a text, is an important means of understanding how individuals and societies constitute themselves and make sense of the larger world in which they live. It can usefully interrogate how mass-mediated commodities create identities and "construct authoritative truths" (Saukko 23) for those who use (or are represented as using) them, thereby illuminating the participatory (or non-participatory) role social actors possess in the creation, reflection, and consumption of those truths. The multiple interpretations of a given "text" frequently look different when they are examined in relation to other texts or social sensibilities; as such, the task of analysis is not to ascertain the "most correct" reading but rather to explore some of the possible and undiscovered interpretations embedded in the targets of textual analysis. This proposition is particularly applicable to the study of mass-mediated commodities that engender strong feelings within the reality TV genre as manifested through images and sounds that "invite the reader to 'feel and feel' and, thereby, feel in touch with the real" (Saukko 109). Accordingly, this research examines *BrokeStraightBoys.tv* as a type of audiovisual telenarrative text and commodity. It utilizes textual analysis to examine the method by which this telenarrative "text" gains social value over time through its conspicuous consumption by its gay male audience. Necessary to this examination is an investigation that determines the degree to which viewers consume mass-mediated commodities like this series, which is created through a corporatized process of production involving financial transactions whose economic profits accrue in only one direction.

As T.V. Reed points out, "Whatever else popular culture may be, it is deeply embedded in capitalist, for-profit mass production" (141). The strength of textual analysis lies in its ability to expose the (1) discourses through which texts communicate their messages, (2) sociopolitical contexts by which those messages are situated or mediated, and (3) lived experiences those messages attempt to represent or replicate. While attempting to get to the "truth" of a particular target, textual analysis facilitates multiple, multidimensional, nuanced, and tentative ways of understanding while frequently employing deconstructive techniques that expose the "historicity, political investments, omissions, and blind spots of social 'truths'" (Saukko 21) that are understood as possessing their own continuously contested but often tightly regulated possibilities. This essay's political economic analysis examines how exchanges of both financial and social capital, along with socioeconomic labor practices, give rise to—or undermine—different kinds of social relations between consumers, employees, and business owners. One of the questions this mixed methodology attempts to answer, therefore, is how do consumers' social relationships to telenarrative commodities such as *BrokeStraightBoys.tv* work in tandem with evolving conceptions of socioeconomic value for an explicitly gay male audience? In this regard, I argue that *BrokeStraightBoys.tv's* value is directly proportional to the belief that the scenes viewers are exposed to are convincingly "authentic" or "real." But what does "reality" mean in relation to "reality TV" today, and who decides? What is "real" and what is not? This has been a perpetual question since the appearance of reality television programming. If the episodes and/or scenes that audience members watch are contrived, what then constitutes the claim of "reality" promulgated and marketed by such series?

Verisimilitude and "Reality" Television

As Mark Andrejevic has noted, one distinguishing element that television networks and series producers emphasize with regard to reality television programs is that "the surveillance of the characters is, for the period they are on the show, comprehensive.... The premise of the show is that the cast members live in a kind of panopticon—not everything they are doing is taped and watched, but they have to live with the knowledge that at any moment, their words and actions could be taped for broadcast" (260). However, in the case of *BrokeStraightBoys.tv*, this phenomenon does not really apply. Throughout the entire first season, the viewer is never exposed to the kinds of uniform surveillance to which Andrejevic refers. The series' format does not reproduce many of the typical surveillance tropes commonly associated with related sorts of series, such as CBS's *Big Brother* (2000–), that it attempts to emulate. Although this essay does not attempt to measure *BrokeStraightBoys.tv* against the ephemeral definition of what constitutes true "reality," I do intend to explore the way this definition "functions to reinforce the logic of a surveillance-based [commodity]" (Andrejevic 260) whose consumption is predicated upon viewers' belief in the veracity of the events that unfold before their eyes, as well as the economic inferences one can draw from such consumption. Moreover, as Andrejevic makes clear, series such as *BrokeStraightBoys.tv* function as a type of cultural exemplar that "ought not be considered in isolation from the socioeconomic contexts within which they emerge and gain a certain degree of acceptance" (260).

Indeed, the attraction to *BrokeStraightBoys.tv* is at least partially related to what Andrejevic contends is the myth offered up by such series, whereby "audience members gain meaningful control over the content of television programming when that programming becomes 'real.' They are no longer force-fed the rehashed formulas pounded out by hack Hollywood scriptwriters.... Content becomes liberated from the inbred coterie of scriptwriters and directors, to be replaced by the spontaneous rhythms of real conflict and real romance" (261) that hallmark *BrokeStraightBoys.tv* across the various episodes of its first season. Series like *BrokeStraightBoys.tv* reinforce the value of this marketing strategy, which equates self-disclosure with freedom and authenticity, while simultaneously suggesting that televisual realness can be guaranteed through the persistent gaze of a camera (Andrejevic 268). This endorsement of the camera's gaze as a validation mechanism of authenticity is the method by which audiences are assured that the images and actions they are being exposed to are "real," as is the case with most reality TV programs. Given that the target audience for *BrokeStraightBoys.tv* is already incentivized (as I have previously established), audience members' reliance on the verisimilitude of the series, episode by episode, takes on even greater social significance.

The series' debut episode, which is titled "Welcome to Broke Straight Boys" and aired on December 19, 2014, is tagged with the following description:

> Broke Straight Boys is a reality-based docu-series that explores the world of "Gay for Pay," a term used to describe when straight men do gay porn for money. The show focuses on the people involved in this taboo and unconventional lifestyle, exploring the dynamic relationships between the owner of Blu-Media, Mark Erickson, his business staff, and the young men who choose to do gay porn to supplement their income by performing for the adult website broke-straightboys.com. As dysfunctional a family as you will ever find, this group of colorful characters *keep you mesmerized at every moment.* From seeing them rehearse scenes in the studio to hearing their unbelievable perspective on life, money, and the pursuit of porn, *you won't be able to look away, even when you want to.* In this episode, a new group of performers arrives at the website owner's mansion for BSB orientation [Here, emphasis added].

From the very beginning, viewers are introduced and acclimated to the expectation that they will be given a behind-the-scenes view of the lives of these actors; the metaphorical language is instructive. It is equally compelling that the description includes the term "docu-series," which invokes the representational belief that the series mimics a hybrid type of documentary. Yet, even in the introductory montage of the series' first episode, viewers learn that "every noise you make is fake, every thrust you do is fake" from the lips of Kaden Alexander, the series' only cast member of color. This disclosure functions in juxtaposition to the series' description of a kind of hybrid documentary to further elaborate upon the "insider's view" gained by one's subscription to the show. Words and phrases such as "colorful characters," "mesmerized," and "dysfunctional" serve as signposts to audience members (and potential viewers as a marketing device) to expect that the series will provide them with a very specific type of performance from its cast members. Moreover, this description further operates to fulfill viewers' expectations that the series will traffic in familiar tropes that can be found within the genre.

In the episode "Welcome to Broke Straight Boys," viewers' expectations are indeed fulfilled when the "boys" are shown being picked up and traveling to their ultimate destination: the home of BluMedia owner Mark Erickson.

This large, modernist home, located in a suburban/rural setting, is emblematic of the reality TV formula with which many viewers are already well familiar. This setting, where the vast majority of the series' action takes place, is reminiscent of the large homes found on *Big Brother, The Real World* (1992–), and other reality telenarratives that rely upon ostentatious displays of socioeconomic wealth (in terms of overall square footage, leisure amenities, and ready accessibility to entertainment opportunities) as an enticement to series participants. The similarities do not end with setting, as viewers soon find the cast members traveling to Las Vegas in episode two, titled "Viva Las Vegas." Its description states, "The guys who are 21 and over take a trip to Las Vegas to promote brokestraightboys.com in the clubs and have some fun" (Here). While they are there, viewers find that their employer spends lavishly on his male employees in terms of nightclub entertainment and a stretch Hummer limousine. These are the prototypical characteristics commonly associated with other reality television series, wherein participants eventually accrue material wealth by virtue of their participation. The same rings true with regard to *BrokeStraightBoys.tv*, with the exception that, in this case, the participants are employees rather than contestants. Indeed, just about a minute into the premiere episode's opening montage, viewers learn that "gay porn pays 10X more than straight porn"; these words are accompanied by endorsements from Denver and Cage Kafig. But the series has a very significant dilemma differentiating between the two categories: Are these employees also contestants in a larger, more complex socioeconomic game of chance wherein those who "win" are rewarded and those who "lose" are punished (perhaps with termination)?

Another common trope of the reality television genre is that losing contestants must eventually leave the house (or other setting) of the series. In episode three, "The Moment of Truth," viewers see Denver leave the house in a conflicted, emotional scene that invokes the dual images of "loser contestant" and "employee termination." Not coincidentally, his departure symbolically communicates the unambiguous message to the privileged few remaining about the need to stay relevant in a highly competitive market of sexual attraction, with its demands for constantly new (and disposable) faces. Contemporaneous with Denver's unexpected departure is the arrival of the only Broke Straight Boy of color, Kaden, an attractive, young African American man with a winning smile and a slight but muscular build. Their exchange of place is not lost on viewers when one examines the significance of this development in relation to the pornography industry and its highly prescribed but somewhat limited availability of racial diversity—until this moment, in terms of the overall composition of the residents of the house, the possibility of having sexual scenes with a man of color has not existed. The racial politics of sexual desire are in many ways directly related to the employability of at least one man in the series. However, the financial consequences of sex work of this kind are also accompanied by an array of adjacent antagonisms that implicate the stability of personal relationships while also calling into question the legitimacy of some men's public performativity of heterosexuality.

I am much less concerned with the economic profitability of the industry as a whole than with the working conditions and financial justifications behind why the actors on *BrokeStraightBoys.tv* appear to be so financially motivated (as they regularly cite money as a primary factor behind their choice of employment) and what influence, if any, money has in terms of advancing a "queerer heterosexuality" among the members of the series' cast. Notably in this regard, Jane Ward states:

> The characterization of straight-identified MSMs [men who have sex with men] as closeted also exemplifies the persistent tendency to view sex *acts* as meaningful and objective indicators of a true sexual selfhood and to gloss over larger questions about the gendered and racialized construction of heterosexual and homosexual categories.... The recent insistence that MSMs are actually closeted gay men constrained by ... culturally internal forms of homophobia has helped to solidify a narrow and essentialist conceptualization of homophobia [415, original emphasis].

Pointedly, "The Moment of Truth" episode finds Kaden out on a date with a white girl, whereupon he incrementally discloses the truth about his chosen profession as a gay-for-pay actor. Sadly, his date reacts very emotionally to this news and abandons him with a contrived excuse, to which he responds that "there are more fish in the sea." At least in this example, viewers are compelled to infer that occurrences like this one are commonplace for heterosexually identified men in similar situations; in this regard, Ward's assertions about the meaningfulness of sex acts as objective indicators rings true not only for some men, but also frequently for their potential partners. Indeed, in the same episode viewers are also introduced to the stories of self-disclosure pertaining to Paul Canon and Jimmy Johnson in relation to their family members and friends and the wide array of reactions that result from sharing such news with those most important in these men's lives.

Accordingly, it is perhaps of little surprise when the series directly challenges audience members' notions of the authenticity and stability of its cast members' heterosexuality in its fifth episode, "Someone's Gotta Go," when viewers end up discovering just how "straight" these "gay-for-pay" actors really are as they "undergo boot camp and a lie detector test" (Here). In this episode, BluMedia owner Mark Erickson and chief operating officer Shannon Prewitt decide to subject their employees to a polygraph examination. The rationale they use for doing so is embodied in Shannon's statement that links the "number one question" the boys regularly encounter on their mandatory public outings with expressed consumer skepticism about the existence and stability of their heterosexuality. Thus, the indispensability of an indisputable heteronormative performativity is linked to the commodification of that identity as a vehicle of profit so much so that, at least in the minds of both the company's owner and COO, scientific proof is required. Pointedly, the polygrapher makes clear that the test can only confirm the veracity of behaviors rather than the assumption of a sexual identity, but it appears to the viewer that, in the minds of the business leadership at least, such information is sufficient for making important business decisions. This perception is confirmed in the eighth and final episode of the first season, "Porn Never Sleeps," when the company's owner makes clear that the hiring process is one that purposely weeds out gay men; the significance of this process to the company's overall business logic is confirmed later in the same episode when producer/director Shane Heiser states, "I think doing the webcam interviews is really crucial because that definitely weeds out the gay guys."

Thus, the overall message that viewers take away from this final episode of the first season is that the convincing appearance of hegemonic heterosexuality is central to the company's profitability and ongoing existence. Earlier in that episode, viewers find Damian Christopher (a BluMedia "creative director") talking with Kaden and conspiratorially asking, "Paul and Damien are close—do you think they're a little bit closer *than they should be*?" (emphasis added), as if to suggest that non-hegemonic heterosexuality demands strict conformity while cast members appear either on the television series or even in the limited privacy of their workplace/home. Christopher's words suggest a rigid and inflexible social policing of both actors to help ensure that they conform to the limiting expectations of hegemonic masculinity and heteronormativity, and they beg the question of why he is so invested in soliciting information of this kind. Is this salaciousness simply a plot device? Do Paul's and Damien's personal, nonconformist, off-screen sexual acts imperil their employment with the company? Moreover, one wonders what responsibility a "creative director" has in regulating employees' off-screen sexual behaviors? Dissatisfied with Kaden's initial response, Christopher continues by stating that he "keeps hearing rumors ... that something's going on with them. Do you think they're together?" To this, Kaden responds, "They do things that 'normal guys' don't do.... I think the gay porn thing opened up a door ... there's definitely..." and, completing his statement, Christopher says, "Something's going on." The entire conversation traffics in the worst kinds of social policing at the expense of both Paul's and Damien's sexual freedom from the ruthlessly imposed confines of hegemonic masculinity and heteronormativity. That this conversation appears to take place outside of both Paul's and Damien's purview further solidifies the conspiratorial nature of the information being discussed as somehow taboo. Ironically, it is the company's owner, Mark Erickson, who states that "It's kind of weird that my two top models are in an affair together.... The members want to see two straight guys in hardcore gay sex.... It will be interesting to see what happens—will the ratings go up, will the ratings go down." The consequences for the business and the livelihood of employees on *BrokeStraightBoys.tv* are therefore intrinsically related to, and predicated upon (for better or for worse), a business logic of viewer demand and personal popularity that caters to sexual fetishization of "authentic" heterosexuality.

Unfortunately, that logic fails to account for the fact that many men who choose to eschew a hegemonic heterosexuality can nevertheless still adequately perform to a reliable sexual conclusion. As Jeffrey Escoffier points out, the effectiveness of video pornography "stems from its ability to satisfy the viewer's expectation that the sex is plausibly 'real' in some way.... A 'documentary illusion' exists in the photographic pornographic genres, which promise to enact certain sexual fantasies and certify them through the 'authenticity' of *erections* ... and *orgasms*" (536, original emphasis), but the fact remains that this sense of authenticity can itself be fabricated with the consumption of today's pharmaceutical remedy, Viagra, and its other analogues. Moreover, the ability of sexually nonconformist men to reliably and successfully deliver a heteronormative sexual performance is most significantly influenced by their fidelity to the applicable sexual scripts. Even in the most ideal of circumstances in which both gay men are performing, there is no guarantee that sexual arousal and orgasm will occur consistently over the many hours of filming required of them. For as Escoffier notes,

> The dramatic fabrication is achieved not only by the performers enacting sexual scenes but also by elaborate editing and montage of the filmed sexual acts themselves. Usually the filming of a sexual scene requires many takes, stops and starts, and requires the performers to regain their erections.... Real sex acts are usually performed, but the video representation of them is more coherent than the actual sexual activity being filmed.... The performed act is interrupted many times to arrange shooting angles and lighting and to allow the actors to "get wood"—to regain their erections.... Thus a fifteen-to-twenty-minute sexual scene that the viewer sees is edited and patched together, with soundtrack added, from footage shot over a six or seven hour period [539, 550].

Given the extensive work involved in this highly choreographed affair, one questions the extensive dedication to the search for, solicitation, and confirmation of a hegemonic heterosexual masculinity embodied in the *Broke Straight Boys* series.

Gay-for-Pay Pornography, Economic Profitability and Social Meaning

The commonsensical definition of "gay for pay" is best understood as a heterosexual man who willingly engages in sexual acts with another (often, but not exclusively) heterosexual man for financial compensation. However, Escoffier contends that "all sexual conduct in the video porn industry is to one degree or another an example of situational sexuality inasmuch as the performers are often required to engage in sexual acts for monetary compensation that they would not otherwise choose to perform and with partners for whom they feel no desire" (534). Discussing the prevalence of gay-for-pay men in the gay porn industry, Escoffier notes that "the prolific director Chi Chi LaRue estimates the number of straight men in gay pornographic videos to be sixty percent" (535). As such, *BrokeStraightBoys.tv* offers a timely intervention by bringing to light this phenomenon during a period of heightened consumption of gay pornography in the digital era.

The popular belief that porn actors' labor cannot possibly be difficult, considering that they are paid a wage to engage in sex acts (that are universally constructed as always and inevitably enjoyable), belies the reality that such on-camera performances (1) require diligent effort and concentration (particularly in gay male porn, which necessitates a constantly reliable erection) and (2) are not always fulfilling emotionally and/or psychologically, despite all appearances to the contrary as the actor's dialogue, facial expressions, and behavior convey the very opposite message of heightened emotional desire and sexual excitement. Indeed, I would argue that this dichotomy only illustrates the highly skilled abilities of the actors involved in constructing a scene of sexual excitement that may, in fact, be entirely devoid of emotional or psychological excitement or enjoyment. The working conditions commonly found in the adult entertainment industry inevitably influence and affect the decisions of actors, and these off-stage conditions are not typically as admirable as the final video products might otherwise suggest. "Indeed, in contrast to their Hollywood counterparts, these actors are not protected by unions [and] they receive no pensions, 401k investment opportunities, health insurance benefits, or percentages of their films' net profits" (Johnson Jr. 185).

Unfortunately, for a variety of reasons and in contrast to other industries, there is substantially less known about the pornography industry (and even less about gay pornography) with regard to issues of labor relations, working conditions, compensation, and other employment-related subjects that normally are well researched and clearly articulated. Georgina Voss makes clear that "the commercial aspects of the industry—industrial dynamics, strategy, technological capabilities, organizational structure—have been given less consideration, and critical examinations of the industry are notably absent, in business studies" (392), despite the fact that the economic profitability of the business is often cited as a primary reason why scholars must engage with it. She further notes that "the business aspects of pornography are rarely the actual focus of academic studies and are often merely the justification for such research" (392). Indeed, I have regularly been met with silence when approaching mainstream pornography companies due to their reticence to participate in academic studies of their work.

Fortunately, viewers who subscribe to *BrokeStraightBoys.tv* are provided a generous amount of detail about the labor practices of BluMedia on the company's BSB website and through the content of the various episodes themselves. In the premiere episode, for example, Shane Heiser states that he and his colleagues conduct "twenty to twenty-five scenes a month" as an indication of the volume of work involved and the financial lucrativeness of the business of gay pornography. In the second episode, Shannon Prewitt notes that the boys are "traveling from January to December at different Pride events around the country to meet our fans and to meet new fans." Moreover, he states that "they work hard from early in the morning to late in the night [and] their job is to sell product," and "the most important part of their job is to make every person that they come into contact with feel welcome."

Also in the second episode, cast member Jimmy explains, "So the scene that we're doing today will probably end up being like forty minutes on the Internet and will probably take, like, an hour and a half to two hours to actually do it." His comment further emphasizes the tedious nature of filming adult sex acts between straight-identified men and the highly choreographed nature of moving-image pornography, which is a very labor-intensive process. Additionally, the boys' labor includes intense periods of hyperactivity throughout the calendar year, which, according to cast member Sergio Valen in episode two, occasionally compresses "two weeks of work into three days." Pointing to the difficulties associated with being gay-for-pay in the industry, Denver states in the series' third episode, "You can't do this forever. Most guys can't even do this for six months before it's over for them. So it's not like it's a career or something"; it is with no small amount of irony, therefore, that Denver leaves the series at the end of that episode. Later in the season during the series' seventh episode, "Straight Boys, Gay Drama," Adam Baer hurts his back because of an incident with Cage, limiting both his and his scene partner's ability to earn money, which further illustrates the fragile nature of their unique work environment. But even with these many limitations, a much larger and more significant obstacle exists for some actors due solely to their racial identity.

Racial Homophily and "Post-Racial" Commodification

In the aforementioned eighth and final episode of the series' first season, "Porn Never Sleeps," which aired on January 23, 2015, viewers hear cast member Damien announce, "I am not racist; I am not sexually attracted to black guys," to which Damian Christopher, BluMedia's gay black male "creative director," responds, "I can be your friend but I can't be good enough ... a black male can't be good enough." "I never said you aren't good enough," Damien adds, during an evening meeting at the house. The episode then cuts away to a subsequent (chronologically later) "confessional" during which Christopher says, "I've tried to move beyond it, and I've tried to not take it personal [sic], but I took it a little personal tonight." Returning immediately to the evening meeting around the patio fire, viewers observe Christopher saying, "It does not feel good for someone to say, 'You know what, I'm good enough to be your friend ... but I'm not good enough to sleep with.'"

Cutting back to the confessional, Christopher continues: "How arrogant do you have to be to say that you're not going to sleep with someone because of their skin color?" Cutting again back to the patio, he continues his argument with Damien by posing the question, "So you're telling me that you've never been in the studio where you've been with another model and you didn't do your job?" (at this moment, the camera predictably pans to the face of Kaden, the only Broke Straight Boy of color in the series during its first season). Damien responds by saying, "Once. And you know what? I did it because everyone talked me through it. You know that guy was colored." A brief aside occurs in the conversation during which Shannon Prewitt informs Damien of his linguistic faux pas, to which Damien appears to offer an honest response, explaining how he was at a loss for an appropriate synonym given the racial ambiguity of his scene partner at the time: "I don't know if he's African American, I don't know if he's Indian, what am I supposed to call him?"

Continuing, Christopher (again in a cut to the confessional) states, somewhat disingenuously, that he's "not here to change [Damien's] mind about who, or what, he's supposed to sleep with. But you're going to tell me that you won't sleep with someone of another color—what does that even say about you?" Cutting back to the patio, Damien continues his explanation by pointing to his disposability: "If you guys want to be mad and whatever, go get a different model. I don't want to do it so I'm not. End of story." Christopher, back in the confessional shaking his head, says, "He's got a lot to learn, a hell of a lot to learn." Back on the patio, Shannon asks Kaden how Damien's statement makes him feel, to which he interestingly observes, "Everyone's always going to take partial offense to somebody not doing something because they're black, but I know black guys that won't have sex with a white girl," at which point the conversation quickly moves away to a brief confrontation between Damien and Cage. In a subsequent confessional, Kaden sums up his personal reactions to the event with, "I could[n't] give a rat's ass—all I want is my money."

The entire event comprises a large percentage of the final episode of the season and reflects the complicated nature of racial politics in sexual choice, especially as they pertain to the adult entertainment industry—an industry notorious for its racial commodification and fetishization. As John Burger pointedly states, "The gay communities are obviously not immune to racism.... These conditions are too deeply imbedded in the white male heritage to be easily eradicated" (54), and, in describing the segmentation in gay pornographic film, he adds, "One is most apt to find, behind these all-black, all–Latin, and all–Asian videos, white capital pulling the strings and naming the names" (55). Most importantly, Burger concludes by observing that "although gay porn may radically rewrite much of history, it unfortunately has not radically positivized the situations of gay men of color in this country" (57).

BrokeStraightBoys.tv is no exception to Burger's assertion, given its singular man of color in the series and no apparent men of color in positions of power or leadership in the company that produces it. Although Damien is critiqued for his ignorance about the issues of racial inequality in the industry, his failure to recognize that "preferences" aren't always rooted in racial bias is equally as compelling as the privileging of whiteness as a racial category. Speaking about Marc Dylan (another popular, but gay, pornographic actor), one web blogger expresses frustration that many in the porn industry are often "trying to shift the problem of racial diversity/stereotyping into a discussion of capitalism, demand, and marketplaces. Sure, if we're going to completely ignore centuries of racial stereotyping and discrimination that have created and maintained narratives of black inferiority, ugliness, and sexual deviance" (CaptainSnarky). While Damien Kyle may be guilty of adopting a logic that "is completely divorced from any understanding of how his white privilege allows him to act as an arbiter of what's 'attractive' or not and how that white privilege is operative in every porn studio out there" (Captain-Snarky), his critics should also recognize that the decisions about who gay-for-pay actors are paired with are not ones entirely of their own making, as viewers see at the end of the eighth episode, when Mark and Shannon actively sift through an array of men and theorize about future pairings. Thus, the logics of the economic market of desire and the capitalist objectives of profitability are just as compelling motivators—and ultimately bear as much responsibility for the perpetuation of the racial status quo—as are the personal preferences of hegemonically white business leaders and consumers. This is something *BrokeStraightBoys.tv* has yet to publicize for its gay viewership, yet it remains something so necessary if the gay "community" is to move forward with a more enlightened consumption of its entertainment commodities.

WORKS CITED

Andrejevic, Mark. "The Kinder, Gentler Gaze of Big Brother: Reality TV in the Era of Digital Capitalism." *New Media and Society* 4.2 (2002): 251–270. Print.

Becker, Ron. "Guy Love: A Queer Straight Masculinity for a Post-Closet Era?" *Queer TV: Theories, Histories, Politics*. Ed. Glyn Davis and Gary Needham. New York: Routledge, 2009. 121–140. Print.

Bronski, Michael. *Culture Clash: The Making of Gay Sensibility*. Boston: South End Press, 1984. Print.

Burger, John R. *One-Handed Histories: The Eroto-Politics of Gay Male Video Pornography*. Binghamton, NY: Haworth Press, 1994. Print.

CaptainSnarky. "A White Gay Adult Film Star Shares His Poorly Formed Views on Racism." *Crasstalk*, 7 August 2013. Web. 6 January 2015. http://crasstalk.com/2013/08/a-white-gay-adult-film-star-shares-his-poorly-formed-views-on-racism/.

Dixon, Wheeler Winston. *Streaming: Movies, Media, and Instant Access*. Lexington: University Press of Kentucky, 2013. Print.

Duggan, Scott J., and Donald R. McCreary. "Body Image, Easting Disorders, and the Drive for Muscularity in Gay and Heterosexual Men: The Influence of Media Images." *Eclectic Views on Gay Male Pornography: Pornucopia*. Ed. Todd Morrison. Binghamton, NY: Harrington Park Press, 2004. 45–58. Print.

Escoffier, Jeffrey. "Gay-for-Pay: Straight Men and the Making of Gay Pornography." *Qualitative Sociology* 26.4 (2003): 531–555. Print.

Gray, Jonathan. "Entertainment and Media/Cultural/Communication/Etc. Studies." *Continnum: Journal of Media and Cultural Studies* 24.6 (2010): 811–817. Print.

Here TV Premium. "BrokeStraightBoys.tv." *YouTube*, 19 December 2014. Web. 5 January 2015. https://www.youtube.com/user/brokestraightboystv.

Jensen, Robert. *Getting Off: Pornography and the End of Masculinity*. Boston: South End Press, 2007. Print.

Johnson, Michael, Jr. "Queer Negotiations Between Love and Work: A Critical Ethnographic Case Study of a Gay Porn Star." *Queer Love in Film and Television: Critical Essays*. Ed. Pamela Demory and Christopher Pullen. New York: Palgrave Macmillan, 2013. 181–191. Print.

Mowlabocus, Sharif. "Gaydar: Gay Men and the Pornification of Everyday Life." *Pornification: Sex and Sexuality in Media Culture*. Ed. Kaarina Nikunen, Susanna Paasonen, and Laura Saarenmaa. New York: Berg, 2007. 61–71. Print.

Reed, T.V. "Popular Culture." *The Year's Work in Critical and Cultural Theory* 19.1 (2011): 141–158. Print.

Saukko, Paula. *Doing Research in Cultural Studies: An Introduction to Classical and New Methodological Approaches*. Thousand Oaks, CA: Sage, 2003. Print.

Thomas, Joe A. "Gay Male Pornography Since Stonewall." *Sex for Sale: Prostitution, Pornography, and the Sex Industry*, 2d ed. Ed. Ronald Weitzer. New York: Routledge, 2010. 67–89. Print.

Voss, Georgina. "'Treating It as a Normal Business': Researching the Pornography Industry." *Sexualities* 15.3–4 (2012): 391–410. Print.

Ward, Jane. "Dude-Sex: White Masculinities and 'Authentic' Heterosexuality Among Dudes Who Have Sex with Dudes." *Sexualities* 11.4 (2008): 414–434. Print.

Sexploitation on YouTube
The Rise, Fall and Rebirth
of the Gay Network

Bridget Kies

Following what Ron Becker has described as a "startling increase in gay-themed programming on prime-time network television in the 1990s" (3), two new networks were launched to cater specifically to LGBT audiences and tap into the newly recognized "gay market" (Sender). Rather than using gay characters and storylines as must-see TV gimmicks to boost ratings, as Becker argues was the case with NBC and other broadcast networks in the 1990s, these new networks would make LGBT-themed programming the entirety of their lineups. Perhaps the better known of the two "gay networks," Logo debuted in 2005 with a lineup of original reality and comedy series, as well as films. The other such network, here! TV (henceforth Here TV), launched two years earlier and continues to offer explicitly LGBT content, predominantly through on-demand and online streaming services.

In some ways, the experiment of queer TV—i.e., television by, for, and about queer people—that began in the 2000s has failed. The gay market that enticed advertisers in the late 1990s and early 2000s proved to be everywhere, including as audiences of broadcast prime-time television, and so exclusively gay televisual offerings on gay networks proved unnecessary to many advertisers. In 2012, Logo announced a shift in programming away from series that explicitly depict LGBT characters and situations; it now airs reruns of popular prime-time sitcoms such as *The Golden Girls* (1985–1992) and *Roseanne* (1988–1997). Here TV continues to offer original programming, but only through a circumvention of television's traditional advertising-revenue model.

Both the rise and the fall of the "gay network" raise important questions about what is meant by the term "queer television." As Michele Aaron argues,

"TV inhabits the domestic sphere, the realm of everyday," whereas the term "queer" denotes something which agitates that mainstream; thus, the "very notion of queer television" seems oxymoronic (69). Similarly, Gary Needham argues that the television schedule presupposes heteronormativity in the way it assumes "temporal coordination of the nuclear family" by having parts of the schedule "correspond to the life timetables of children and child-rearing activities … and eventually [having] the family united every evening in front of the box during prime time's evening hours" (145). In contrast, Alexander Doty argues that certain television series can be read as queer through homosocial bonds between central characters; as such, television offers queer pleasures to both gay and straight audiences (3). Amy Villarejo similarly argues that television is and always has been queer to some extent, because television time is not just the moment at which we watch but also "a mesh of temporalities of real life, recording, transmission, repetition, and seriality" (118). Both Doty's and Villarejo's arguments rely upon readings of LGBT characters and homoerotic subtext from television history, examples primarily intended to push boundaries with straight audiences. On the whole, television remains a routine part of domestic life that depends on the broadest appeal and, as such, has proved itself inherently "not-queer."

Yet in the fiercely competitive television market, queer audiences remain a potentially lucrative base. The explosion of cable channels in the 1990s and 2000s and of online viewing platforms in the 2010s has meant that microcasting to certain subgroups within the LGBT community is one viable strategy for success. In the case of Here TV, that subgroup is almost exclusively gay men. Time-shifting technologies, on-demand portals, and streaming services such as YouTube allow for the queering of viewing practices that avoid the normativity of the television-scheduling grid; viewers can watch what they want, when they want. Because viewers pay for this convenience through monthly subscription or pay-per-view fees, a network like Here TV can continue its non-traditional model of programming and scheduling. In this essay, I examine the rebirth of the gay network, which I argue has been made possible through Here TV's strategic use of new distribution modes that eschew the traditional advertising-driven economic model. I demonstrate how Here TV continues to offer programming that depicts nonnormative sexualities and lifestyles, despite limited audience size and limited budgets—a feat that is worthy of further examination for challenging both traditional industry practices and common scholarly perceptions of television as incongruent with queerness. I use in particular the meta-sitcom *From Here on OUT* (2014) as a paradigmatic example of Here TV's queer programming.

The Rise and Fall of Logo

As an explicitly gay network, Logo debuted in 2005 with a lineup of reality programs, comedies, and films. A subsidiary of Viacom and MTV, Logo populated its time slots with kitschy, campy, queer fun programming. For example, from 2007 to 2009 the network aired *Rick & Steve: The Happiest Gay Couple in All the World*, a stop-motion animation comedy that experimented with form as much as it did with traditional sitcom narrative tropes. *Rick & Steve* also capitalized on the celebrity of cast members known and appreciated by the LGBT community, including the openly gay actor Peter Paige, who had gained a queer following from his work on Showtime's groundbreaking drama *Queer as Folk* (2000–2005); comedian Margaret Cho, known for her outspokenness on the subject of LGBT rights; and stage and screen actor Alan Cumming, who has described himself as pansexual, bisexual, and non-monogamous in various interviews ("Exclusive!"; Walsh). Original series like *Rick & Steve* relied upon in-jokes and allusions that specifically referenced the LGBT community, often without explanation for viewers who may not have been in the know.

As Ben Aslinger has chronicled, Logo's strategy for delivering LGBT audiences to advertisers through programming that reflected the community was often undermined by "textual choices in specific programs that reinscribe[d] class, race, and national hierarchies in queer cultures" (108). Logo's mission of narrowcasting to viewers with a range of sexualities was fundamentally at odds with its business model. The most valued audiences for any network reliant upon advertising revenue are those with the most spending power; in Logo's case, this translated to "positing gay audiences as upscale, white, and brand loyal" at the expense of viewers of different races, ethnicities, economic backgrounds, and sexualities (112). In order to court nervous advertisers, Logo often had to silence or censor some of its sexually explicit content. Just as advertisers targeting the gay market favor white, middle- and upper-class gay men in particular (as they tend to be the ones with the most disposable income), so too did Logo's programming come to reflect only this one segment of the LGBT community (Sender 10).

In 2012, Logo announced a shift in its programming strategy away from explicitly LGBT-themed content and toward what it called "lifestyle programming" (Ciriaco). Its lineup, as mentioned previously, began to feature reruns of popular sitcoms such as *The Golden Girls* and *Roseanne*, both of which are also rerun on several other cable networks. Notably, both series feature LGBT-identified secondary characters and, at the time they original aired, challenged representations of sexualities on television; both also have tremendous queer followings. However, neither series was created *by* the LGBT community *for* the LGBT community, as had been the case with Logo's original programming. In press releases explaining the shift, Logo representatives cited research suggesting that LGBT people no longer look to sexual identity as a determining factor in their television viewing choices. Rather than offering programs that explicitly depict the LGBT community, Logo now primarily broadcasts "straight" series that have historically appealed to members of the LGBT community.

This shift in Logo's programming coincided with increased LGBT representation across broadcast and cable networks. The 2012–2013 GLAAD media report, for example, found that approximately four percent of television characters across all networks identified as LGBT, about the same percentage as American adults who self-identify as LGBT (Gates and Newport; Gouttebroze). At the time of Logo's announcement, members of the LGBT community could see themselves in numerous places on television, especially in prime-time broadcast series such as *Glee* (2009–2015) and *Modern Family* (2009–).

Despite Logo's claims about what LGBT viewers prefer to watch, there is little doubt the rebranding was a cost-saving measure. Airing reruns is more cost effective than developing, producing, and/or purchasing rights for an original series that may not succeed. The new lineup may also appeal to those who had not previously watched the network, including viewers who identify outside the LGBT community. While its original mission led Logo to become too targeted—to affluent gay white men—the network's new strategy instead emulates those of broadcast networks by offering series that have broad appeal to a variety of viewers, beyond the original LGBT target audience.

In contrast, the other gay network, Here TV, has maintained a strategy of being gayer, queerer, and less normative. Here TV was a forerunner in the use of pay on-demand content, which has enabled the network to maintain its express focus on LGBT themes. Cheekily advertising itself as "the *only* gay network in America" following Logo's rebranding, Here TV continues to offer original series, made-for-TV movies, and independent films that foreground explicitly LGBT characters. Series such as *Dante's Cove* (2005–2007) and *The Lair* (2007–2009) feature actors and minor celebrities who are known to the LGBT community. Movies based on Richard Stevenson's Donald Strachey mystery novels tell the story of an openly gay private investigator and star Chad Allen, an openly gay actor. By continuing to create media by, for, and about the LGBT community, Here TV's programming strategy is in direct opposition to Logo's and demonstrates that queer television is indeed feasible.

Homonormativity in Prime Time

Since the 1990s, a decade when television exploded with images of gay life, gay characters and stories have persisted in both broadcast and cable television (Becker). However, the majority of the resulting depictions are normalized into monogamy, parenthood, and domesticity. As defined by Lisa Duggan, homonormativity is a "politics that does not contest dominant heteronormative assumptions and institutions, but upholds and sustains them, while promising the possibility of a demobilized gay constituency and a privatized, depoliticized gay culture anchored in domesticity and consumption" (50). Increasingly, gay characters in U.S. television are homonormative and look just like their straight counterparts: they buy houses, get married, raise children, etc. The process of watching these characters is also homonormative in that it encourages domesticity (i.e., staying home to watch TV) and the consumption of the goods and services advertised during commercial breaks.

In addition to propagating the values of domesticity and consumption, prime-time broadcast television's depiction of the LGBT community tends to exclude certain lifestyles, races, and economic classes. As with Logo's original lineup, prime time favors upscale, white gay men. Perhaps two of the best known gay characters at the present moment, Mitch (played by Jesse Tyler Ferguson) and Cameron (played by Eric Stonestreet) of the ABC sitcom *Modern Family*, are white and middle-class, and, through their shared residence, adopted daughter Lily (played by Aubrey Anderson-Emmons), and recent legal marriage, the two have assimilated into a normative lifestyle patterned after the two heterosexual couples in the same series. As Steven Doran notes, *Modern Family*'s portrayal of "homodomesticity"—i.e., the shared domestic life and gay parenting performed by Mitch and Cameron—"suggests that the project of LGBT activism has been achieved" (96–97). Although assimilation may look at the outset like acceptance, "homodomesticity silences and erases the possibility of queer alternatives" (Doran 97). In particular, being successful at homodomesticity means appearing straight and embodying the prescribed gender norms that much LGBT activism has devoted itself to undoing (Doran 103).

Challenges to gender identity have been a component of television content from the medium's early days (e.g., Milton Berle appeared in a dress as often as Lucille Ball did in pants), but such challenges typically existed for the sake of comedy, with characters returning to their "proper" state at the end of the sketch, joke, or episode. Until recently, transgender characters were almost entirely absent, with the exception of serving as the occasional punchline to a joke. Tellingly, the two series that have received critical acclaim for their portrayals of transgender characters, *Orange Is the New Black* (2013–)

and *Transparent* (2014–), are produced and screened outside the traditional broadcast model through Netflix and Amazon.

Finally, in addition to domesticity and gender normativity, LGBT characters in prime time are typically portrayed as wholly monogamous or chaste. As U.S. society has adopted a favorable impression of same-sex marriage, reaching a majority in favor as of 2011, more and more gay couples have wed on television and live in domestic bliss (Newport). But many of these happily wedded characters are, on-screen at least, in sexless relationships featuring only the slightest of hugs and occasional, quick kisses. Broadcast television does not depict non-monogamous gay relationships or anonymous gay sex as anything but problematic. For example, the young gay man Connor Walsh (played by Jack Falahee) on *How to Get Away with Murder* (2014–) often uses sex to his professional advantage, absent a favorable moral compass (Bernstein).

In the post-network era, the move to web and on-demand content has interesting repercussions for the portrayal of LGBT identities. Although flexible gender identity is not common on Here TV, which microcasts particularly to cisgender gay men, the network's various series actively work against other aspects of homonormativity. Characters in such series live in worlds where male nudity and casual gay sex are unabashedly depicted—even expected.

Quality TV, Female Nudity and the Heterosexist Male Gaze

While traditional broadcast networks tend to deny open expressions of gay sexuality, cable channels, in contrast, depict gay sex, sometimes quite vividly. Because network television is restricted with regard to language use, sex, and violence, cable and premium cable channels often expressly include these elements in order to attract audience members with their "transgressive" content. As Janet McCabe and Kim Akass observe, this transgressive content is also legitimated through high production values—and the high price subscribers must pay—in order to enable the audience to feel elite, separate from the low-class rabble who must watch broadcast television (66). Among the members of that elite audience are individual viewers who identify as LGBT; however, with few exceptions, what is termed "quality TV" on premium cable does not deliberately target members of the LGBT community. Depictions of gay sex in premium cable series differ from those in series for Here TV in terms of the intended viewer for whose gaze that sex is filmed.

Television critics and bloggers have noted that the series most often praised as being "quality" series, or part of the current "Golden Age" of television, are the ones that feature retrograde patriarchs, such as *The Sopranos*

(1999–2007) and *Mad Men* (2007–2015), and are typically aimed at male audiences. Michael Newman and Elana Levine tie the legitimation of "quality" television series to "cultural hierarchies and hierarchies of all kinds" within which some televisual offerings are denigrated in order to "justify the elevation of others" (36). Perhaps unsurprisingly, therefore, the troubled patriarchs of premium cable are regarded by television critics and popular audiences as anti-heroes of the "Golden Age," whereas daytime soap operas and reality competition series such as *The Bachelor* (2002–) are often cited as noteworthy examples of what makes television a "mind waste." In other words, series that feature masculine characters for straight male audiences are "quality" televisual offerings; what is not "quality" are series that traditionally target female audiences.

In addition to ostracizing female audiences, "quality TV" on cable ostracizes queer audiences for whom the voyeuristic gaze onto the nude female body is untitillating or perceived as problematic. As Hannah Mueller argues, there is a "disconnection between contemporary cable shows and their female and queer audiences that is facilitated by the contemporary discourse on 'quality TV'" (1). As "quality TV" becomes "increasingly entangled with strategies of transgression and masculinization," it follows that the kind of nudity seen in "quality" premium-cable series increasingly reflects not only a male gaze, but specifically a heterosexist one (Mueller 2). Across HBO series, "diegetic logic … permits the inclusion of spaces where naked women pose for a male audience" (Mueller 6)—for instance, in strip clubs and brothels— and these women are uniformly beautiful, with a lack of body diversity. In contrast, nude male bodies are often "hairy, dirty, ageing, overweight, wrinkled, and sometimes they are meant to be revolting" (Mueller 13). Clearly, it is the female body that is expected to attract and arouse viewers. For viewers who find such exploitation of the female body unappealing, HBO is something to both sexually and technologically turn off.

Gay TV, Male Nudity and the Gay Male Gaze

In contrast to broadcast television's fear of depicting gay sex and premium cable's exploitation of women's nudity, series on Here TV often depict gay men with healthy sexual appetites and active sex lives. Full frontal male nudity and depictions of non-monogamous sex are common and clearly intended for the gay male gaze. Admittedly, this state of affairs overlooks lesbians and other members of the LGBT community who are uninterested in gazing at men's bodies, as well as straight and/or otherwise identified women who enjoy that type of gaze. However, casual nudity and sex on Here TV iterate the possibility of media content that does not portray assimilation or normativity. Although Here TV's programming does not fit the standard definition of contemporary "quality TV" (i.e., high production values and cinematic aesthetics), it is nonetheless an important development in the trajectory of LGBT televisual representation.

Across Here TV's corpus of television series, there are certain commonalities. First, gay men make up the bulk of characters on any particular series, with women often an afterthought. Those gay men are all physically attractive, with muscular bodies that are regularly on display; characters are often shirtless, if not completely nude. (There is far less female nudity and sex between women.) In discourses surrounding Here TV's various television series, actors, producers, and fans regularly discuss which actors are gay in real life and which are not. While straight men who "play gay" in Hollywood films or "quality TV" series are often celebrated for their accomplishments (presumably because "playing gay" is an especially difficult task for a heterosexual actor), straight actors appearing on Here TV are the exception. Instead, the network favors casting openly gay actors to play openly gay characters.

A particularly ripe example of the values and themes of this unique network is the meta-sitcom *From Here on OUT*. A backstage comedy about a producer making a series for Here TV and trying to land the cover of *Out* magazine (which is owned by Here TV's parent company, Here Media), the series subscribes to many of the conventions of LGBT television at the same time as it critiques them. Within the narrative of the series, there is rampant male nudity and indiscriminate sex, representations of women that highlight the gay male community's often contradictory attitudes toward women, and a succession of tropes seen in LGBT films and television programs (as well as in traditional sitcoms). *From Here on OUT* utilizes a show-within-a-show format to highlight, rather than ignore, the challenges that LGBT media face and are often criticized for: minuscule budgets, tiny audiences, and poor production values, including those pertaining to writing and acting.

In the premiere episode of *From Here on OUT*, titled "Nudity Required!," Taylor (played by Austin Robert Miller), the fictional teenage head of Here TV, decides to green-light a spy drama entitled *Guy Dubai: International Gay Spy*. It first season is planned to include two episodes, to be produced on a shoestring budget. Producer Jimmy (played by *From Here on OUT*'s actual series creator and executive producer, Terry Ray) must also serve as writer and director because of the budgetary limitations. Such stipulations call attention to real-world constraints associated with making television offerings for Here TV. The network's well-known supernatural melodrama *Dante's Cove*, for example, featured only two long episodes in its first season and five each in its second and third seasons. Its half-hour spinoff, *The Lair*, managed thirteen episodes in its third (and final) season, but the previous two seasons each contained fewer than ten episodes. Here TV's various series are routinely panned by critics and viewers because of their low production values, the result of having small budgets. Both *Guy Dubai* and *From Here on OUT* are clearly made with budgets that are minuscule when compared to those of typical broadcast or cable television series. The actors in *Guy Dubai* frequently narrate action sequences with the concluding note, "I wish you could see it, but we can't afford to show you," a meta-commentary that is as tongue-in-cheek as it is sincere. Although *From Here on OUT* has a bigger budget than the fictional *Guy Dubai*, its small cast, limited sets, and short season all speak to the economic constraints under which explicitly gay-themed television offerings are typically made.

Within the fictional *Guy Dubai*, frequent male nudity seems as gratuitous and titillating as it does on other gay-themed series such as *Dante's Cove* or Showtime's *Queer as Folk*. While *From Here on OUT* comments on how exploitative this nudity is through *Guy Dubai*'s inane plots, it is simultaneously contributing to that exploitation because, after all, its actors appear nude in order to "act" in *Guy Dubai*. In the aforementioned premiere episode of *From Here on OUT*, executive Taylor insists to producer Jimmy that *Guy Dubai* must feature nudity because it is the primary reason viewers watch gay television. As a result of this network directive, *Guy Dubai*'s cast members are often underdressed (typically without shirts), and extras "accidentally" lose their clothes during action scenes. (As previously mentioned, the title of this episode *is*, after all, "Nudity Required!")

In campy action sequences as well as scenes of sex, Here TV offers plenty of nudity like premium cable networks—but always featuring beautiful *male* bodies rather than female ones. Whereas sex between men in "quality television" is rarely portrayed as "anything but an act of violence" (Mueller 11), sex between men in gay television is intentionally for the gay male gaze. Nude male bodies must be smooth, muscular, and tan; they exhibit the same level of perfection and lack of diversity as women's bodies on premium cable. These sorts of portrayals are certainly not unique to Here TV, however—Showtime's *Queer as Folk*, for example, regularly featured male-male sex in backrooms and bathhouses, and while the sexual positions varied, as did the sexual partners, the bodies featured on-screen were uniformly young, taut, and beautiful.

The trend of simultaneously shocking and titillating via vivid depictions of gay sex began with *Queer as Folk* and disrupted the tradition of the gay eunuch seen in many Hollywood films and on broadcast television. Series on Here TV continue to depict gay sex as graphically as *Queer as Folk* did. *Dante's Cove* featured a sex club that had little to do with the series' narrative but was a convenient way to show flesh and simulated sex. The pilot episode of *The*

Lair included a scene in which the main character, Thom, took a shower, with languorous shots of soap and water sliding down actor David Moretti's nude backside. Moretti has conceded that the scene served no real narrative function but was necessary to appeal to the gay male target audience (Scholibo).

The nude male body in gay television is, in many ways, an equalizer to female nudity in "quality television." In *From Here on OUT* (and/or the fictional *Guy Dubai*), it is the men who are exploited for their bodies. Male nudity in gay television often coincides with gay sex, because on the whole there is a lot of gay sex in gay television. Whereas gay characters in broadcast television series remain sexless and male-male sex in "quality" premium cable series (in other words, "straight" series) is most often about hierarchy and rape rather than lust, gay sex in gay television series is distinct in that it shows men engaging in sexual acts for pleasure. They do not have to be married or monogamous; they do not have to be chaste.

Nevertheless, male nudity and gay sex in gay television are still regularly exploitative and gratuitous. As in the aforementioned shower scene from *The Lair*, such nudity often does not advance the narrative. Full frontal shots of extras in the meta-series *Guy Dubai* and in the sex club of *Dante's Cove* serve a different—and, I argue, equally valuable—function. With nude men constantly in the background, series on Here TV reassert the network's queerness. It is impossible to watch any Here TV program and lose sight of the fact that it appears on a network for gay men. As Christopher Pullen has demonstrated, women also constitute an audience for media that depict gay men due to their "shared political vision, and the connectivity between feminism and queer identity politics" (ix); no doubt, many women also enjoy looking at the spectacle of men's bodies in gay television, apart from any political alliance with the content they might feel. However, while network executives and advertisers are indeed aware that these additional audience members exist, gay television is not principally made for them. Its depictions of indiscriminate gay sex and its denigrations and/or absence of women are intended primarily for the gay male gaze.

A key difference between the exploitative nudity and gratuitous sex on premium cable and on Here TV involves where this nudity and sex can be found. Here TV can regularly feature explicit gay sex because it keeps that content far from the eyes of those who might readily be offended by it: on YouTube, behind pay walls, and on a subscription-based cable channel. Graphic depictions of sex serve to compensate viewers for the cost of subscribing and to reaffirm the "gayness" of the network brand, much like HBO and Showtime must offer profane language, female nudity, and violence to their target audiences.

Pornography and Gay Television

Whereas "quality" television series revel in artful cinematography and lavish production design, series on Here TV intentionally embrace the limitations imposed by their restrictive production budgets. The end result, once combined with scenes of graphic male nudity and male-male sex, is something akin to amateur or low-budget pornography. Because so much of pornography resides online in today's media ecology, there is also a connection with how users regularly access content. Streaming a series on Here TV's YouTube channel can happen in the same browsing session as streaming videos on popular gay pornography websites. Additionally, Here TV offers some content for free in order to entice viewers to pay for a subscription to access even more, better videos, a strategy that directly follows the model employed by most pornography sites.

The correlations between gay television and pornography also extend to the talent. Here TV makes no secret of the fact that its various television series frequently cast former porn stars. This strategy is twofold: (1) gay porn stars have their own fans, who may follow them to other projects; and (2) the aesthetic demands of pornography are not unlike those of gay television. Gay porn stars typically possess the beautiful, flawless, muscular bodies that gay television series require. They are regularly expected to perform wearing few or no clothes, so gay television's requisite nude scenes may not require the same emotional resilience of them as they do of other actors. Indeed, actor Frankie Valenti (aka porn star Johnny Hazzard) specifically comments in *The Lair*'s second-season DVD commentary that acting in a gay television series is easier than doing pornography because he gets to cover his genitals and only has to simulate arousal and orgasm. *The Lair*'s Dylan Vox (formerly porn star Brad Benton) finds little difference between doing pornography and "mainstream" acting: in both, "you just show up, do your job, and then leave," he has said (qtd. in Wilson).

It is difficult to imagine a similarly porous border between pornography and prime-time broadcast television, in which gay sexuality is routinely erased. This extends beyond the narratives of individual series to the publicity and discourses surrounding openly gay actors. Frequenting clubs, using Grindr, and watching pornography (much less appearing in it) are simply not part of the dominant image of gay actors on broadcast television in the current age of assimilation and homonormativity. For example, when actor Jim Parsons of *The Big Bang Theory* (2007–) came out, mainstream media coverage emphasized his monogamy: "Mr. Parsons is gay and in a ten-year relationship" (Healy). Actor Neil Patrick Harris' real-life gay identity was tempered by his on-screen performance of the virulent heterosexual Barney Stinson in *How I Met Your Mother* (2005–2014); conversely, the character's unapologetic womanizing was tempered with the extratextual reality of Harris as a devoted partner and father of two. In both examples, elements of normativity help to render the actor's gay identity more palatable to conservative audience members.

Porn-stars-turned-actors make up one facet of casting "gay for pay" on Here TV. Nonetheless, straight actors also take roles as gay characters, with this kind of "gay for pay" calling attention to the economics of the entertainment industry. Regardless of whether a straight actor sees "playing gay" as a greater challenge than playing straight, actors like to work, and they may find themselves faced with playing someone of a different sexuality in order to keep doing so. Because networks like Here TV cater to the tastes and interests of the LGBT community, the political ramifications of straight actors in gay roles may invoke pushback: Why cast a straight actor when there are plenty of openly gay ones who are willing and able to play the same role?

Both within its narrative and extratextually, *From Here on OUT* takes up the subject of straight actors playing "gay for pay." Within the series, producer Jimmy casts the hunky Sam Decker (played by T.J. Hoban) in the role of Guy Dubai but, despite the network's directive that the lead must be played by a gay man, Sam is straight. Because Jimmy needs an actor and Sam needs a job, the two conspire to keep Sam's heterosexuality a secret by masquerading as a couple. As Jimmy is fortysomething and bald while Sam is youthful, muscular, and tan, their relationship meets with many puzzled expressions from colleagues and reporters. The improbability of Sam finding Jimmy to be attractive reinforces body image stereotypes within the gay male community. More significantly here, however, is how the closet has been reappropriated for a straight man. In a circle of exclusively gay actors, writers, and executives, straight-identifying Sam is the one who fears being outed. This reversal of "closet logic" certainly situates *From Here on OUT* in a queer universe and reiterates its status as television made for queer audiences.

The series' commentary on the politics of casting is further complicated by the fact that, in real life, Hoban (who plays Sam) also identifies as straight; unlike Sam, however, Hoban is able to be open about his sexuality. He has thus far managed to avoid provoking the ire of gay audience members who want to see gay actors in leading roles by maintaining a cordial relationship with the LGBT press—he poses shirtless in publicity photos in order to allow fans to ogle his idealized body and speaks candidly about how he sees "playing gay" as just one of many acting challenges. In an interview with the *Wisconsin Gazette*, a biweekly LGBT newspaper, Hoban explained that the "straight closet" in which his character Sam finds himself is partly what attracted him to the role. As for being surrounded by male nudity and gay sexuality, Hoban admits he is at times uncomfortable but added, "I've always been taught that when it comes to acting, those things that make you uncomfortable are the things that usually get the best out of you. Instead of shying away from them, tackle them" (qtd. in Shapiro). Hoban's acknowledgement of his discomfort reads more like the earnest confession of a friend than the hostile masculine posturing of actors in earlier eras who desperately needed to assert their heterosexuality while "playing gay." Actor Chris Potter of Showtime's *Queer as Folk*, for example, quipped in a 2000 interview that he had to spit and rinse his mouth after kissing scenes, which rankled executives and fans so much that Potter's character was written out of the series and replaced with an openly gay actor, Robert Gant (Streitmatter 130). Although T.J. Hoban still speaks of "playing gay" as a challenge, he, like his character Sam, is open to and embracing of that challenge.

The Here TV reality series *Broke Straight Boys* (2014–) similarly explores the phenomenon of straight men "playing gay," this time for pornography. Although acting "gay for pay" in this series is primarily a means to financial solvency (rather than a challenge to one's craft, as Hoban indicates), some of the participants confess to developing an appreciation for the challenges of performing gay sex. By airing a series with this premise, Here TV further links gay television to pornography.

What About Women?

Here TV's flagship series *Dante's Cove* increased the number of women in its cast over the course of its three-season run, with nearly half of its third-season cast composed of women. The central storyline of the third season reached its climax as both male and female witches had to unite in order to stop an evil supernatural entity from destroying the fictional island on which the series was set. Such unity between men and women is somewhat unusual on a network that caters to its gay male audience far more than to any lesbian or other women viewers. Far more commonly, women characters are extraneous to the central storyline or are in contentious relationships with the gay male heroes. (*The Lair*, for example, began with one woman, actress Beverly Lynne [playing character Laura Rivers], as a series regular but she was soon killed off.)

Women of various sexual identities are frequently viewers of television and cinema aimed at gay men. Although (as previously mentioned) television executives and advertisers are aware of this constituency, women are often not the targeted demographic for gay media. Logo's rebranding in 2012 heralded a greater recognition of its women audiences, especially those women who do not identity as LGBT. In contrast, Here TV aggressively courts its gay male audience, and women who choose to watch are merely bonus subscribers. While there is interest among media scholars and advertisers in deciphering why women watch programming aimed at gay men (see, for instance, Christopher Pullen's *Straight Girls and Queer Guys: The Hetero Media Gaze in Film and Television*), my goal here is not to rehash the common explanations. Instead, I want to note how the reality that women viewers are an afterthought to gay men shapes portrayals of women across Here TV. Because its portrayals are intended primarily for gay men (and are usually created, written, and directed by gay men), they are more reflective of the complicated and often contradictory relationship gay men have with women than with the reality of women's lives.

There are two women characters in *From Here on OUT*: Dottie (played by Juliet Mills), an elderly woman who once served as the nanny to the young network executive, and Divina (played with exquisite comedy by Suzanne Whang), a Korean maid who aspires to be a star. Dottie prefers a good foot rub to sex and wears an ankle-length flannel nightgown to bed. She is too old to be interested in sex—a reflection of the popular cultural unwillingness to see senior citizens as sexual beings as well as the typical gay man's desire to not be confronted with images of female sexuality. Divina is cast in a supporting role on *Guy Dubai* only because she offers the use of a house that she cleans as a free set; she contributes little to the plot of the spy series. Like Dottie's, Divina's body and sexuality are subjects of scorn. In an episode of *Guy Dubai* set in Scotland, a kilt inspector responsible for ensuring that no one wears underwear beneath a kilt is disgusted when he checks under Divina's skirt. Although the male cast members often appear shirtless and many male extras fully nude, neither woman ever does. In the fictional world of Here TV seen through the making of *Guy Dubai*, as well as in the real politics involved in the making of *From Here on OUT*, there is little room for female sexuality. In opposition to "quality TV" and its series that employ gratuitous female nudity for the straight male gaze, series like *From Here on OUT* go to great pains to avoid female nudity, as Here TV's target audience is expected to be, like the kilt inspector, uninterested in—if not disgusted by—women's bodies.

Although the women are confined to supporting roles, it is nevertheless clear that the men, given the choice, would not banish them. The young network executive, Taylor, adores Dottie for her nurturance and often turns to her for advice and support. Without Divina's scheming, Jimmy would never be able to produce *Guy Dubai* on time and on budget. Although he finds her tiring and her acting terrible, Jimmy knows he needs Divina in order to make the show a success. The world of *From Here on OUT*, therefore, is one in which gay men must contend with the presence of women. Gay men, the series tells us, cannot survive in an entirely homosocial environment, a concession that allegorizes the reality of the network's own audience.

Conclusion

The various series made for Here TV, as particularly noteworthy examples of explicitly gay television, feature frankness about gay sexuality that is impossible on broadcast television. Their frequent male nudity, casting of both porn stars and straight actors, and forthright depictions of male-male sex have thus far proved unachievable except through convergence technologies such as video on demand and YouTube subscription channels. Whereas broadcast television is limited by the need to entertain and pacify the many, alternative networks like Here TV can effectively target smaller niche audiences. As a result of broadcast television's dependence on audience size and reliance upon advertising dollars, its representations of LGBT life are much more limited. In contrast, Here TV is able to offer queer alternatives to homonormativity and domestic stasis by circumventing the normative advertising/broadcast model of television. With both its content and its on-demand model, Here queers what television can be.

WORKS CITED

Aaron, Michele. "Towards Queer Television Theory: Bigger Pictures Sans the Sweet Queer-After." *Queer TV: Theories, Histories, Politics.* Ed. Glyn Davis and Gary Needham. New York: Routledge, 2009. 63–75. Print.

Aslinger, Ben. "Creating a Network for Queer Audiences at Logo TV." *Popular Communication* 7.2 (2009): 107–121. Print.

Becker, Ron. *Gay TV and Straight America.* New Brunswick: Rutgers University Press, 2006. Print.

Bernstein, Jacob. "How to Get Away with Chutzpah." *New York Times,* 13 November 2014: E9. Print.

Ciriaco, Michael. "Logo's New Programming Slate Reveals Shift Away from Gay-Centric Shows." *Queerty,* 21 February 2012. Web. 20 January 2015. http://www.queerty.com/ exclusive-logos-new-programming-slate-reveals-shift-away-from-gay-centric-shows–20120221.

Doran, Steven Edward. "Housebroken: Homodomesticity and the Normalization of Queerness in *Modern Family." Queer Love in Film and Television: Critical Essays.* Ed. Pamela Demory and Christopher Pullen. New York: Palgrave Macmillan, 2013. 95–104. Print.

Doty, Alexander. *Making Things Perfectly Queer: Interpreting Mass Culture.* Minneapolis: University of Minnesota Press, 1993. Print.

Duggan, Lisa. *The Twilight of Equality? Neoliberalism, Cultural Politics, and the Attack on Democracy.* Boston: Beacon Press, 2003. Print.

"Exclusive! Alan Cumming Opens Right Up." *Me-Me-Me TV,* 31 August 2007. Web. 20 January 2015. http://www.me-me-me.tv/2007/08/31/exclusive-alan-cumming-opens-right-up/.

Gates, Gary J., and Frank Newport. "Special Report: 3.4% of U.S. Adults Identify as LGBT." *Gallup,* 18 October 2012. Web. 1 December 2012. http://www.gallup.com/poll/158066/ special-report-adults-identify-lgbt.aspx.

Gouttebroze, Max. "GLAAD's Where We Are on TV Report: Highest Percentage Ever of LGBT TV Characters on Broadcast TV." *GLAAD*, 5 October 2012. Web. 1 December 2012. http://www.glaad.org/publications/whereweareontv12.

Healy, Patrick. "Stalked by Shadows (and a Rabbit)." *New York Times*, 23 May 2012. Web. 20 January 2015.

McCabe, Janet, and Kim Akass. "Sex, Swearing, and Respectability: Courting Controversy, HBO's Original Programming and Producing Quality TV." *Quality TV: Contemporary American Television and Beyond*. Ed. Janet McCabe and Kim Akass. New York: I.B. Tauris, 2007. 62–76. Print.

Mueller, Hannah. "'At Least Let Us See Them Before You Cut Them All Off!' The Gendered Representation of Nudity in Contemporary Quality TV." Console-ing Passions. University of Missouri, Columbia. 11 April 2014. Conference presentation.

Needham, Gary. "Scheduling Normativity: Television, the Family, and Queer Temporality." *Queer TV: Theories, Histories, Politics*. Ed. Glyn Davis and Gary Needham. New York: Routledge, 2009. 143–158. Print.

Newman, Michael Z., and Elana Levine. *Legitimating Television: Media Convergence and Cultural Status*. New York: Routledge, 2011. Print.

Newport, Frank. "For First Time, Majority of Americans Favor Legal Gay Marriage." *Gallup*, 20 May 2011. Web. 20 January 2015. http://www.gallup.com/poll/147662/first-time-majority-americans-favor-legal-gay-marriage.aspx.

Pullen, Christopher. *Straight Girls and Queer Guys: The Hetero Media Gaze in Film and Television*. Edinburgh: Edinburgh University Press, 2016. Print.

Scholibo, Corey. "Interview with a Vampire." *Advocate*, 14 August 2007: 60. Print.

Sender, Katherine. *Business, Not Politics: The Making of the Gay Market*. New York: Columbia University Press, 2004. Print.

Shapiro, Gregg. "T.J. Hoban Is a Straight Man Playing Gay in a New Here TV Series About a Straight Man Playing Gay." *Wisconsin Gazette* 17 April 2014. Web. 20 January 2015. http://www.wisconsingazette.com/interview/tjn-hoban-is-a-straight-man-playing-gay-in-a-new-here-tv-series-about-a-straight-man-playing-gay.html.

Streitmatter, Rodger. *From "Perverts" to "Fab Five": The Media's Changing Depiction of Gay Men and Lesbians*. New York: Routledge, 2009. Print.

Villarejo, Amy. *Ethereal Queer: Television, Historicity, Desire*. Durham: Duke University Press, 2014. Print.

Walsh, Jeff. "Alan Cumming: Interview." *Oasis Journals*, 23 November 2007. Web. 20 January 2015. http://oasisjournals.com/2007/11/alan-cumming-interview?page=0%2C3.

Wilson, Drew. "A Conversation with Dylan Vox." *MileHighGayGuy*, 27 March 2010. Web. 20 January 2015. http://www.milehighgayguy.com/2010/03/conversation-with-dylan-vox.html.

About the Contributors

Anna **Ciamparella** is a Ph.D. candidate in comparative literature at Louisiana State University, where she conducts research in various languages (including English, French and Italian). Her research interests include cosmopolitanism, modern poetry and queer studies.

Renee **DeLong** teaches first-year composition and LGBTQ literature at Minneapolis Community and Technical College. Her research interests include the examination of visibility/hypervisibility issues in LGBTQ mainstream media and the push for racial equity in composition studies and pedagogy.

Julia **Erhart** is the associate dean (academic) in Humanities and Creative Arts at Flinders University. Her research interests include LGBT representations in movies and television and feminist re-writes of the historical past in fiction films, biopics and documentaries.

Kylo-Patrick R. **Hart** is chair of the Department of Film, Television and Digital Media at Texas Christian University. He is the founding co-editor of the academic journal *Queer Studies in Media & Popular Culture* and the author of several books about media, including *The AIDS Movie: Representing a Pandemic in Film and Television* and *Queer Males in Contemporary Cinema: Becoming Visible*.

Michael **Johnson**, Jr., is an instructor in the Department of Critical Culture, Gender and Race Studies at Washington State University. His research interests include constructions of masculinity, Foucauldian deployments of power and resistance among sexualities and the intersections of queer and ethno-racial (re)presentations in media and their political economic production.

Bridget **Kies** is a Ph.D. candidate in Media, Cinema and Digital Studies at the University of Wisconsin–Milwaukee, where she researches masculinity and gay male sexuality in popular media. Her academic research has been published in *Intensities: The Journal of Cult Media*, *The International Journal of the Book*, *Transformative Works and Cultures* and elsewhere.

Dragos **Manea** is an assistant lecturer at the University of Bucharest, where he teaches seminars in British and American literature, translation and academic writing. His research interests include the adaptation of history, cultural memory and the relationship between ethics and fiction.

Zachary **Snider** teaches courses in film, literature, speech and writing at Bentley

University. Before becoming a professor, he worked as an entertainment journalist in Los Angeles, New York City and across Europe.

Gael **Sweeney** teaches courses in creative nonfiction, cultural studies and rhetoric in the Writing Program at Syracuse University. She has published on diverse topics including Hugh Grant's British masculinity, Elvis as a white trash icon, and the queer significance of *The Lion King*'s Timon and Pumbaa.

Don **Tresca** received his master's degree in English from California State University–Sacramento, where he specialized in 20th-century American literature and film studies. He has previously published essays pertaining to Clint Eastwood, Stephen King and J.K. Rowling.

Looi **van Kessel** is a Ph.D. student in comparative literature at the Leiden University Center for Arts in Society. His current research focuses on the representation and deconstruction of sexual subjectivation in the novels and plays of the American author James Purdy.

Thomas J. **West** III is a Ph.D. candidate in English at Syracuse University. His dissertation explores the ways that epic films construct a complex interplay between antiquity and modernity, seeking to provide spectators various visceral experiences of time, history and embodiment.

Index

213